The Book of
NIDDERDALE

Aspects of a Yorkshire Valley

NIDDERDALE MUSEUM SOCIETY

First published in Great Britain in 2003.

British Library Cataloguing-in-Publication Data.
A CIP record for this title is available from the British Library.

ISBN 1 84114 247 6

HALSGROVE

Halsgrove House
Lower Moor Way
Tiverton, Devon EX16 6SS
Tel: 01884 243242
Fax: 01884 243325
email: sales@halsgrove.com
website: www.halsgrove.com

Frontispiece photograph: *Coronation procession in 1911, near the bottom of High Street.*

Printed and bound by CPI Bath Press, Bath.

Preface

In 1998, four members of Nidderdale Museum Society wrote a series of articles for the *Nidderdale Herald* on various aspects of the dale's history. At the time, there were many requests that they should be put into a permanent format and they form the nucleus of this book, with another 12 sections added.

As a result of the material being written by four people with different interests, each section varies considerably in style and content. Some areas and topics are dealt with fully, but there are also gaps. The book does not claim to be a complete history of the area – that was dealt with in 1968 by *A History of Nidderdale*, in which three of the members were involved. This is a miscellany of a few aspects of the dale's life through the centuries.

We have had help and encouragement from many people, including Mrs Anne Ashley-Cooper, Dr Geoffrey Blacker, Mr Brian Ives, Professor Bernard Jennings, Miss Joan Knightson, Dr Christopher Metcalfe, Yorkshire Water and members of Nidderdale History Group and Nidderdale Museum Society. To them, and anyone we may have inadvertently omitted, our most grateful thanks.

Photographs

Most of the originals of these photographs are in private hands, the rest belong to Nidderdale Museum Society. They are not available for reproduction.

We are grateful to the following for lending photographs: Mary Barley, Eileen Burgess, Valerie Faulkner, Joyce Hawkesworth, Linda Kendall, Joyce Liggins, Elsy Moss, John Richmond, Richard Shillito, Joyce and Muriel Swires, George Wainwright and Harrogate Museums and Arts.

The reproductions of David Rose's watercolours are by kind permission of Harrogate Museums and Arts.

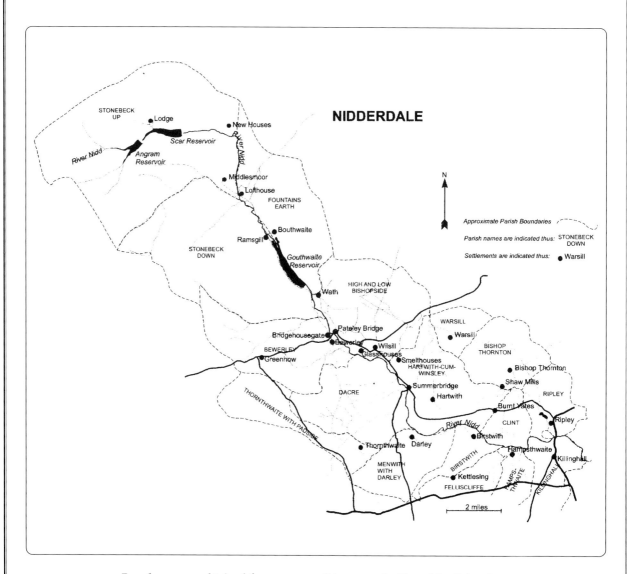

NIDDERDALE

N

Approximate Parish Boundaries

Parish names are indicated thus: STONEBECK DOWN

Settlements are indicated thus: ● Warsill

STONEBECK UP

● Lodge

● New Houses

Scar Reservoir

River Nidd

River Nidd

Angram Reservoir

● Middlesmoor

● Lofthouse

FOUNTAINS EARTH

● Bouthwaite

Ramsgill ●

STONEBECK DOWN

Gouthwaite Reservoir

● Wath

HIGH AND LOW BISHOPSIDE

WARSILL

● Warsill

● Pateley Bridge

Bridgehousegate ●

● Beverley

● Wilsill

BISHOP THORNTON

BEWERLEY

● Greenhow

● Glasshouses

● Smelthouses

HARTWITH-CUM-WINSLEY

● Bishop Thornton

● Shaw Mills

● Summerbridge

● Hartwith

RIPLEY

DACRE

● Burnt Yates

CLINT

● Ripley

THORNTHWAITE WITH PADSIDE

River Nidd

● Birstwith

● Thornthwaite

● Darley

● Hampsthwaite

● Killinghall

BIRSTWITH

MENWITH WITH DARLEY

HAMPS-THWAITE

KILLINGHALL

● Kettlesing

FELLISCLIFFE

2 miles

Based on maps obtained from www.multimap.co.uk. Traced by Brian Ives.

Contents

Introduction

It gives me great pleasure to commend this latest achievement of what has become a characteristic Nidderdale activity, team work in regional and local history. Most of what we know about the rich historical legacy of the dale has been researched and presented by local people, beginning 45 years ago with the formation of a WEA tutorial class in Pateley Bridge. The members produced three successive editions of *A History of Nidderdale,* and also used the profits of the first edition to help establish the prizewinning Nidderdale Museum.

Large areas of the dale had common experiences: they were covered by extensive hunting forests; colonised by monastic granges; and involved in the major local industries of lead mining and flax/linen textiles. Social movements such as the rise of Methodism flowed through the dale with no regard for township boundaries. For these reasons *A History of Nidderdale* concentrated on broad themes, looking at the dale as a whole, as did the study *Kith and Kin: Nidderdale Families 1500–1750* (1995), the work of Summerbridge WEA tutorial class under the leadership of Dr Maurice Turner.

Building on these foundations, local historians have now turned their attention to a mass of absorbing detail, often linked to old photographs, the collection and preservation of which is an achievement in itself. In addition to the human interest associated with local families and people who have left their mark on Nidderdale, there is here a strong sense of place. I am sure that many readers will be inspired to visit the buildings and other landscape features described within this volume, for example, to use their imagination to re-people the timber villages established for the builders of the massive reservoirs in the upper dale. The authors of this book, most of whom were members of the original 1958 class, have deepened our understanding of local history through their painstaking research and imaginative presentation.

Bernard Jennings, Emeritus Professor and former
Pro-Vice-Chancellor of the University of Hull, former National President of the
Workers' Educational Association, editor of *A History of Nidderdale.*

Chapter 1

UP THE DALE

TOP OF THE DALE
Mary Barley

At the top of the dale are the two large reservoirs, Angram and Scar, which collect water for the city of Bradford. I have always been fascinated to know who lived in the settlements before the reservoirs were built and it was my interest in vernacular houses and their owners that inspired the weeks of research, together with a friend, into family records, wills and inventories, hearth-tax returns and censuses.

The land had been granted to Byland Abbey in the twelfth century, and some years after the Dissolution of the Monasteries it was acquired by the Yorke family. They leased shooting rights in 1549 and in 1603 purchased the whole of Stonebeck Up township.

At this time, the houses would have been of cruck construction, probably with wattle-and-daub walls, and the fire would have been in the centre of the room. A lease of Scar House for 3,000 years to Peter Horner in 1606 informs us that:

The old messuage house to the range wall between the old east end and the new west end, and the said range and one pair of crucks being the partition between the old and new end, and one house standing in the common garth called stables and peat house, and a swine cote, garden and all the herb garden under the sun side of the old messuage house, sheep fold and barns and several closes and cattle gates.

This tells us that, by the beginning of the seventeenth century, the house had some stone walls and the fireplace had been taken from a central hearth to a range on the side wall. The roof was probably covered with ling (heather). It would have been a single-storey building with small windows. For this property, Peter Horner paid a yearly rent of 40s. and two fat hens at Christmas and 40s. on any change of tenant. 'Sun side' means south side – terminology from the

days of open-strip fields. At a later date the house would have been encased in stone, with flags on the roof held in place by sheep bones.

In his will, Francis Topham of West Houses left window cloths and loose boards, both of which were portable. The boards would have been slatted across the beams for storage or children's sleeping quarters and accessed by a stee. This was a ladder fastened to a beam at one end, with a hook by which it could be fastened on to another beam when not in use. Window cloths indicated that there was no glass in the house. Both were mentioned because they were moveable goods.

There were five settlements in the area: Angram, West House, Lodge, Heathen (Haden) Carr and Scar House, plus scattered farms at Cockley Gap and Pry House. Lodge and Scar House were not below the reservoir water-level but were abandoned at a later date.

Angram Farm, c.1890.

Angram had two farms and lay at the confluence of Stean Beck and the River Nidd. Occupants included Christopher Horner (1719), Christopher Ripley (1726), Richard Stephenson (1735), Thomas Horner (1767), Anthony Hannam (1838), and Anthony Horner's son (1887), until Bradford Corporation's purchase in 1897. In 1726 Christopher Ripley, yeoman, left High Angram to his granddaughter Elizabeth Ripley and to his wife, Anne, he left Low Angram and its contents for her lifetime – the total value was £17.13s.6d.

The next settlement down the valley was West Houses, built on a promontory just north of Angram dam wall. There appear to have been three messuages here, together with Cockley Gap. Tenants included George Horner in 1606, Thomas Foster in 1606, Richard Horner in 1628, Thomas Horner in 1656, Isabel Horner in 1695, John Horner in 1704 and John Nicholson in 1722. Cockley Gap had Thomas Atkinson in 1839 and Anthony Horner in 1841.

In 1709 Roger Paley left £136.8s.4d., of which £4 was 'for putting his youngest son to a trade'. He also

7

Left: *West Houses Farms, with Cockley Beck Farm in the centre distance.*

Below: *The road near Lodge, leading over Deadman's Hill to Coverdale.*

Left: *Lodge Chapel with an early-nineteenth-century house. The ruin amongst the trees was the Yeoman's House.*

left 22 beasts and a bull with sheep valued at £106. His funeral expenses were £13. In 1713 Thomas Topham left £95.15s.2d., which included 90 sheep and 27 beasts. John Beckwith, in 1750, signed his will with an 'X' and described himself as a butcher.

In 1775 Anthony Horner left a detailed will giving land to two sons, Thomas and Anthony, both to have the right 'to get limestone in each other's land from the quarry and to break and burn the same in the kiln at Little Close.' He left lands at Cosh, Kettlewell and Angram to other sons.

Lodge consisted of three dwellings and one cottage and lay on the trading tracks which went over the moor into Coverdale and via Angram to Kettlewell. Early in the nineteenth century one of the houses was rebuilt and a Wesleyan Chapel was added in 1858. It was not submerged under Scar reservoir but most of its farms were left to ruin, with some stone removed for other uses, and only one remained with walls high enough to measure, so a friend and I named it the Yeoman's House. We only saw one dated lintel from the Yeoman's House – IH 1744. Did Joseph Horner add the extension to the house when he took his new bride to Lodge?

Tenant leases were granted to Christopher Horner (who had two hearths), George Benson and Anthony Watson, all in 1606; Thomas Watson, who had one hearth in 1664; Joseph Horner (1739); James Stott (1769); Elizabeth Horner (1772); Squire Brockhell (1785); John Breare (1808); Richard Allen (1835); Thomas Brockhell (1839); and William and Benjamin Brockell (1872). When Bradford Corporation took over, they sublet two dwellings, one to Elias Harrison and the other to Thomas Simpson and later to Robert and Thomas Wellock.

Lucas, in his *Studies in Nidderdale*, says that in 1872 'A flood carried away the newly erected bridge over the Nidd at Lodge, which had cost £500 to build.'

Wills and inventories show some interesting details. Christopher Horner, in 1695, left just over £10. Among his assets were a reckon, tongs, axes and spelt, which was an inferior type of wheat grown on higher ground.

Two years later, another Christopher Horner left his farm to his wife Elizabeth for life and then to his son, George. His stock was valued at £66, but his debts were over £37.

Anthony Watson signed his will in 1709 and had £350 worth of sheep and wool, and by the time his debts were paid there was almost £119 in hand. His son, Thomas, who died in 1728, surprisingly had no sheep, although he had a second farm and his assets were valued at £100.

Anthony Knowles, aged 22, was drowned when returning from Ripon market. He was 'sick of body but sound of mind' when he prepared his will, but it was not signed. He was unmarried and kept no servant in the house. Letters swearing as to the authenticity of the handwriting and his state of mind were found in the house by Christopher Horner within a few days of the death. His inventory showed assets of £111, and the will went to probate and was proved.

When John Kidd made his will in 1751, he left his wife £1 a year, providing she remained unmarried. He also added 'Contagious Distemper raging'. One wonders how rinderpest reached such a remote corner of the Yorkshire dales. The outbreak had a depressing effect on the price of grain nationwide – two years earlier the country's compensation bill had amounted to £7,000.

Simon Horner left 26 beasts and 290 sheep in 1773, together with other assets all to the value of £147.10s. Joseph Horner, whose initials are on the lintel at the Yeoman's House, and who died about the same time, gave to his wife, Elizabeth:

The west end of my Dwelling House known as the old end as long as she remain my widow. John Horner, my son, to put it in repair and she to keep it so. When the youngest child do reach 21, all my leasehold land and appurtenances there belonging to be sold in a fair sale to the highest bidder and the money to be divided amongst them all.

Hayden Carr (also known as Haden or Heathen Carr, but for the sake of clarity within this publication shall be referred to as Hayden Carr) was the fourth

The rear of the Yeoman's House of 1744, in a painting by David Rose.

Hayden Carr, painted by David Rose.

settlement from the top of the Nidd Valley. In the 1890s a small dam was built here, but it was later submerged under Scar House reservoir, along with the settlement.

There were four dwellings, occupied by some of the following, the names being taken from the Yorke leases: Richard Horner, Leonard Horner, Elizabeth Horner and her son Roger, and Leonard Craven, all in 1606; Thomas Horner (1617); George Horner (1647); Henry Hammond (1682); Isobel Horner (1695); George Brockell (1769); Thomas Mawer (1770); Squire Brockell (1785); John Thompson (1795); John Brockell (1795); Matthew, William and Thomas Mawer in trust (1799); Moses Brockell (1838); Richard Allen (1853); John Verity (1859); John William and Matthew Verity (1880); and finally Bradford Corporation acquired the house and land in 1894.

The earliest will found for Hayden Carr was for Elizabeth Langsroth, widow, but few details were given. Later, in 1683, Henry Hammond, yeoman, who signed his will and had land in Bradley as well as Hayden Carr, left four horses and a little galloway, linen, wool and books.

Squire Brockell left a will in 1795 and bequeathed 'the old dwelling house at Heathen Carr to my wife Elizabeth, my executors to keep it in repair if she wish to live in it after my decease.' He also left a clock, a rare item in wills from these years. Some time before this, Squire Brockell had purchased the Yeoman's House in Lodge, 'He not to enter the said house until the death of Elizabeth Horner'. Elizabeth's husband, Joseph, had died in 1772 – as mentioned in the Lodge wills.

The houses shown in David Rose's painting appear to be late-eighteenth or early-nineteenth century, and this is confirmed for at least one house by Thomas Mawer, yeoman, whose will in 1799 bequeathed to his wife, Elizabeth, for life:

... the dwelling house where I now live and the chamber above it, also the peat house and stable with loft over it and to have full liberty of erecting buildings on the beck side of the messuage without interruption, on land farmed by my sons where the kiln was. Also concerning the new erected messuage or tenement with turf house.

Pry House with Hayden Carr reservoir in the background.

The ruins of the kiln can still be seen when Scar reservoir is low. Usually the widow was allowed property only if she did not remarry, according to most of these wills.

We then read from the leases of the changes in ownership. In 1877 Christopher Other of Coverham Abbey purchased a dwelling and 118 acres at Lodge and 'part land and sheep gaits on Dale Head Moor.' This was after the property had passed through various owners residing mainly in Wensleydale. In 1887, Anthony Horner mortgaged leases of West Houses with the Swaledale and Wensleydale Bank in Leyburn. In 1890 it was purchased by Christopher Other direct from the bank, together with shooting and fishing rights. These he left to his daughters Jane Winn of West Burton and Ann Wright of Heysham who eventually sold the estate to Bradford Corporation in 1904.

SHEEP WASHING
Eileen Burgess

One of the things which most intrigued me when we first started the Nidderdale Museum in 1975 was a collection of postcards entitled 'Sheep washing'. They showed men standing in water, watched by crowds of people dressed in their Sunday best.

Sheep washing goes back to monastic times. Fountains and Byland Abbeys both had lands in the upper dale where they established farms to supply wool, cheese and butter, originally just for their own use and then, as production increased, for sale. These granges were managed by lay brothers until the Black Death, and afterwards increasingly by tenants on supply leases – they delivered specific amounts each year to the abbeys, and the rest was their own profit. After the Reformation they continued in their holdings, still using many of the techniques introduced by the monks.

The Cistercians had found that clean wool brought a higher price than dirty, so they washed the fleeces to rid them of grit, surface dirt and parasites. The quickest way to do this was to dam up a stream and push the sheep through it. Having been trained to do this by the monks, the farmers continued the practice through the centuries.

By Victorian times, it had become a social as well as a practical gathering, with the families of each hamlet coming together to do the job. About two weeks before the sheep had to be shorn, the men would make a dam with stones, earth and sods across a beck about 3 or 4 feet high, so that it would keep the water back to about chest height. A few days later, the shepherd and the farmers would gather to collect the sheep from the moor. They started off soon after daybreak, probably at about four in the morning, and brought them down to the 'wash dub'. Two or three young, strong men went into the water and spent the day up to their waists, or higher, in it.

Left: *Collecting Gouthwaite sheep for washing. Notice all the onlookers behind.*

Below: *Stean Moor sheep washing, 1908. The men in the water would suffer from rheumatism for the rest of their lives.*

Bottom: *Burn Gill sheep washing in 1906, with 'Grandad' Carling and his horse on the right.*

In mid-June the high pastures could still have snow on the ground, so the workers were plied with whisky to keep out the cold. Even so, many suffered from rheumatism for the rest of their lives – seldom were they able to do the task another year. Other men came along to push the sheep down into the bath, where they were submerged and rubbed until all the loose dirt was removed, and to sort them out as they emerged from their ducking.

Meanwhile, the rest of the families turned up with their horses and carts loaded with children and food. They could have travelled three miles or more to encourage their men folk, so they were determined to make it an occasion. Friends and relations were invited to take part in the fun. They came dressed in their finery – the women with their splendid hats, the men in their chapel suits and the children in their best pinafores and stiff collars. For some remote and very poor families, like the Newboulds who had many children and lived high above Heathfield, it was the only outing they had.

The youngsters ran off to play with their friends while the old men encouraged the workers and the women organised the picnic. They brought rabbit pies, cooked ham, gooseberry pies, homemade ginger beer, lemonade, elderflower champagne and bottles of hot tea for the washing men.

The men took off their wet clothes – no waterproof waders in those days – and put on dry ones for the picnic. Did they have a third set in the cart for going home when the job was done, I wonder?

Sheep washing continued until well into the 1930s, when dipping was made compulsory. It was the end of a focal point of the upper-dale life – a respite before the hard work of shearing and haymaking when everyone was involved.

THE RESERVOIRS
Eileen Burgess

During the 1880s Bradford needed more water for its growing population and wool industry. It had utilised the available supplies in the area around the city and so began to look further afield for the soft

Hayden Carr.

water which was suitable for washing the lanolin from the fleeces. In 1890 an Act of Parliament was passed to give Bradford the right to construct four reservoirs at the head of Nidderdale – Angram, Hayden Carr, High Woodale and Gouthwaite. The sites chosen made use of the natural landscape, by using the moraines formed where glaciers had melted in the Ice Ages, leaving large barriers of rock and rubble across the valley to form the bases of the dam walls.

The first reservoir, Hayden Carr, almost at the head of the dale, was constructed in the 1890s by Morrison & Mason of Edinburgh, who also had a contract for the pipeline to Chellow Heights, Bradford, a distance of over 32 miles. They had a construction yard at Heathfield for the tunnel, with a railway to transport material to the sites. In addition, there were workshops and huts in Bridgehousegate, where the garage is at the time of writing.

At the same time, John Best & Son, another Scots firm, won the contract for Gouthwaite, the compensation reservoir, which would guarantee a supply of water to those with rights lower down the valley – mill owners, anglers and so on. The first sod was cut by Bradford Corporation's chief engineer, James Watson, on 13 September 1893. The stone came from Spring Wood Top, 500 yards away. Horses were used instead of locomotives to transport materials.

Accommodation for the core workers was found in houses and farms in the surrounding area. Heathfield and Pateley schools admitted many children and the Independent Chapel in Bridgehousegate, since it was nearest in type to the Presbyterian places of worship the Scotsmen knew, flourished. Some local men were also employed, as the lead mines had closed some years previously.

When the construction was nearing completion the dam was filled, but the rain was so heavy over three days in October 1899 that it overflowed, destroying huts, plant and cement sheds. The reservoir was finally completed in June 1901, at a cost of £240,000, twice as much as the original estimate.

As part of the work, Gouthwaite Hall, which had been divided into three farms after the Yorke family had moved down to Bewerley, was pulled down and re-erected as separate houses above the new line of road up the dale. A handsome house was built for the reservoir keeper, with a boardroom in which the visiting councillors and officials could be entertained whenever they inspected the works.

Meanwhile, the London-based Power & Traction Ltd had gained an order in 1901 to construct a railway of 2 feet 6 inches gauge from Pateley to Lofthouse and two years later Bradford invested in the scheme, subsequently taking over the entire project. Although the North Eastern Railway advised that it should be installed as standard gauge, in the event 3 feet was initially used. A road was also constructed from Lofthouse to Angram.

Above: *Pry House with Hayden Carr reservoir in the background. Some walls of Pry House can be seen when Scar House reservoir is very dry. Hayden Carr dam wall was 60 feet long and 20 feet high.*

Right: *Gouthwaite reservoir trench.*

Right: *Wath Woods Quarry. Stone is being cut for Gouthwaite reservoir, 1895.*

Below: *Rubble and timber in the Gouthwaite reservoir trench, 1893.*

Right: *Gouthwaite nearing completion in 1901.*

Below: *The disastrous flood at Gouthwaite, October 1899.*

Left: *Gouthwaite Lodge – 'The Aldermen's Rest'.*

Nidd Valley Light Railway, with the first train arriving at Pateley Station.

*Nidd Valley Light Railway. The Lord Mayor of Bradford (Alderman Gadie?) is about to take
the controls, at the end of Gouthwaite reservoir. The occasion was possibly the cutting of the first sod
for Scar House reservoir*

Bunty engine hauling goods. Notice the third line for the narrow-gauge engine with the standard trucks.
The postcard is date stamped 2 November 1905 and has a love poem signed 'From a friend in London'.
It is addressed to Miss M.J. Metcalfe at Intake Farm, Middlesmoor.

The firm employed on Angram was again John Best & Son, who made a yard at Lofthouse. On 13 July 1904, a party of 150 from Bradford City Council watched the Lord Mayor cut the first sod of the Nidd Valley Light Railway (NVLR). They went in carriages up to Lofthouse where they mounted 15 navvy wagons and were taken up on the Bests' light railway to Angram.

As the work progressed, standard-gauge rail was also laid, so goods could be transferred directly from the North Eastern Railway at Pateley Bridge. Passengers were carried as well as goods and stations were constructed at Pateley, Wath, Ramsgill and Lofthouse, all to the same design. The offices were on the ground floor with living quarters upstairs, reached by an external stone staircase. The connection with the North Eastern Railway took place in 1907, although passengers were not allowed to travel on the link section, except for a very few excursion trains – they had to walk the half mile across the town between the stations. There were usually four trains a day each way in summer and three in winter, with an extra train on Wednesdays and Saturdays, and none on Sundays.

A small village was constructed at Angram for the workers, with a school and houses for the missioner and policeman. There were also three bungalows, ten huts for the workers, a canteen with bedrooms above and a couple of shops. A small hospital, with Dr Holmes in residence, was further down the dale.

On the opposite side of the valley was the engineer's office which remained until it burned down in 1929.

The dam wall was not the usual earth bank, but concrete pillars and huge rough stones, faced with dressed stone, which came from a quarry opened above Scar House on the south side of the valley, with an inclined railway to bring it down the steep hillside.

Although James Watson was the chief engineer, he was based at Bradford. His deputies on the sites were H. Duncan at Pateley and E.S. Barlow at Angram, although the latter lived at Gouthwaite and went up by horse gig to his office at Lofthouse. Allan Best, son of the contractor, lived in Scar House.

On Saturdays, the people living at Angram and in the farms around had a special train to Lofthouse, so they could catch a connection to shop in Pateley or walk over the moors to Masham. Men living on the farms had to walk up to the site. The weather could be very severe and they could be cut off for weeks by snow. In February 1907 the exceptional weather meant no work at all, so each day the contractors provided basic soup and bread to the men.

Angram was almost completed by 1916 and many of the men enlisted, but clearing the equipment from the site continued until 1920. During this time, Bradford decided to abandon the scheme for the High Woodale dam and make a much larger one opposite Scar House which would incorporate Hayden Carr. It was started in 1920 with direct labour under the control of James

Cutting the first sod of Angram reservoir.

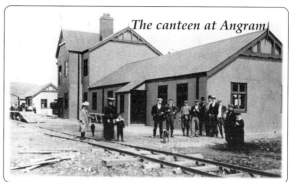

The canteen at Angram

Above: *Work in progress at Angram.*

Right: *Cranes working on the construction of the wall at Angram reservoir.*

Left: *An inspection of Angram by the Bradford Corporation Water Works Committee.*

Below: *The new road up the side of Gouthwaite. The gentleman driving his horse is possibly Mr E.S. Barlow, site engineer at Angram, coming home to Gouthwaite from his office at Lofthouse.*

Right: *An inspection of Angram by the Bradford Waterworks Committee.*

19

Watson's successor, Lewis Mitchell, with John Busfield as resident engineer, succeeded by William Newlands four years later, and George Renton as assistant.

A new village was planned with ten hostels for 64 men, each with self-contained accommodation for the landlady and her family, servants' rooms, kitchen, men's large dining-room, bathrooms, lavatories, lockable sleeping cubicles and drying room for wet clothes, etc. They were a tremendous improvement on the primitive conditions usually provided for the navvies. The men paid 8d. a night in the hostels and were provided with a cooked breakfast, packed lunch, and cooked evening meal, presumably at an extra charge. The navvies mostly came from Ireland in the summer months.

East View was the first block of houses to be built for married workers, with Mr Holmes the schoolmaster and PC Tate among the first residents. Three other sets of bungalows were erected and let with rents varying from 7s. to 9s. a week. They all had a bathroom and toilet, scullery, pantry, storeroom, coal house, hot and cold water and electricity for lighting and ironing, facilities which very little of the working-class housing in the rest of the dale provided. The buildings were of timber with red asbestos tiles and

blue ridges; each had a small garden with flowers and rhododendrons. They were redecorated regularly inside and out to the occupiers' tastes. Unfortunately, in winter the pipes froze and water had to be carried from a spring, which luckily never failed.

There was a large assembly of other buildings. The bakery could produce 200 loaves an hour and a laundry washed the sheets and tablecloths from the hostels. There were six shops – a hairdresser/newsagent, greengrocer/fishmonger, drapery, grocery, butcher's and cobbler's – plus a fish-and-chip shop, sub-Post Office and bank.

The recreation hall had billiard tables and reading- and writing-rooms with a library. The cinema, whose projection room is the only building left on the site at the time of writing, had a stage and dressing-rooms used each year for the Pateley Bridge Operatic Society's performances of Gilbert and Sullivan. Whist drives and dances were held every Saturday. The canteen had separate sections for different grades of workers and a house for its manager. There were also tennis-courts, but the men had to go to Ramsgill for football. The hospital built for Angram was used, augmented by another, with Dr Campbell in charge during the 1920s/'30s.

The Mission Church was transferred from Angram to Scar. Mr E.W. Coplestone, a lay reader, was in charge, taking Anglican and Free Church services on alternate weeks. He acted as an intermediary between the corporation and the workpeople and their families – he was good at getting financial

Above: *The Crescent at Scar.*

Right: *Workshops and offices at Scar.*

support for activities. He also wrote a church magazine which provided an excellent record of the religious and secular activities in the community. The vicar of Middlesmoor administered communion once a month. Father Hammond, the Roman Catholic priest, came weekly and celebrated Mass in the canteen. It is said that on Saturday mornings he stood at the top of the steps above the pay office with his hat out for contributions, which helped pay for his church to be built in Pateley in 1936.

The community life at Scar was very strong – whole families lived and worked there. Jack Haines, who was born in the village, was employed there, along with both sets of grandparents, his parents and many aunts and uncles. The Drummonds had come originally to Gouthwaite with six sons, then went to Angram and finally Scar. Several of the children brought up there recall their happy childhoods in *Scar Village Remembered,* wandering freely and safely, although they were expected to behave themselves – their fathers' jobs depended on good behaviour from the whole family. The employers also contributed to the well-being of the community by providing excellent welfare and social services. Each year the children were taken for a day at the seaside and were given a wonderful Christmas party. When one little boy, George Shackleton, was lost, all the men were ordered to search for him – unfortunately, by the time he was found, it was too late.

When William Newlands became chief site engineer, one of his assistants was David Rose, a very talented artist. He painted many evocative watercolours of the work and the dale, but his great forte was the cartoon portrait. It was said of him that if he did not know the name of one of the 1,000 men working on the site, he drew a line sketch on his cuff, and the man was instantly recognised. Some of his work is in Bradford Industrial Museum and a large collection is kept in the Harrogate Mercer Gallery, although it is not always on show because of its fragility.

The NVLR was improved in 1920 with curves being smoothed out and loops made at Lofthouse and Woodale. The tunnel opposite Manchester Hole was cut for ascending trains, but descending ones still used the outside curve which had derailed several heavily loaded trains.

Right: *Scar workman in a cartoon by David Rose.*

The tunnel near Manchester Hole, which was used by the up trains – the down trains continued to use the outer bend, which was the scene of several derailments.

A group of stonemasons.

Construction of the pipeline which was used to carry water to Bradford, c.1910.

Scar House.

The first sod of Scar was cut in 1921. Trenches 30–35 feet wide were dug down to 60 feet below ground level in the bottom of the valley, with massive foundations and concrete piers to carry the wall. Stone for facing came from Carle Fell on the north slope above the site, with an incline to bring it 400 feet down to the site. During the construction 20 steam cranes and three steam navvies were used.

The tunnel from Scar House to How Stean Beck was constructed by the Hoare family. The father had worked all over the world and started work on the tunnel in 1929. Only a few months later, he and his wife died within five days of each other. Bradford Corporation honoured the contract with his young sons who had between 50 and 60 men working in shifts throughout the 24 hours. The engineer in charge was G.W. Butler and the men were accommodated in B Hut. Only one man was killed. And the sections met within inches!

Between 1924 and 1929, 800 people were working on the project in winter and up to 1,100 in summer, some of whom had to be housed in the villages, as far down as Pateley. After 1929, the numbers declined as the various stages of the work were completed. The same year passenger services on the NVLR ceased.

When completed, the masonry dam was 1,825 feet in length, rising 170 feet above the river. When the reservoir is full the maximum depth of water is 154 feet 6 inches, deeper than any other in England, holding 2,200 million gallons and covering 172 acres, with a catchment area of 7,240 acres of moorland.

The official opening took place on 7 September 1936 and later that year the reservoir-keeper's house was built. The NVLR was closed down, once the equipment had been sold. The farms were cleared and allowed to fall into ruin, although several of the buildings were used for military purposes during the Second World War. The mission hut was taken to Heaton, Bradford and the canteen became Darley Memorial Hall.

Alderman Gadie was the chairman of Bradford Corporation Water Works Committee and the dam became known as Gadie's Folly. However, he was vindicated many times during drought years when Leeds and other towns rapidly became short of water and Bradford had to supply them.

A SEDITIOUS PLAY AT GOUTHWAITE HALL
Eileen Burgess

The old Gouthwaite Hall was demolished when the reservoir was constructed in 1901. It was the home of the Yorke family until they moved down to Bewerley. Originally a monastic farmhouse, it was rebuilt in the later-sixteenth century as a gentleman's residence, with the comforts and fashions of the time.

One of its features was a pair of priest holes, one on either side of the main bedroom, for although Sir Peter Yorke and his son Sir John were both conforming Anglicans, as the law required, their wives were active Catholics. Peter's wife, Elizabeth, was the daughter of Sir William Ingilby of Ripley Castle and

Gouthwaite Hall, scene of the seditious play.

the sister of Francis Ingilby, the Jesuit priest martyred at York for his faith. John's wife, Juliana Hansby, also came from a good Catholic family. Keeping to the old faith was a dangerous and costly business – heads of families were fined heavily for each Anglican service or rite they missed, so they tended to conform outwardly but allow the rest of their household to worship in private as Catholics. Priests travelled the country in disguise, from one safe house to another, celebrating Mass in upper rooms away from prying eyes, with vestments and utensils carefully hidden away between visits. They and their congregations were in constant peril, for being or even harbouring a priest was a capital offence. In spite of this, Catholicism flourished, particularly in Nidderdale, which was one of the most fervent areas in the country.

One cover frequently used for priests was that of a member of a band of strolling actors, taking plays around to gentry houses. Staying for a few days, they could take services, hear confessions and baptise children in secret. One such company had been operating from Egton, near Whitby, since 1601, led by two brothers, Christopher and Robert Simpson, who had an alibi as travelling cordwainers (high-class shoemakers). At Christmas in 1609 they visited Gouthwaite to present one of four plays – *King Lear*, *Pericles*, *The Three Shirleys* or *St Christopher*. Sir John and Lady Juliana chose the last and invited about 100 of their friends, tenants and servants to

share the performance. However, unknown to the hosts it was decided to include an interlude in the entertainment. At least two family members, Christopher Yorke and Christopher Mallory, were given parts in a disputation between an Anglican minister carrying a Bible and Catholic priest carrying a cross, about who would go to heaven and who to hell. Needless to say, the Anglican was dragged below by the Devil, whilst the Catholic ascended with angels singing.

Those present were highly amused, saying to their friends later that had they seen it and would never set foot inside a Parish Church again. However, one person was not so enthusiastic – Elizabeth, a former servant at Gouthwaite who had recently married William Stubbs, the newly appointed curate of Pateley Bridge. Stubbs was a protégé of Sir Stephen Proctor who had bought Fountains Abbey and some of its estates, including those in Nidderdale.

Proctor was a fervent Protestant, a Puritan, and extremely quarrelsome. With his father, he was very interested in metallurgy and wished to develop the potential of the lead, coal and iron deposits in the upper dale. He was constantly at war with Sir John Yorke and his cousin, Sir William Ingilby, over boundaries and mineral rights, and was almost paranoid about their threatening his life, although it must be said that they were far from angelic! Therefore, when William Stubbs reported the seditious play to Proctor, who was a magistrate, he tried un-successfully to arrest the players and Sir John Yorke. However, Proctor had himself fallen foul of the authorities, since he had been collecting overdue fines by using extortion and other undue pressure, so they took no notice.

It was another two years before Yorke and Ingilby were arrested, together with family members and several servants and tenants. Charges of being implicated in the Gunpowder Plot of 1605 were also laid against them. These were plausible, because all the plotters except one were closely related to the Ingilbys and all had been in the neighbourhood shortly before the treason was discovered. However, only the charge connected to the performace of a seditious play was upheld. Sir William Ingilby was released within a few months, but Sir John was kept in the Fleet prison in London for yet another two years.

As a result of the difficulty of transporting witnesses to London, a journey which could take a week or more, most of them were examined in Ripon. The few people who supported Proctor told tales of being subjected to abuse and ridicule, intimidation and bribery. The Stubbs pair came in for more than their share. On his way to church, the curate was shouted at and reviled 'Out villain thief – the devils go with thee!' Peter Smith told Elizabeth that her husband would have 'his ears cut off and preach at Paul's Cross with a paper on his head!' She had even been offered the bribe of a living of £100 a year for her husband if he would withdraw his charge, but as the actual sum handed over had only been £2 for him and 5s. for herself, she hadn't accepted it! Robert Joy, a mason who had been working on the building of Gouthwaite and a key prosecution witness, said his brother had implored him to retract his evidence as he would be put off his land by Sir John Yorke. Several witnesses said that Sir William Ingilby had been party to these pressures and had abused his position as a Justice of the Peace.

The Court of Star Chamber accepted that Sir John and Lady Juliana had only chosen the *St Christopher* play and had known nothing about the interlude. However, they should have stopped it, instead of applauding the actors. It was libel, so they were fined £1,000 each and his brothers £300 each, with various tenants being fined smaller sums. The judges said they would not examine the matter of hiding priests, which was an ecclesiastical matter. It was the longest trial about a dramatic production ever held in Star Chamber. The next day Richard Yorke, one of Sir John's brothers, was imprisoned in the Fleet gate-house, presumably as a surety. No payments were made for three years and Sir John and Lady Juliana were kept in the Fleet Debtors' Prison at their own expense – not the disgrace it might have seemed, as many Catholic gentry were similarly housed! In February 1617 they were released and the fines were all reduced to a total of £1,200, which Sir John under-took to pay himself. In order to do so he granted extraordinarily long leases to 14 tenants, retaining only hunting and fishing rights.

Incidentally, the players had returned to Gouthwaite the February after the play and presented what is believed to be the first provincial performance of Shakespeare's *King Lear*.

Stephen Proctor continued his legal wrangles whilst he built Fountains Hall, but the two projects so impoverished him that he died in debt. As he had no heir, his friend and ally, Sir Timothy Whittingham, bought his estates at a much reduced price.

Sir John and Lady Juliana had no children, so the estate passed to a nephew and down his family line. In 1674 the Yorkes bought the Bewerley estate and even-tually moved their residence there. Gouthwaite Hall was split into three and let to tenant farmers. When the reservoir was completed in 1901, the hall was taken down and re-erected as separate houses on the western side of the road. Many features were preserved, partic-ularly the window and door lintels, giving the houses a period air, yet looking relatively modern.

Lead mine at Lofthouse, 1905.

Far left: *Harald Bruff, Norwegian civil engineer who loved Greenhow, its miners and their dialect.*

Left: *Mrs Bruff.*

Below: *Greenhow is notorious for its harsh climate – in the cold winters of the early-nineteenth century the roads were regularly blocked by huge snowdrifts.*

Left: *Bradford Corporation No. 2 Shaft. A rich seam of lead was discovered when the pipeline from Angram reservoir to Bradford was constructed. The First World War brought a need for lead, so the mines were reopened. Harald Bruff came to manage them.*

Chapter 2

GREENHOW

HARALD BRUFF & KELD HOUSE
Eileen Burgess

When the great pipeline from Angram and Scar reservoirs to Bradford was being constructed in the early-twentieth century it hit a rich seam of lead ore at Craven Cross. As a result, Harald Bruff, a Norwegian, came to Greenhow to superintend the reopening of the mines in 1915.

He was very interested in the local dialect, recognising the many links with his own Scandinavian tongue, and was also fascinated by the tales the old miners told of their experiences, and those which had been handed down from their fathers. He became one of the committee members of the Yorkshire Dialect Society in the 1930s and published several of the stories. He was also very active in community life and acted as secretary for Greenhow war memorial and the Recreation Ground. In 1994 Nidderdale Museum was fortunate to receive some of his papers, including correspondence and first drafts of his publications.

Harald's wife was also Norwegian. As a young girl she had made a sampler – not the Victorian cross-stitch type we normally see, but a true sample of all the processes and stitches she would need in later life. It is about 5 feet long and 6 inches wide, of several different grades of natural linen, worked in blue. The pieces are joined with a variety of seams, there are buttonholes and the whole is decorated with traditional Norwegian embroidery patterns. It is exquisitely done and was completed before her twelfth birthday. It is preserved in the museum, although not exhibited.

The Bruffs lived at Keld House, almost the last house on the right in Greenhow, just before the bend which takes the road out across the moor to Grassington. One of Harald's strangest stories concerned this house.

The occupants at one time had a young orphan boy living with them. The woman was very unkind to the child, who was frequently banished to an outhouse, beaten and starved. His misery in the bleak climate of Greenhow must have been intense. He could be heard sobbing in the outhouse by passers-by – and eventually he died.

Harald Bruff believed he had heard the child several times and a few weeks before Harald died it is said he saw the child, holding out his arms to him.

Keld House must have had many other tales to tell over the years. The site dates back to monastic times, when it was an outpost of Fountains Abbey, a base for the development of the lead mines. At that time and until the early-seventeenth century there were no other houses at all in Greenhow. The miners lived down in the valley hamlets, such as Hardcastle, where it was sheltered and there was a water-supply – the rain quickly penetrates the limestone and runs away far below the surface, leaving most of Greenhow dry. For the small group of lay brothers who lived there, it could be a fairly lonely existence, although they would have had travellers passing along the 'high road to Craven', as it was called.

The way across the moor was marked with crosses, the first – Craven Cross, only a few yards from Keld House – also marked the boundary where the manors of Appletreewick, Bewerley and the Forest of Knaresborough met. Some of the travellers would be fellow monks on the way from the vast Fountains estates in the upper dales of the Wharfe and Aire where great flocks of sheep were pastured on the limestone. In autumn spectacular herds would be driven across to winter pastures or for slaughter. The animals were kept chiefly for their wool, although the milk was also used to make cheese. They were the foundation of the Cistercian wealth, enabling the order to build the magnificent monasteries which, in 2003, we can only visualise from their majestic ruins.

Even in monastic times the house would have been built of stone, since wood was scarce on the hilltop. Small fields around would make paddocks for driven animals resting overnight, while their drovers slept in the house. The brothers would also oversee some of the lead mines being worked by direct labour or hired servants. In the later years of the monasteries, a tenant would be in place, and this continued after the Dissolution of the Monasteries in 1539.

Stephen Proctor, who bought the Fountains estates in the early years of the seventeenth century, was very interested in the development of the lead mines and applied for permission from the Crown to build houses for miners on Greenhow. Each one had land attached, providing a subsistence of milk and oats to supplement the erratic wages available to

27

Dedication of Greenhow war memorial. Harald Bruff was a prime mover in the design and construction of the war memorial.

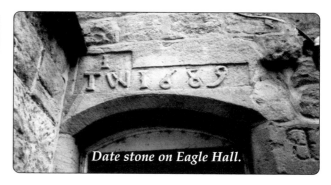

Date stone on Eagle Hall.

White, who had mineral rights and royalties in Bewerley Parish.

In 1678, Samuel Taylor of Wallingwells, Nottinghamshire, and his heir Henry Richard Taylor repaired the monastic chapel at Bewerley for use as a school and endowed it with £10 a year. Later, in 1683, this same Henry Richard Taylor and his uncle, Richard Taylor of Newall, had a gallery erected for their own use in St Mary's Church, Pateley Bridge. By the marriage in July 1698 of Thomas White to Bridget, only daughter and heiress of Richard Taylor MP, the estate came to the Whites of Wallingwells. John, the eldest son of Thomas and Bridget, died unmarried and the second son succeeded. He married twice, dying in 1772, and his eldest son Taylor White inherited. On Taylor's death in 1795 his eldest son Thomas Woollaston White succeeded and was created a baronet on 20 December 1802.

Eagle Hall got its name from the crest of the White family, an eagle rising with expanded wings from a ducal coronet. This can still be seen carved in stone over a tall arch in the courtyard. Over a window is the date 1689 with the initials T.W.

From the middle of the nineteenth century, Thomas Thorpe and Matthew Newbould lived there. Mr Thorpe, who was descended from an old local family, had a stationery and printing business in Pateley. In 1863 he printed and published *Nidderdale* by William Grainge, the first book issued from a Nidderdale press, and he also printed and published the *Nidderdale Almanac* for 17 years. A violinist and singer, he was also organist at St Cuthbert's Church, Pateley Bridge, for about 20 years. Unfortunately, his business failed and he died April 1884, aged 56.

In around 1860 the Eagle Hall property had passed to T.F. Burnaby, who sold about half of it to Hanley Hutchinson of Grassfield House. George Metcalfe bought a detached farm on which he built Castlestead. The rest was auctioned by Mr Topham at the Town Hall, probably the Oddfellows' Hall, Pateley Bridge on Wednesday 20 November 1867. The auctioned property consisted of several farms and farmsteads, 'The Miners Arms', woods, rich minerals, lime and other valuable stone, a powerful stream with trout, and Hardcastle Moor containing 2,397 acres.

In 1870 the whole estate was bought by Miss Elizabeth Rawson of Nidd Hall, who shortly afterwards rebuilt Eagle Hall. She left the property to

lead miners. The mines expanded and the population rose throughout the eighteenth and most of the nineteenth centuries.

The exhaustion of the most accessible deposits had closed several mines by the 1870s. Attempts at their revival were checked by a fall in the price of lead as Spanish then American ore found its way onto the market. This ore was much richer in silver than the British ores and the precious metal paid for the cost of extraction, so the lead was sold very cheaply. As a result, the local industry collapsed and the mines were almost deserted until, around the turn of the century, the pipeline revealed considerable unworked deposits.

The demands of the First World War meant that home-produced ore was again needed. Harald and his wife lived at Keld House for several years, but moved to York when he went to work on the railway. However, they continued to return for weekends, and kept their interest in the community until his death in 1945. They had one child, Ruby, who married a Swede and lived in Stockholm, Washington and then Paris, where she died.

Keld House, which had become very dilapidated, was rebuilt during the 1990s, so perhaps the ghost of the unhappy child has finally been exorcised.

EAGLE HALL

Muriel Swires

Eagle Hall occupies a south-facing site about half a mile from Pateley Bridge on the road to Greenhow. It was formerly the seat of the families of Taylor and

The Lodge at Eagle Hall, 1904.

The grounds of Eagle Hall.

Left: *Sod cutting at Eagle Hall for the reservoir in the grounds, which took Eagle Level water and stored it for Pateley Bridge.*
The lady standing on a platform in the centre is Lady Mountgarret.

Parish Church, Pateley Bridge

Rev. W. R. H. WRIGHT, M.A., C.F. (T.), Vicar.

PROGRAMME

of the

GRAND GYMKHANA

Held at

EAGLEHALL

PATELEY BRIDGE

on

SATURDAY, AUGUST 15th, 1931

Opened at 2-30 p.m. by

THE RIGHT REV. THE LORD BISHOP OF RIPON

PROGRAMMES	::	ONE PENNY

Above: *Sledging the coffin of Dr Barwick down Eagle Hall Lane in 1947.*

Left: *Programme of the Grand Gymkhana at Eagle Hall, 1931.*

her great-nephew, the Hon. Henry Edmund Butler, the eldest son and heir of Viscount Mountgarret of Nidd, who with his wife Mary Eleanor lived in the hall for several years. According to Speight in *Upper Nidderdale* (1906), he used it first as a shooting lodge.

Gardens were laid out in front of the hall and shrubs and heathers planted along the drive from the lodge. Around the lakes and lining the drive there were wonderful displays of azaleas and rhododendrons and the marshy part near the lakes was a picture with flowers of the primula family. Paths were laid out and covered with gravel, but sadly, at the time of writing the grounds are overgrown. The Lodge was built in 1888 and is inscribed with the date and the initials H.E.B.

In 1893, the Home of Rest was built further up the hill towards Greenhow, to be used as a convalescent home and maintained by the 14th Viscount Mountgarret 'for the benefit of deserving persons resident within the city of Bradford.' It was also used by local people – my Auntie Annie spent several weeks recuperating there after suffering from double pneumonia in 1923. Before the Second World War conditions were regularly surveyed by Mr Davies, a government inspector who married the matron when his wife died. During the war babies and children under the age of five were housed there. There was a shortage of staff in the summer of 1942 so my friend, Joyce Longster, and I walked every night from Pateley to help bath the babies. Joyce actually lived in the house for three weeks during her vacation from college. Olwen Beresford was the matron from 1946 when there were 33 children in residence. She left in October 1948 to marry John Wright and was succeeded by Sister Appleby. The home was auctioned on Friday 12 July 1968. It had a private chapel and after the sale Sam Firth transported the altar stones to the Parish Church in Pateley where Fred Spence senr used them to build the altar in the Lady Chapel. When the building was converted to private houses it was renamed Arthursdale Hall but, after further construction work, is called Nidderdale Hall at the time of writing.

In St Cuthbert's Church, Pateley Bridge, there is a brass plaque inscribed to Mary Eleanor Butler of Eagle Hall. She died on 12 May 1900 and left money for the maintenance of a district nurse. The money covered not only the nurse's uniform and salary, but also the necessary medicines and medical equipment. Nurse Eggers was the last nurse to benefit and completed her 20 years of service in 1947.

For many years Miss Barwick and her brother lived at Eagle Hall. She was the Girl Guide Commissioner and the Rangers met weekly in a room over the stables under her leadership. When I was the local Brown Owl I remember going with Tawny Owl (Joyce Longster) to gather bluebells and greenery from Eagle Hall grounds to decorate the Brownie lorry in the procession to Bewerley Park.

Girls' Friendly Society dancing on the lawn at Eagle Hall in 1932. The leaders are Edith Atkinson and Cherry Spence and the girl on the left is Renee Swires, next her sister, Joyce.

Miss Barwick also contributed each year to our Brownie jumble sale. Gymkhanas and fêtes were held in the grounds to raise money for the church. There were displays of country dancing by members of the Girls' Friendly Society run by Edith Atkinson and Cherry Spence. Stalls and games were set up around the lawn. When her brother died, Miss Barwick left the hall, which remained empty. Then, in 1950, Miss Bennett and her sisters opened it as a boarding-school for girls, and boys under the age of eight, with an average number of 50 pupils on roll. The name given to the school was 'The Carradyls', meaning 'the wooded hollow among the hills'. Miss Bennett had been the headmistress at Bolton Percy before moving to Eagle Hall, where she stayed for 14 years. Sadly, her sister Hazel died whilst there, but she and her other sister, Mrs Elizabeth Knowles, told me what pleasure they had from the lovely flowering shrubs in the grounds.

They remember the eels in the lakes and the paths in the woods. The two small lakes in the grounds are below an old lead-mine entrance and are believed never to have frozen over because of the warmth supplied by the water flowing from under the ground. This supply is known as Eagle Level, which has a fine carved stone over the entrance with the inscription 13 July 1825, the date it was opened. It was the source of Ripon-Pateley Rural Council Regional Water Scheme and provided a piped supply to the area. In 1959 it was taken over by the Claro Water Board which drew more than a million gallons of water each day. In 1972 mining engineers surveyed the 8,000-foot-long tunnel. After 173 years in operation, Yorkshire Water abandoned this source in 1998 because parasites were found in it, although it was one of the few supplies with natural fluoride content.

Mrs Edwards bought Eagle Hall from Lord Mountgarret and was the last person to live in it as one dwelling. She sold it piecemeal and in 2003 not only the hall, but also the buildings around the courtyard, have been converted to private houses.

Chapter 3

BEWERLEY HALL

Muriel Swires

In 1674 the Yorke family left Gouthwaite and bought the manor of Bewerley, moving to establish their family seat there. John Yorke (1733–1813) was responsible for changing the earlier Bewerley Hall. He built two east towers on the old house and added the morning-room and the room above it. Later, in 1832, another John Yorke made further alterations, enlarging the bow-windows and re-fronting the south side. He built on the third tower and the east wing. At the time of writing all that is left is one of the stone towers, without its conical cap, in the garden behind the chapel.

The main approach to the hall was by the Lodge (built in 1832) at the entrance to Bewerley Park. The long drive is still there, winding through the Nidderdale Agricultural Society's showground.

As the picture *(above right)* shows, the hall was surrounded by extensive lawns and gardens and some years ago two elderly ladies, who had been the first two women gardeners employed by Squire Yorke during the First World War, visited the museum.

The gardens at Bewerley Hall and the monastic chapel.

During the years spent at Bewerley, members of the Yorke family were responsible for laying out walks in Ravensgill and Fish Pond Wood and for building the Two Stoops in the first decade of the nineteenth century. Although a folly, this was of practical benefit

The entrance to Bewerley Hall.

Bewerley Hall.

Above: *The Three Stoops. During a period of economic depression, c.1800, John Yorke of Bewerley Hall gave 4d. and a loaf of bread daily to each man building the mock ruin. On 17 November 1893 one stoop blew down in a gale, so since then it has been known as Two Stoops.*

Above: *The tower at Bewerley Hall is the only original part of the hall remaining.*

Below: *The beck in Bewerley Park.*

A Sunday-school treat in Bewerley Park. The hall can be seen in the background.

Bewerley Hall in 1905. Thomas Brown is on the far left, centre row.

to local labourers and farm workers during a time of depression because each man was paid 4d. and a loaf of bread daily – just enough to keep starvation at bay.

Schools owed much to the generosity of the Yorke family, particularly those at Bewerley and Bridgehousegate. Several churches also received benefits. In St Cuthbert's Church, Pateley Bridge, the fine organ was given by Thomas Edward Yorke in 1899. There is also a stained-glass memorial window to the Yorke family, made by the firm Wailes of Newcastle, which cost £63. Their coat of arms was granted to Richard Yorke (1430s–98) and the motto was taken from Psalm 18 – *'Per Meum Deum Transilio Murum'* – 'with the help of God I can scale any wall'.

When Thomas Edward Yorke died in 1923, aged 90, the estate had to be sold. He was buried in the family vault beside his youngest son and sister Fanny, as were other members of the family. A cross in Nidderdale marble marks his grave.

The sale catalogue in the museum describes the hall as an imposing structure. The ground floor's main rooms were the ballroom, morning-room, drawing-room and domestic quarters. The first floor had 15 bedrooms. Nearby were the laundry, wash-house, bakery, coal house, storerooms and stables.

The 70-acre park was bought by John Todd of Northallerton who later sold it to the Nidderdale Agricultural Society. In 1939, 19 acres were trans-ferred for £1,900 to be used as a camp school. The many other properties included Bewerley Chapel, Pateley Bridge Auction Market, the Yorke Arms Hotel, 36 farms and practically all the cottages and buildings in Bewerley. The estate also sold a 9,000-acre grouse moor at Heathfield and Ramsgill as well as mineral rights, manorial rents, quarries, fishing and shooting rights. The sale lasted three days.

So, after nearly 400 years in Nidderdale, the association with the Yorke family ended. All that survives of Bewerley Hall is the grassed-over site on which the building stood, the north-east tower, the knot-garden and three stained-glass windows which are in Nidderdale Museum.

Today Bewerley Chapel remains. It was given by Dame Mary Yorke in 1678 to be used as a school which continued until 1818 when Squire Yorke gave two cottages in Bridgehousegate to be converted for a school and house for the schoolmaster. However, Mrs Yorke disapproved of the master so she kept Bewerley School open until his death in 1830. After being used for several different purposes, including a joiner's workshop, it was restored for worship in 1965, a gem of peace and quiet.

JOHN BRADFORD

Some time ago a collection of papers and books was sent to me which had belonged to John Bradford. They are handwritten and contain much interesting information and are now in Nidderdale Museum.

Right: *John Bradford in 1808.*

Below: *John Bradford's family. Pictured are his great-great-uncle John Appleby, great-aunt Emma and grandfather Race. The photograph was taken by the Pateley Bridge photographer, Percy H. Marsden.*

John Bradford was born in 1782, the son of the agent at Hornby Castle, the seat of the Osborne family, dukes of Leeds. In the collection are two of his school books dated 1797 and '1798 Hornby'.

John joined the Army with a commission of ensign at Richmond in Yorkshire on 8 August 1807. The photograph *(top)* is taken from a painting done in 1808 and shows him in his uniform. Enclosed in the collection are two letters, one from his sister and the other from his father, written to him when he was in the Army. An excerpt from his sister's letter says:

... your birthday was not forgot by us. I purpose going to Richmond tomorrow to procure calico for a dozen shirts which I will get Nancy Townshend to make with the greatest expedition...

From his father's letter, written three weeks later, we learn that:

Your calico shirts are in great forwardness, and I expect by the time this reaches you, they will all be finished, half a dozen of them being ruffled before your letter arrived, the other half dozen will be plain, with two night shirts of the same kind of stuff but coarser.

Why he left the Army is not known but by 1814 he was living in Pateley Bridge and was agent to Squire Yorke of Bewerley Hall. In his book of 1814 we get quite a detailed picture of the duties of an estate agent. Here are a few selected entries:

Two Guineas Reward
Whereas some evil disposed person or persons, did some time last night cut and injure the leaden pipes, which convey water through the Fish Pond Wood to Bewerley Hall, now this is to give notice that whoever will give information of such offender or offenders they shall upon conviction receive a reward of two guineas. Bewerley Hall July 21, 1814.

Bewerley Moor
This is to give notice that if any person or persons are detected burning the ling upon the moor or commons within this manor they will be prosecuted according to law. By order of John Yorke Esquire, Lord of the said Manor. John Bradford. 7.3.1815.

Bewerley Hall, March 10, 1816. M.J. Whaites
You will have the goodness to ship 500 pieces of Major Yorke's lead marked JY for Hull and consign the same to Simon Horner, Jun., Esq. and you will acquaint me with the weight thereof and also what number of pieces remain on the Wharfe at Ripon, J.B.

March 27, 1816. Joseph Smith
We think it proper to appraise you that if you do not quit the cottage house which you occupy under Mr Yorke in Bewerley, we have his express direction to proceed to eject you.

Bewerley Hall, June 1817
All persons not having business at the hall are particularly requested to refrain from walking about the grounds...

Turnip stealers
Whereas some evil disposed persons are in the habit of pulling turnips, breaking down fences and doing other damage to the tenants of John Yorke...

Sabbath breaking
Whereas complaints have been made that certain persons not only break the Sabbath but also molest and disturb the inhabitants of the Chapelry in the exercise of public worship on the Lord's day, particularly at Greenhow Hill.
  This is therefore to give notice that any person or persons who will give information to the chapel warden of such offenders steps will be taken to put the law in force... Chapel Wardens: John Bradford and George Whitley.

There are many more interesting entries relating to water rights, boundary disputes and threat of evictions to tenants unable to meet their dues.

At yearly Court Leet meetings in Bewerley Chapel, as well as at Ramsgill and Appletreewick, tenants were requested to attend to pay their rents.

John Bradford ended his days at Kell House and died there in 1845. He is buried in St Cuthbert's churchyard, Pateley Bridge. His relatives, the Applebys, continued to live at Kell House throughout the nineteenth century; they were stone merchants and quarry owners. Miss Elizabeth Appleby was the last of the family and after her death all the antique furnishings were sold by auction in the house on Wednesday 11 July 1900. Among the 301 items for sale were rare specimens of old oak and Chippendale furniture. There was also an elaborately carved brown oak side-table, supported by six turned pillars having moulded rail and carved frieze, dated 1600 and said to have come from Gouthwaite Hall. It was priced at 31 guineas. This sale catalogue was also among the papers and is now in the museum.

Right: John Bradford's aunts, the Misses Appleby.

Kell House on Ripon Road, where John Bradford ended his days.

Left: *The fox-head well in 1852, before its removal to the top of Pateley High Street.*

Right: *Bridgehousegate well is now used only for flowers.*

Left: *The well in Bewerley village.*

Below: *Bewerley village in the 1890s. The lady on the left is at the well, waiting for her bucket to fill.*

Chapter 4

WATER, WATER, EVERYWHERE
Muriel Swires

In and around Pateley Bridge there are many wells and horse troughs, some of them still functional but no longer used, others blocked up. One of these, standing in the flower-beds at the top of the High Street at the time of writing, used to be situated in Souter, between Well House and Woodclose, and for generations it served the people living there. The date inscribed on it is 1852 and the spout was a lead fox head, made in Todd's foundry at Summerbridge. The original has been removed and is now preserved in the Nidderdale Museum.

In the 1920s a local doctor living at Fog Close considered this water the purest he knew and drank it as often as possible. Obviously, no one worried or was even aware of lead poisoning in those days. In 1980 it was decided to restore and move the well to where it is at the time of writing, with the permission of the owner, Mr Geoffrey Buller, the work being done by Harrogate Borough Council's Parks and Gardens Department. Mr Charles Smith, the metal-work tutor at Upper Nidderdale High School, made the perfect copy of the fox-head spout which can be seen at the time of writing.

In Bridgehousegate there are two wells which also had fox-head spouts made at Todd's foundry, but these have long since disappeared. The house which stood opposite these wells until 1977 had 'Wells Cottage' engraved in the stone lintel over the door. In 1876 the headmaster at Bridgehousegate School received complaints from people using the wells that the children coming to school were washing there and making the water unfit for even the horses to drink. Consequently, orders were given that 'a pail of water be always placed in the school yard for washing.' At the time of writing the wells just feature flowers and plants.

I don't remember either the Souter or the Bridgehousegate wells in operation, but I do remember the Bewerley one in use. It had a metal frame placed across the stone basin and the ladies put their buckets under the tap and while the buckets filled they enjoyed a chat and exchanged gossip. It was quite a social occasion and, no doubt, a welcome break from housework. Mr Alan Foxton recalls taking a handcart with a large milk churn to fill at this well for washing days. He also remembers on Sundays taking a jug to fill for the midday meal.

In 1873 the Medical Officer, Dr Edward Warburton, in his report for Pateley Bridge Board Of Guardians, stated that there was plenty of water, but it was too far from the houses around the High Street and so people were taking it from open watercourses in the street. He said only six houses had piped water and he attributed freedom from epidemics to the merciful providence of God. A few years later an epidemic did break out, which stimulated a campaign for a piped supply. However, the owner of the most suitable spring refused to have it tapped. Bishop Keld, at Blazefield, was the next possibility, but George Metcalfe pointed out that this was now serving the mill and village of Glasshouses. He did offer Lady Well, high above Fellbeck, but the cost of piping it four miles was prohibitive to a population which had hitherto paid nothing. There was much arguing and correspondence in the *Nidderdale Herald*. In the end the owner of the original source relented, but it was several years before the matter was finally settled.

THE DAM STAKES, PATELEY BRIDGE

Fine summer evenings in the 1930s saw many people lining the riverbank at the Dam Stakes, Pateley Bridge. They were watching the swimmers and would-be swimmers enjoying themselves. The changing hut provided was paid for by Mr Marshall, a farmer of Hartwith Top, and built by the brothers Alan and George Thorpe. Up to this time the swimmers had to undress behind the bushes and leave their clothes there, so the provision of somewhere to change was greatly appreciated. Season tickets cost a shilling. One half of the hut was for the boys, the other for the girls. Attached to the walls inside were narrow wooden seats, and on the floor were duckboards. Above were many hooks, and it was often a scramble to find an empty one on which to hang one's clothes. Outside the air resounded with shrieks of laughter and noisy splashes. Some nights Police Sergeant Light would be at the water's edge holding a long pole or long string with a webbed harness attached to it for the purpose of guiding and encouraging the beginners.

My cousin and I decided to knit our own bathing costumes. Mine was in dark brown wool and hers in orange and white. Little thought was given to how the wool would absorb the water. Imagine, then, our

The opening of the bathing hut, Pateley Bridge, on 19 July 1929.

On the steps used for diving and jumping into the river. From the top: *Muriel Swires, Nora Harwood, Peggy Harwood.*

Muriel Swires on the steps of the bathing hut, 1935.

dismay and the feeling of horror when, after we had jumped proudly into the river in our new knitwear, the costumes slowly sagged down to our ankles! Then there was the further embarrassment of having to struggle out dragging the waterlogged garments clinging to our bodies and the sigh of relief when we reached the safety of the hut without attracting too much attention.

No changing hut was needed by the holiday-makers because alongside the Dam Stakes, on the extended railway line, LNER coaches were stationed. They could be hired weekly by people travelling to Pateley Bridge by train.

Near the changing hut was a spring diving-board and on the opposite bank a tree had been pruned to accommodate further diving bases and a swing. A ladder was provided to reach the highest level, but this was for the more adventurous and able swimmers.

The sense of achievement when you first swam across the river to the deep side and the thrill as you climbed onto the swing before plunging into the depths below were unbelievable. No swimming since has given the same feeling of exhilaration that I experienced after dips in the River Nidd at the Dam Stakes.

A little way upstream a thick rope was fixed across from bank to bank and firmly anchored. This was the division between the swimming and boating areas. Mr Reg Longster, who owned the land on the Recreation Ground side, hired out rowing-boats and a punt. He also opened a small kiosk selling sweets, etc. Boating became a popular pastime. My friends and I enjoyed many happy hours rowing on the river and one friend had a clumber spaniel who insisted on being in the boat with us, not only drenching us whenever he shook himself but also dangerously rocking the boat, with the inevitable result.

Sadly, these happy times ended with the outbreak of war in 1939, when the local Home Guard found a use for the hut and removed it. Later, in the summer of 1943, tragedy struck when a boy lost his life trying to rescue a girl who had got into difficulties in the deep water, and the following year a Scout drowned in almost the same place.

Left: *In the river at the Dam Stakes, Pateley Bridge, 1934.*
Left to right: *Joyce Lowcock, Nora Coates (holding her dog, Bill), Renee Skaife, Muriel Swires, Joyce Longster.*

Below: *The paddling pool in the Recreation Ground, Pateley Bridge.*

Left: *Construction of the Southlands estate, 1964.*

Below: *Manchester Square. On the left is the Midland Bank with Mrs Green's paint shop, later the hairdressers', in the centre and Todd's hardware shop (an Indian restaurant in 2003) on the right.*

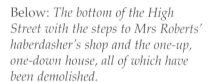

Below: *The bottom of the High Street with the steps to Mrs Roberts' haberdasher's shop and the one-up, one-down house, all of which have been demolished.*

Chapter 5

PATELEY BRIDGE

HIGH STREET
Muriel Swires

Some gaps in the High Street that give access to the Southlands car park were once filled with shops. According to H. Speight, in *Upper Nidderdale* (1906), at the bottom of the High Street was a quaint building with a clock on its gable. This, he said, had been an inn called the Miners' Arms, kept by Matthew Dickinson in the early-nineteenth century. It was thought unsafe in 1906, but it was not until 25 August 1947 that it finally collapsed. In 1900 four premises occupied the area where the flower-beds are at the time of writing: Ingleby Thorpe, watchmaker (in the building that fell down); John King, bootmaker and clogger (he later moved to the opposite side of the street); James Ingleby, hairdresser (the barber's pole of red-and-white stripes can be seen on many old photographs of this section of the street); and Percy H. Marsden, photographer, tobacconist and stationer.

The fifth building is still extant and was the premises of Charles Todd, cycle agent, ironmonger and general dealer. He sold wringing machines, sewing machines, bicycles, tricycles, churns, chains, bedsteads, mattresses, door mats, baskets, brushes, oil-lamps, stoves, oils, paints, varnishes, toys, glass, china, earthenware and fancy goods. He also hired out cycles. His son Walter followed in the business and at the time of writing the building houses an Indian restaurant.

When I knew these buildings in the 1930s and '40s, Dave Lawson had the tobacconist's up the steps at the bottom of the street, William Marshall the cobbler's, Albert Johnson the one-up, one-down house and Mrs Roberts' haberdasher's shop was up the second flight of steps next to Walter Todd's hardware shop.

Quite often on Saturdays the open space was filled with stallholders like 'Pot' Morrison who sold every kind of potware imaginable. Originally the Market Hall had been at the bottom of the High Street on the opposite side, where the Bridgeway Store and Restaurant stand at the time of writing. The address of John Bell & Son, general drapers, clothiers and outfitters, was 'Market House', Pateley Bridge.

Several old shops (one occupied by Mrs Kaberry for 50 years) were demolished to make way for the Midland Bank in 1894. To widen the street the bank was set back 5 feet from the old frontage – the

bank insisted on this and paid a cheque for £100 for it to be carried out. In the yard under the arch was Mr Wray's warehouse, later removed for a garage for the bank manager. Facing this was Mrs Green's painting and paper-hanging business. In the 1930s this became a hairdressers' run by two sisters, Alice and Mary Light. The younger one was a great fan of the film star Norma Shearer and on the wall on the right as you entered the salon was an enormous poster of her with an Eton crop haircut, the fashion of the day. On the right of this establishment the row of houses was locally known as Todd's Yard, but in *Robinson's Directory* was entered as Harker Square. Behind Todd's shop was access to the station yard and the rear

Pateley Bridge High Street in the 1920s.

41

Above: *The bottom of the High Street with the signal-box and level-crossing gates. The large gate on the right was the entrance to the station yard.*

Right: *The cobbled street with the Black Bull, which was demolished to make way for Southlands car park.*

Left: *Bay Horse yard. In the background is the gable of the tourist office and the Black Bull yard. On the right is the back of the Bay Horse Hotel, including the lean-to. On the extreme right is part of the rear of the fish-and-chip shop.*

High Street with the oldest buildings on the left.

John Hardy outside his butcher's shop in 1920.

entrance to the station platform. I can recall many mornings when scurrying children dashed through this gap to catch the train for school in Harrogate.

Further up the street is the main entrance to Southlands car park. Here, until the 1950s, were the Bay Horse Inn and the Black Bull. Both were demolished together with the seven houses in Maltkin Yard and part of Ripley Row. The two inns looked onto the stone cobbles of the High Street, which were covered with tarmac in the 1950s. At the beginning of the century the Bay Horse Inn not only provided accommodation for cyclists, wines and spirits of the best blends, cigars of the choicest brands and dinners, but it also had in the yard (behind) a dame-school for very young children. Later in the 1920s and '30s it had a popular fish-and-chip shop approached via steps at the front.

Little evidence remains of these old buildings at the time of writing, but in their place we have flower-beds and a large car park and the entrance to the housing estate also called Southlands.

THE PATELEY BRIDGE COCOA HOUSE
Eileen Burgess

Cocoa houses were established in the 1870s to combat the heavy drinking which took place in pubs, the refuge for working men from their overcrowded cottages.

In 1879 the Hon. Henry E. Butler of Eagle Hall called together the ministers of the town, John Yorke of Bewerley Hall and certain other worthies, with

The Pateley Bridge Cocoa House with the fire-engine parked alongside.

Ripley Oddie as secretary, to form a steering committee to establish a cocoa house in Pateley Bridge. After canvassing the townspeople, they negotiated for premises in a new building adjoining the gasworks in Millfield Street. A limited liability company was formed with £1,000 possible capital in £1 shares, directors having to hold a minimum of five. The prospectus stated that the purpose was:

... wholesome refreshment and social recreation with no intoxicating liquors. Open from 6am, for men going to work, to 10pm. Coffee, tea, cocoa 1d, per mug, bread, cheese, rolls and butter, etc., on sale. Newspapers and periodicals in reasonable numbers. To be registered as a lodging house.

The Mechanics' Institute transferred into the building, bringing its library and reading-room and paying a rent equal to its income.

Just about everyone who considered himself anyone subscribed – the list is a mirror of the relative social standing of the subscribers. Mr Butler himself bought 200 shares, Mr Yorke and George Metcalfe 25 each, the professional men 10, and the small traders one each, but the average was five.

The house furnishings are listed in detail in the minutes. The centre room on the top floor was equipped as a six-bed dormitory, and the partitioning could still be seen until the mid-nineteenth century. There was one private bedroom on the middle floor, which also held the boardroom and reading-room. The ground floor had a bar and recreational facilities such as chess and a billiard table.

J.W. Green from Halifax was appointed manager at 15s. a week, for which he was expected to be caretaker, barman and librarian as well as supervising the general conduct of the place. His wife had to cook and clean as required, with no other help than that they found themselves.

Why it was called the 'Royal Cocoa House' we do not know, but it sounded prestigious! The opening celebrations took place on 4 February 1880, starting with the Pateley Bridge Brass Band meeting the noon train. Mr John Yorke made a short speech at the entrance and dinner was served at 1p.m. – 1s.6d. for ladies, 2s.0d. for gentlemen – to musical accompaniment. The band members then had their dinners and played again over teatime. They then led a procession up to the Oddfellows' Hall on Church Street for an evening meeting.

The directors took it in turns to supervise the manager and the board met monthly. Party catering was a profitable feature, but Mr Butler complained on one occasion that he had brought friends and they had been unable to obtain refreshments. Green was ordered sternly that he must always keep a supply of tinned meats available and be prepared to send out for a chop or steak if required.

The gasworks soon proved to be an inconvenient neighbour – the retort house abutted onto the building, so there was an ever-present risk of fire, and provisions could not be kept in the bar. Eventually the retort house was moved and the Cocoa House was enlarged – Mr Butler lending the funds. The problem was then reversed – the bar was too cold! A series of stoves was tried, with little success.

The extra space provided an assembly room for concerts and social gatherings. Local organisations could use it for meetings and rehearsals.

Unfortunately, from the outset, the venture did not succeed as had been hoped. Almost immediately there was a downturn in trade generally, and wages were reduced. There were problems with bad debts – a man called Newstead left without paying his board-and-lodging bill.

In March 1882 J.W. Green left, his place being taken by George Hawkin who had a bread round and a large family. He was appointed at 12s. a week, perhaps not too bad when there were several mouths being fed. The older girls could help with the work, but the younger children were to be kept firmly out of sight. When, on one occasion, the family wanted to take a day-trip to the sea, Mrs Hawkin and the girls were graciously given permission to go, but Hawkin himself had to stay behind and mind the shop – there was no provision at all for holidays.

In March 1884 the first and only dividend of five per cent was paid. A total of 815 shares had been taken by 104 people, of which 382 were fully paid up. Of those who received dividends, 20 returned theirs as gifts.

Later that year there was a quarrel with the Mechanics' Institute, which the directors wished to control directly. There was a very acrimonious meeting, reported in full in the *Nidderdale Herald*, with opposition led by the Metcalfe family. The Institute withdrew, taking its library and periodicals with it. As the 'Articles of Association' specifically stated that a library was to be available, something had to be done quickly. An appeal was made for people to give books and a grand gala was organised in Bewerley Park.

Special trains from Doncaster, Bradford and Leeds were laid on, the Stanningley Band leading a procession of travellers from the station to Bewerley Park. Tours of Ravensgill Woods, Guisecliffe and Bewerley Hall gardens were offered and there were refreshments and band concerts, ending with dancing until 8p.m. A profit of £40 was made, but the great mystery is how the event was ever organised, since more than half of the board were out of the area for the entire preparation period of five weeks.

Trouble was also brewing domestically. For some time the board had had suspicions about George Hawkin and the amount of food supposedly consumed by his family. In July 1885 he was asked to account for 21 rolls of butter, each weighing 1½lb, and 115lbs of ham, when the average weekly takings were about £6. He was offered the chance of resigning after Pateley Feast, which he did, but left the till £4 short. His successor was an ex-soldier called Lewis, who stayed only a few months and was also very unsatisfactory. At the same time J. Shuttleworth threatened court action for an unsettled plastering bill. In addition, the income-tax collector was demanding tax for all the years of operation, which the board refused, offering to pay only for the one dividend declared.

Matters improved temporarily when the next manager, a Mr Haviland who had previously worked at Eagle Hall, took over. He raised standards in both house and food, and in nine months took £42 more than the whole previous year. Unfortunately, running the library of books which had been collected interfered with his other duties, so borrowing times were cut to Wednesday and Saturday, 3 to 7p.m.

One of the attractions of the Cocoa House had always been the billiard table, but as soon as the King's Arms installed one, the takings at the temperance venue halved – alcohol still had its attractions. By March 1888 the receipts were lower than the expenses and there were arrears of rent and an unpaid loan of £248. The Hon. H.E. Butler took over the running himself as he felt that there might be more trade once the reservoir construction began – as he was in sole charge there were no more board meetings.

By 1893 he was no longer resident in Pateley Bridge and, although there were suggestions that the High Street might be a better venue, further outside calamities – epidemics of influenza and smallpox and a disastrous flood – brought the deficit to £100 and so the company and the Cocoa House closed. The Liberal Club took over the following year, eventually becoming the Social Club, which still occupies the ground floor at the time of writing. The minutes of the well-meaning, if patronising, venture were kept in Oddie's office until it closed in 1984 and were then given to Nidderdale Museum.

PARK ROAD
Muriel Swires

Several changes took place in Park Road, Pateley Bridge during the twentieth century. At the High Street end, the chemist's shop was for many years Mark Harrison's Nidderdale Supply Stores. In 1914 he was selling:

... quarter pound tins of cocoa for 4 ½d., guaranteed pure machine cut bacon, prime hams of rich flavour, Robinson's specialities of Peppermint Candy 1s. per lb., Magnet Toffee 8d. per lb, Home-made Ginger Wafers 8d. per lb, Calmuta Ceylon Tea 1s.8d., 1s.10d., and 2s. per lb.

It continued as a grocer's until 1957.

Between the chemist's and the Willow Restaurant was a dwelling and it was here the Mechanics' Institute met after leaving the Cocoa House in 1884. From the 1920s until the late '50s, the Willow was a sweet shop, then a bakery for a short time.

The row of cottages from here to Colbeck Lane was Tanners' Row, and one cottage still retains '4 Tanners' Row' on its door. These one-up, one-down cottages would, at one time, have housed the tanners,

Right: *Number 4 Tanners' Row.*

Left: *Part of Tanners' Row which was demolished to make way for the car park behind the Talbot in 1968/9. The shop with the shade over its front was Mrs MacLellan's greengrocery shop.*

Right: *Laying the date stone of the Memorial Hall in 1959. Left to right: Revd Woodmass (Congregational minister), Jim Fisher (builder), Major Collins, Jack Richmond (builder), Councillor Harold Lowcock (chairman of the committee).*

Left: *John Green and Harold Moorhouse outside the Universal Stores, which is the site of Scott House and Falcon House at the time of writing.*

whose job it was to tan the outer skin of bullocks in a solution of tannin from oak bark, a very smelly operation. The cottages at the end were demolished in the 1960s to make way for the entrance to the Talbot car park. Mrs MacLellan had her greengrocer's shop here before moving into the High Street.

Where the Memorial Hall stands at the time of writing was Fawcett's Field. James Fawcett was a builder and contractor during the First World War and for many years after. The Memorial Hall was built to commemorate the local men and women who served in the two world wars.

Across the road are two houses built in 1998, named Scott House and Falcon House, and so called because the builder was the son of Sir Peter Scott, the naturalist, and grandson of the explorer, Robert Falcon Scott. He carved motifs to commemorate them – two geese, a map of Antarctica and a dragonfly.

In 1913 Joseph Summersall had a garage with waggonettes here. In the same year Thackrey Summersall owned a draper's business in the High Street. He bought a large wooden hut from Angram, used as a mission hall during the construction of the reservoir, and placed it on the site. The building was taken over by the board school just across the road (now St Cuthbert's Primary School) for teaching practical subjects. One half was used for woodwork lessons with Mr Grant and the other half for cookery classes with Miss Fisher.

In the early 1920s, Thackrey Summersall converted the hut into 'The Universal Stores', advertising that it sold 'Everything required for Household Furnishing and Requisites'. Eventually, the building deteriorated and the roof became unsafe. Mr Summersall employed Edward Stoney to build a smaller one and erect it on the same site. When Jimmy Ross was manager in the 1930s you could buy anything from tennis rackets to carpets to menswear.

John Walker owned the hut in the 1940s and '50s and continued to sell household goods and menswear until his retirement, when his son, Dennis, took over. The premises were managed alongside the shop in the High Street, both in Summersall's and the Walkers' time, with the High Street shop selling ladies' clothing. The green hut was demolished in 1997.

Returning to the High Street, there is a blocked doorway facing Park Road which led upstairs to the priest's room where the vestments were kept and where the priest would robe before proceeding up the hill to St Mary's Church. In 1849 Edward Thackrey paid a tithe for the room. Mr John Walker told me, in 1964, that it still belonged to the Parish Church and he was still paying an annual tithe of 5s.

Where the mail vans are garaged at the time of writing was, before 1859, the Primitive Methodist Chapel. Two staircases led up to it, one for the men and one for the women. After 1859 it became two cottages with a butcher's shop below. Jack Sinclair, the poacher, is said to have lived there in his old age,

Hilton Pickard at his printing press, a Britannia Hand Press made by Porters of Leeds.

before going into the workhouse. At the corner with Back High Street, Hilton Pickard had a printing press and for many years printed programmes, tickets and posters for all the local events.

THE CINEMA
Muriel Swires

The cinema stood on what is at the time of writing part of the playground of St Cuthbert's Primary School, where the staff park their cars. Alongside had been a garage and taxi service run by Bob Weatherhead and Jack Suttill, which they started in 1919. Later, Mr Weatherhead moved his garage to Souter, where he lived, and Mr Suttill became a driver for the West Yorkshire Road Company on the Pateley Bridge–Harrogate route. The original garage buildings were still standing when the cinema was built.

Here also was the base of the Pateley Bridge Motor and Motor Cycle Club. These motorbike and motorbike-with-sidecar owners held regular rallies. I have a silver spoon won by my father in one of them and several trophies are displayed in Nidderdale Museum.

The cinema in Pateley Bridge, pictured here in the early 1930s, finally closed its doors to the public in August 1963.

THE BOOK OF NIDDERDALE

Pateley Boys' Brigade outside the cinema in 1934. Left to right, back row: Harold Lowcock (leader), Edwin Millward, Joe Derrick, Alan Heaton, George Hawkesworth, Norman Geldart, Maurice Pickering, Eric Heaton, Peter Thorpe, Jimmy Ross (second in command); middle row: Kenneth Geldart, Dick Richmond, John Wray, Archie Baines, Arthur Ibbotson, Stanley Longster, Tommy Stoney, ?, Walter Gibson; front row: Brian Wray, Jim Storey, George Hackney, ?, Selwyn Baines, Cyril Swires, Len Marshall, Norman Atkinson.

Judging the fancy dress in the Feast Field in 1935. In the background the cinema, school house and the 'Hut' on Park Road can be seen.

Sir William Nicholson of Summerstone Lodge had the cinema built in 1929. The date stone commemorating this is still there and reads 'W.N. & S. 1929'. The letters refer to William Nicholson & Son, a Leeds building firm. On completion Sir William was presented with a very fine large silver cigarette box, which now belongs to his great-nephew, also William. The building was constructed entirely of concrete, apart from one large stone at the rear. The fuel tank holding the diesel for the generator was taken from an aeroplane which had crashed on the moors. Mr Redgrave was the first manager and George Shillito operated the projector. Films were shown three nights a week on Thursday, Friday and Saturday, with Saturday having three showings – a matinée and two evening performances.

Each week the films were collected from Leeds by Christopher Summersall, the coal merchant, who brought them to Pateley on the back of his wagon. Sometimes he was very late and so you can imagine the panic getting everything prepared in time!

Left: *Dick Whittington (Joyce Longster) with his cat. The picture was taken in Simm Hutchinson's studio on Greenwood Road opposite the cinema.*

Below: *Barbara Irving's children's dancing class performing* Dick Whittington *on the cinema stage in 1934/5.*

There are some display cases on the wall in the long corridor at the museum which were used to advertise forthcoming films at the cinema. Mr Shillito provided part-time work for many local boys as his assistants – John Richmond, Roy Keighley, John Wilkinson, Bruce Storey and Norman Slater among them. Inside the building, apart from the projection room, there was a balcony with seating for 100 people, and the auditorium with seating for 182, although several of the front rows were later removed. Then there was the stage with two small rooms behind and a large basement downstairs.

The opening of the cinema was of great benefit to the local Operatic Society. Until this time their shows had been given in the Oddfellows' Hall, the building, a private house at the time of writing, next door to the Playhouse. Their first production here was the Gilbert and Sullivan opera *Ruddigore*, followed by *Patience* and their last, *The Gondoliers*.

The large cast for the shows used the small rooms behind the stage for the principals' dressing-rooms, but the chorus had to change together downstairs with no privacy whatsoever. In 1949, however, rods were fixed and curtains slung over to provide separate cubicles for teams competing in the Nidderdale Drama Festival.

In 1937 the newly formed Pateley Bridge Dramatic Society staged its first three-act play, *The Farmer's Wife*. The society rehearsed in private houses, the parish room, the assembly rooms, The King's Arms and others until they finally used the long room up the steps in the yard of The Crown.

With the outbreak of war the cinema was used as a base for many functions including ARP and Home Guard activities as well as first-aid demonstrations and lectures. Special variety concerts were given to raise money for the war effort, including 'Salute the Soldier Week', 'Wings for Victory Week' and 'Merchant Navy Week' among others. Mrs Hardy staged pantomimes. Most of Mrs Hardy's wartime concerts were rehearsed in the Red Shield Club, at the rear of the council offices.

The annual Police Ball and other whist drives and dances were held in the cinema. When all the seats were removed for these occasions one had to take care not to trip over the metal connecting fixtures on the floor.

After the war the Dramatic Society reverted to its two productions each year. It was 'all hands on deck' preparing the stage because after the late film on Saturday night the screen had to be dismantled and

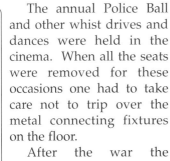

Left: Little Women, *a Dramatic Society production in 1948. Left to right:* George Hackney, Edgar Blagg, Madge Sutton, Ian Jefferies, Joyce Longster, Thelma Mann, Margery Todd, Muriel Swires.

Right: Boyd's Shop, *Pateley Bridge Dramatic Society's production on the cinema stage, 1951. Left to right:* Margery Todd, Brian Wray, Olive Dougill, ?, Alice Blamire, Bob Lowry, Michael Kelsey, Madge Sutton, Mabel Millard (seated), Ronnie Blamire, Arthur Johnson, Muriel Swires.

FRI. and SAT.   Nov. 22 and 23
ELEANOR POWELL in

Honolulu

Metro-Goldwyn's big scale music and dancing production.

WED. and THURS. Nov. 27 and 28
MICKEY ROONEY
in Mark Twain's

The Adventures of Huckleberry Finn

FRI. and SAT.   Nov. 29 and 30
ANNA MAY WONG and
J. CARROL NAISH in

The Island of Lost Men
Also
William Boyd as Hopalong Cassidy in
RANGE WAR

THE CINEMA
Pateley Bridge.

PROGRAMME
For NOV., 1940.

Times of Showing :
SATURDAYS at 5-50 and 8-0 p.m.
OTHER NIGHTS at 7-15 pm.

(Programme subject to alteration without notice).

FRI. and SAT.   Nov. 1 and 2
ALLAN JONES, MARY MARTIN
and Walter Connolly in

The Great Victor Herbert

Story of America's greatest composer.

WED. and THURS.   Nov 6 and 7
RONALD COLMAN and
IDA LUPINO in

The Light That Failed
By Rudyard Kipling.

FRI. and SAT.   Nov. 8 and 9
MICKEY ROONEY, LEWIS STONE
and Cecilia Parker in

Out West with the Hardys
A Metro-Goldwyn success.

WED. and THURS.   Nov. 13 and 14
RAY MILLAND and
ELLEN DREW in

French Without Tears

Don't miss this great British Comedy.

FRI. and SAT.   Nov. 15 and 16
LAUREL and HARDY'S
best Comedy!

Bonnie Scotland

WED. and THURS. Nov. 20 and 21
Paramount's full-length Cartoon in Colour.

Gulliver's Travels
Greater than "Snow White and the Seven Dwarfs."

Two cinema programmes from November 1940 and July 1941.

WEDS. and THURS.   July 23 and 24
GEORGE SANDERS and
SALLY GREY in

The Saint in London

Fiction's greatest character "The Saint" comes to London in pursuit of justice.
Also Lucille Ball in
PANAMA LADY

FRI. and SAT.   July 25 and 26
CLIVE BROOK
JOHN CLEMENTS
JUDY CAMPBELL in

Convoy

Don't miss this record-breaking British film.

WED. and THURS.   July 30 and 31
ANNA NEAGLE in

Nurse Edith Cavell
with George Sanders and
Edna May Oliver
Don't miss this outstanding film.

THE CINEMA
Pateley Bridge

PROGRAMME
For JULY, 1941.

Times of Showing :
SATURDAYS at 5-45 p.m.
and 8-0 p.m.
OTHER NIGHTS 7-15 p.m

Programme subject to alteration without notice.

WED. and THURS.   July 2 and 3
LITTLE BILLY LEE
HELENE MILLARD
and
"SNOWFLAKE"
in

God Gave Him a Dog
Paramount's great drama

FRI. and SAT.   July 4 and 5
BOBBY BREEN
LEO CARRILLO
HENRY ARMETTA in

Fisherman's Wharf
Also George O'Brien in
RACKETEERS OF THE RANGE

WED. and THURS.   July 9 and 10
JON HALL and
LYNN BARI in

Kit Carson
A big scale outdoor adventure film.

FRI. and SAT.   July 11 and 12
CHESTER MORRIS
WENDY BARRIE
C. AUBREY SMITH and
KENT TAYLOR in

Five Came Back
A highly dramatic film
Five to live—four doomed to the perils of the jungle—who would you save?

WED. and THURS.   July 16 and 17
GEORGE FORMBY in

Come on George
with Pat Kirkwood & George Carney
Great comedy of the turf.

FRI. and SAT.   July 18 and 19
CAROLE LOMBARD
CARY GRANT
KAY FRANCIS in

In Name Only
Three big stars in the year's most powerful drama

A Police Ball in the cinema. The photograph was taken from the stage and shows the edge of the balcony.

on Sunday morning the men had every bit of scenery and furniture to transport to the cinema while the ladies coped with costumes, properties and make-up, etc. There was hustle and bustle everywhere as the aim was to have the stage ready for a dress rehearsal in the late afternoon.

The amusing incidents and minor crises during these times were numerous. In *Queen Elizabeth Slept Here* the men pouring water from above to give the impression of the rain leaking through the roof didn't realise it would trickle down to the footlights until they saw the steam rising. One member of the society was prone to giggling and once started had difficulty stopping. In one scene of *The Ghost Train* she was supposed to be sleeping under a blanket, but to the consternation of the rest of the cast on stage the blanket started heaving and shaking. George Ellison devised revolving jars for the ghost train and they gave a most convincing effect of a train passing the two windows, but one night a wrong cue was given and both jars were started simultaneously from opposite sides and crashed in the middle.

Bookings for the plays were taken in the café of the Station Square fish shop. The last play presented on this stage was *Barnet's Folly* in March 1963.

When interest in films waned, Sir William Nicholson offered the building to the town for use as a village hall, but his offer was turned down. So George Shillito rented it and introduced bingo. New films were shown, after which Mr Edgar Hardcastle took over as bingo caller, but little interest was shown so this ceased in August 1963 and the cinema finally closed.

The West Riding County Council bought the building with the intention of converting it into a hall and gymnasium for the secondary school next door. However, it was found to be structurally unsound and was eventually demolished.

CHURCH STREET
Muriel Swires

As early as 1693 Church Street was recorded in the parish registers as Bend Lane. Other sources refer to it as either Ben Lane or Masons Lane.

In the 1950s, the buildings in the street were listed as being of special architectural interest. The east side was described as a charming row of eighteenth-century cottages with Georgian bow-windows, although they were demolished in 1959. The roof timbers and stone roof slates from one cottage were bought to re-use on the extension to a house because they were in such good condition and are still 'going strong' at the time of writing. The remaining shops are early-nineteenth-century stone-built houses with stone roofs and doors with simple stone surrounds. There are arched carriage entrances at both sides, opposite each other.

At the east side, just off the photograph *(see top left overleaf)* Dr Lumsden's surgery was on the corner until 1932 and later it was Edgar Hardcastle's shoe shop. Next door was the Oddfellows' Hall, built in 1855 at a cost of £700. It has been converted into private dwellings, but it started life as a meeting-place for members of the Independent Order of Oddfellows. This was a friendly society, operating a

Ben Lane, pre-1930s, before the bow-windowed
cottages were removed and the car park made.
In the foreground is the Primitive Methodist Chapel,
which is the Playhouse at the time of writing.

The Oddfellows' Hall, which is private
apartments at the time of writing.

Below: *The Playhouse was built in
1859 as a Primitive Methodist Chapel
and was used as the Salvation Army
Citadel between 1936 and the early
1960s. It was opened as a
theatre in 1968.*

Above: *Old yard under the arch on the west side of
the street, to the rear of the Apothecary's House.*

An advertisement under the arch on
the east side of the street.

The sign for The Cross Keys was on the corner of the
building. This eighteenth-century inn was first
called The Cricketers' Arms and then
The Shoulder of Mutton. The last landlord was
Mr George Naylor. This building has been
converted to private houses.

scheme for sick benefit and accident compensation, which was popular with quarry workers. It was established in Pateley Bridge c.1840 or earlier and there were between 200 and 300 members.

According to the *Ripon Chronicle*, on 21 June 1856 the Pateley Bridge Primitive Methodists assembled in the Oddfellows' Hall to take tea and 240 tickets were sold. This was repeated the following June when 210 members attended.

At a public meeting on 23 November 1882, the Pateley Bridge Choral Society was formed. *The May Queen* by S. Bennett was performed in the Oddfellows' Hall on 3 May 1883. The hire of the hall was 10s.6d. Miss Winkworth from Leeds was engaged as soprano for a guinea and Mr H. Parratt from Ripon as principal tenor, also for a guinea. The pianist was Mr Townsend from Leeds. This performance resulted in a loss of

£1.11s.10d., so it was decided to repeat *The May Queen* using local talent, which they did on 22 August 1883, with Miss Skaife as pianist and Mr T. Wilson as conductor. This time it made a profit. The following year a concert of Mendelssohn's *Hymn of Praise*, glees and songs made a profit of more than £5 and was very highly praised in the local press. There was a balcony at the back but the stage had to be erected for each performance. In 1884 a Broadwood grand piano was bought for £12.10s.0d., which had formerly belonged to Edward Yorke Esq. of Bewerley Hall – up to this time Miss Wise had lent her piano, free of charge.

Other activities took place in the hall: children from Bridgehousegate School held concerts there and St Cuthbert's Church had fancy bazaars in aid of the church improvement fund. The price of seats at a concert in 1889 was 1s.6d. for reserved chairs in front of the platform, 6d. for the gallery and 3d. for the body of the hall. In the 1920s Gilbert and Sullivan operas were performed including *HMS Pinafore*, *Iolanthe* and *Ruddigore*.

The Playhouse *(see opposite)* was built in 1859 as a Primitive Methodist Chapel which closed in 1933 when the Methodist connections united nationally. The Salvation Army was there from 1936 to the early 1960s and the Pateley Bridge Dramatic Society bought the building in 1963, converting it into a beautiful little theatre.

MARKET HALL
PATELEY BRIDGE.

VISITORS to Pateley Bridge should not fail to walk round the Market Hall. Best and Cheapest place in Town for PRESENTS of every description.   .   .   .   .   .

Left: *An advertisement for the Market Hall.*

Below: *The Market Hall, c.1910.*

The view from the church tower. In the foreground is the Market Hall and Court House (now a private dwelling).

Above: *Fog Close House, 1859, where John Snow, the famous epidemiologist, lived and worked before going to London. The Parish Church of St Cuthbert can be seen on the left.*

The shop next door in the early 1930s was Mrs Ibbotson's drapery before she moved into the High Street. Mr Arthur Geldart then had it as a grocery.

Moving down the cobbled street, the third bow-window belonged to Mrs Winn's sweet shop. Under the arch it is still possible to read part of the advertisement for Wellington Shirting. The last door led up the stairs to Mrs Sutton's café. Her cake shop had its frontage on the High Street. Across the street on the west side was Mrs Layfield's sweet shop, with the windows once looking onto Ben Lane now blocked. The main shop window still faces the High Street at the time of writing. It claims to be the oldest sweet shop in England. Enter the arch on this side and you come into a cobbled yard. Immediately on your left is perhaps the oldest house in the town with its very early door surround, tiny blocked fire window and small mullions. The original door is in the museum.

All that remains in Pullan Square is a stone plaque dated 1781 showing where Thomas Pullan, one of the earliest local Methodists, lived. Here is also the rear of Colbeck House, built in 1892 for the Oddy family, which is the Masonic Hall at the time of writing.

The cobbles were covered in the 1950s when those in the High Street were also resurfaced.

Chapter 6

A COMMUNITY AT WORK

THE BLACKSMITHS
Muriel Swires

Walk down Back High Street, Pateley Bridge, in the 1930s, and you would have seen the children congregating around the entrance to the blacksmith's shop on the corner. Sometimes there would be two or three horses waiting to be shoed. While the new horseshoe was being heated in the forge, Mr Harrison would scoop out the offending hoof and boys would collect the chipped-out bits to use in their catapults.

There was a certain fascination with watching the red-hot shoe being attached to the horse's hoof with the cloud of rising smoke, accompanied by a hissing sound and a horrible smell of burning. The

blacksmith's job was not an easy one and could sometimes be dangerous if the horse was nervous and restless. Apart from shoeing horses, the blacksmith did many other seasonal jobs. Children went to him to make their iron hoops and crooks for a favourite game of 'booling'. Some days, when the horses couldn't be brought to his smithy, Mr Harrison took a horse-drawn cart with a portable forge to the farms.

Before the days of tractors and other vehicles horses were essential in many walks of life; they were especially important for the farmers in the dale. They were also needed for transport on the roads. All the inns in Pateley Bridge had stables for coaches and horses. In 1968, when the decision was taken to make

Pateley Bridge smithy in 1941. William Harrison is pictured with Alan Iveson and an unknown man looking on.

Bewerley blacksmith's shop, c.1926.
Blacksmith J.T. Swires (left) and his eldest son, Francis,
are pictured with wheels awaiting their metal rims.
The man on the right is Clifford Hudson.

Blacksmith's Cottage, Middlesmoor.

a car park at the rear of the Talbot Hotel, stables providing accommodation for 15 horses and several coaches had to be demolished. The stables behind the King's Arms Hotel have been converted to shops, making a very attractive courtyard.

Formerly most of the carts and wagons had wooden wheels with iron rims, which were fitted by the blacksmith.

In Bewerley there were two blacksmiths' shops. Up to October 1924, when the Bewerley estate was sold by auction, Mr Swires paid an annual rent to Squire Yorke of Bewerley Hall for the smithy and buildings, which were constructed of stone and slate

Above: *Dacre Banks blacksmith, c.1910. Pictured are,* left to right: *Dick Rainforth (apprentice), Sam Moorhouse (blacksmith), Sarah Moorhouse, ?, Mrs Moorhouse, ? and Harry Abbott with the horse.*

and consisted of forge, store, gig house and cowhouse with standing for four. This smithy was finally closed in 1936 and the buildings converted into a bungalow. Mr Swires moved to Hill Top Farm, Bewerley, and he and his son Clifford went to Scar village to inspect the foreman's hut there, with a view to buying it. They did so, and it was moved to Hill Top for use as the blacksmith's shop.

Next door to Mr Harrison's smithy on Station Square was a popular sweet shop. It was small and almost tucked into the corner but the shelves held jars and jars of tempting goodies. As children we affectionately called it 'Gracie's' because the lady managing it was Mrs Grace Marshall. It was very handy for people waiting for the buses.

At the other side of the smithy was the entrance to the Feast Field. Here, every September, came the annual fair with stalls, roundabouts, swing boats and many other amusements. Feast Saturday and

Stockdales' blacksmiths, Birstwith, c.1910.

Show Monday attracted hundreds of local people and visitors. Trying to find someone in the crowd was like looking for a needle in a haystack. The whole place was seething with bodies and the air was filled with music and shrieks and the smell of frying fish and chips and hot dogs. Often the field was ankle deep in mud and straw had to be scattered to make it easier for people to walk.

During the rest of the year the field was used for other purposes but most of the time it was empty. The 'Rose Queen' was sometimes crowned here and fancy-dress parades were judged, like the one held to celebrate the Elizabeth II's coronation in 1953. A circus occasionally pitched a marquee on the site.

In May 1955 the blacksmith's shop and the sweet shop were demolished to make space for a bus station. This was soon completed and opened to the public in April 1956. Buses had been in service here from 1910 onwards. In the 1920s the well-established firm of Longster Bros was running school buses in the area as well as other regular services. Then, in 1928 the West Riding Yorkshire Road Car Co. took over. They offered an excellent service for many years but as more and more people travelled by car the station was used less so that by 1989 it became redundant. It was pulled down (and a bus stop with shelter erected in its stead) to make way for the building of the new health clinic. The old name lives on in the Feast Field Health Centre.

No longer can we walk down Back High Street and look over the Feast Field wall to picture images of swing boats and the fair, or the horses queueing at the smithy, but instead we see a row of houses, Blacksmith Court and Blacksmith Mews, which in name at least remind us of the past.

Above: *Haymaking at Wilsill, c.1910,
with the hay ready to take to the barn.*

Left: *A sledge-load of hay.*

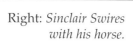

Right: *Sinclair Swires
with his horse.*

Below: *Sheep fair at
Pateley Bridge, c.1910.*

Above: *The office at Scotgate Ash Quarry.*

Right: *Entrance to a mine level at Lofthouse, 1904.*

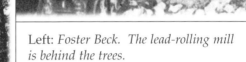

Left: *Foster Beck. The lead-rolling mill is behind the trees.*

Above: *An early motor car visiting the dale.*

Left: *Nidderdale Brewery, c.1860, soon after a major rebuilding in 1855, when it became John Metcalfe and Sons instead of J. & G. Metcalfe.*

Below: *A bird's-eye view of the brewery at the height of its prosperity in around 1890. Artistic licence has been employed in this picture, as it appears much larger than it was in reality. It does, however, show the details, such as the double-decked stables in the far yard. William Metcalfe's rival brewery can be seen in the far distance.*

Below: *Nidd Valley Brewery at Bridgehousegate, William Metcalfe's rival brewery, with its chimney on the extreme left.*

Chapter 7

GLASSHOUSES

Eileen Burgess

NIDDERDALE BREWERY

The Nidderdale Brewery was run by the Metcalfe family for nearly 140 years. In the photograph *(opposite)*, behind the trees on the left, can be seen the chimney and buildings before they were demolished in 1963. The drawing is an artist's impression of them at the height of the brewery's prosperity in the early 1890s. It should, however, be treated with great caution, since the far yard is only behind the Pateley Club, and not nearly at the bottom of the street as the drawing would suggest!

In 1771 Elizabeth Ragg, daughter of a Pateley Bridge tallow chandler, married Thomas Smith, a flax dresser of Hartwith. Two years later Thomas died but fortunately Elizabeth's father inherited the George and Dragon Inn (built in 1664 and usually known as The George) near the top of the High Street in Pateley Bridge, so she was able to support herself and her daughter with a home and income. Elizabeth became so successful at brewing that in 1777 she applied for a licence as a commission brewer, whereby she could sell her ales to other establishments. In order to accommodate the extra equipment needed, she bought adjoining property and water 'of remarkable purity' was piped from a spring on Panorama Walk 200 metres away.

It was through this venture that she probably met her second husband, George Metcalfe, an excise officer. They married in 1779 and were devoted to each other – there is a touching note from Elizabeth telling George not to worry, so long as they and the children were well, nothing else mattered. They were true partners in everything, although, since Elizabeth bore seven more children in the first ten years of her second marriage, George probably took over the day-to-day business affairs. We do tend to forget that, before the Victorian period, women were frequently equal partners with their husbands in commercial enterprises.

Elizabeth's first husband had been a flax dresser, and soon after their marriage George and Elizabeth were active in this field also. The flax was transported from Hull as a return load for lead being exported from the local mines. George and Elizabeth invested in the Smiling Fancy Mine on Greenhow, four miles away, and because lead required coal for smelting, they had shares in a local coal mine as well.

Four of their children were still surviving when their father died in 1798, and Elizabeth was once more alone. Until the two boys, John (15) and George (10), grew up she continued the businesses by herself. According to her grandson:

It is well known my grandmother managed her house well and engaged in brewing and kept many flax hecklers to provide linen for the spinning wheels for many miles around.

She rode to Hull each summer, taking one day for the journey of at least 60 miles there, one day for her business with lead, flax and grain merchants, and a third to ride home again. The block by which she mounted is still in the yard behind the inn.

One interesting short note in the firm's records is from John Bailey, a hop merchant in Skipton, 15 miles away, dated 15 May 1804, about blockading in the Napoleonic Wars – 'This packet of hops I should have sent to you earlier, but it has been detained by a French privateer.'

As John and George grew up they were gradually initiated into all their mother's concerns and by 1812 she was ready to take them into partnership. While George specialised in textiles at Shaw Mills, John seems to have been the one more interested in the brewing of ale and was keen to develop it from a very small output of 16 barrels a week, as the following year he entered into a long correspondence with John Richardson of Wilton about the secrets of making porter. Richardson was demanding 36 guineas for his information despite John pointing out that, as he only brewed 16 barrels a week, this could hardly be a profitable investment. In 1821 he made an entry at the Excise Office in Ripon of 'One Malt House, one Cistern, one Kiln, one Working and one Withering floors, likewise four rooms for the storing of Barley and Malt' – this is the only description of the buildings as they were at this time. He did continue to develop and tidy the premises, pulling down an old blacksmith's shop at the corner of the site, which improved the general approach down into Pateley. A malt kiln was operating just across the road, adjacent to the flax-heckling shop.

John had two surviving sons, George and William. As in the previous generation, George paid more attention to textiles, whilst William became involved in the brewery, although both were well acquainted with all aspects of the family's affairs and together they bought Scotgate Ash Quarry. By 1855 George senr had lost interest in the brewery, particularly since considerable reinvestment and rebuilding was required, although he retained a financial stake, and the brewing business was henceforward known as John Metcalfe & Sons.

The new buildings were erected on the eastern side of the site, going round the corner from the George Inn to the Ripon Road, whilst the lower half was converted into stables and warehouses. More men were taken on – from only 5 at the time of the 1851 Census to 17 some 30 years later, before the final enlargements were carried out.

In 1859 John had a stroke and was unable to take any further part in the business. When he died two years later his sons expected to be made full partners with their uncle in all the combined ventures. George senr disapproved of William, who was fond of gambling and drinking, and refused to allow him into the mill. When both nephews protested he declared he was the only partner, but secretly arranged a deal with George to exclude William. The younger brother asked that he might be at least allowed to buy or manage the brewery. When they refused, he stormed out of the family home for ever, on Pateley Feast Saturday in September 1862.

He had, however, already acquired some wealth and invested it in building a rival establishment, The Nidd Valley Brewery, across the river in Bridgehousegate. Unfortunately, there were problems with the water-supply and so it was never really successful. This brewery can be seen in the top right-hand corner of the drawing on page 60.

When George senr died in 1865 he left all his half financial share of the businesses to George junr. William decided to claim the quarter share left him by his father and, as he and his brother could not agree as to how the complicated mesh of property and business was to be divided, they started a long and costly legal battle, which went into arbitration in Leeds. The result was declared very much in George's favour – out of the property and assets valued at £25,000, William received £2,250, but only after expenses of £1,000 for George and £2,000 for William had been paid. William was thrown completely off balance and never spoke to his brother again, except to threaten, and possibly attempt, to shoot him, for which he was bound over for two years. Nearing the end of the period he renewed his vow, terrifying the family governess with his threats when he accosted her in the town. As it happened he died before he could carry out the threats, refusing to be reconciled even on his deathbed.

The new brewery was sold to two brothers. One, William Pullan, had been William's brewer and continued to manage it successfully. The other, the

landlord of the Somerset Hotel in Harrogate, went bankrupt and pulled his brother down with him.

When no buyer had appeared after six months, George bought the premises, but used them only for storage and as a base for the local Rifle Volunteers when they formed in the 1880s, so it became known as the Drill Hall. It was used as a public hall, and later as a gym and dining-room for the Bridgehousegate School a few yards away, until 1968 when it was closed on grounds of safety, and was eventually turned into flats.

George continued to develop the original brewery, refurbishing much of the premises in 1883. As well as the manufacturing buildings and a suite of offices, there were cask-washing sheds, hops stores, cooperage across the road and other workshops. The foundations can be traced in the garden at the top of the High Street. In the lower yard behind the George Inn were the double-decker stables for ten dray horses – because of the steep slope of the land both levels could be entered directly from the ground. The inn was closed and made into a house for the head brewer or travellers.

The range of products and their markets were expanded so that by the 1890s they were being exported all over Britain, and to France and Germany. At the end of the century the company

The brewery tower and the fermenting house in 1890 – compare this with the earlier drawing.

Anthony Busfield with a brewery wagon, 1907.

was producing a wide range of mild and pale ales, stout, porter and bitter pale ale, which was their best seller. By this time George had acquired several other inns, sometimes as a result of unpaid debts. In George's detailed account of the property holdings in the mid-1890s there are five inns in Pateley: The Crown, King's Arms, Shoulder of Mutton, Black Bull and Star, as well as the Birch at Wilsill, Prospect (Darley), Queen's Head (Kirkby Malzeard) and Joiners' Arms at Hampsthwaite.

In all their businesses, the Metcalfes were known for their fair and benevolent treatment of their workers, being always ready to listen to suggestions for their welfare and liberal with their treats. In addition to subscribing regularly and generously for the brewery workers' own supper, the third George responded to an idea from the cashier that a party for the wives and families would be appreciated. He provided a knife-and-fork tea for 70 men, women and children with a magic-lantern show and other entertainment. Light refreshments, tobacco and drinks were also on offer, although 'not one became overbalanced and all left at midnight.' The head

Above: *The approach to the High Street, c.1900. The earlier Wesleyan Chapel is on the left, the brewery chimney and buildings are behind the trees.*

Left: *The brewery just before its demolition in 1963.*

brewer and traveller, Henry Richardson, stayed with the Metcalfes for 37 years, retiring to take over a public house in Ripon.

As George's older sons grew up they, too, were incorporated into the concerns, with John specialising in brewing and the fourth George in spinning. A younger son, Herbert, was also interested in brewing and went to South Africa to learn more secrets of the trade. Many people find it hard to reconcile the fact that the Metcalfes were staunch Methodists as well as brewers, but the teetotal movement did not really take hold until the 1880s. They believed in moderation, not total abstinence, and continued to serve the Methodist Church as Sunday-school teachers, trustees and officials until almost the end of the century.

In 1896 the brewery became a private limited company and about the same time went into the bottling business. After their father's death in 1898, Herbert joined John and attempted to modernise the processes, but some methods were not appropriate and did not succeed. There was also a clash of personalities and, combined with the difficulties experienced in the spinning and stone trades, the businesses went into terminal decline and the brewery was closed in 1912, when the family went bankrupt.

John Smiths bought the premises but appear never to have used them for brewing. They were later used as a furniture store by an eccentric old man called Freddy Campbell, and became increasingly decrepit, until eventually they were condemned and pulled down in 1962. Now all that remains of the upper buildings is an oddly shaped garden at the top of the High Street with flagstones marking the lines of the walls. In the lower yard part of the stable block is a private dwelling, but the George Inn has returned almost to its original function, being the Pateley Club in 2003.

CASTLESTEAD

Coming into Pateley Bridge from Harrogate or Ripon and looking down to the valley floor, we can see a mansion – not enormous but impressive nevertheless with its Gothic turrets.

It stands on a bend of the River Nidd, high on a terrace. This is Castlestead, built by George Metcalfe (grandson of George and Elizabeth, m.1779) in the middle of the nineteenth century, half a mile from Glasshouse Mill which his father and uncle had acquired in 1828, and which he was effectively managing. The land was reputed to be the site of a Roman encampment, but whether it was a Romano-British villa or farm is not known. A later farmhouse was erected nearby.

George Metcalfe married in 1855 and moved into Grassfield Cottage, on the Low Wath Road, with his bride, Isabella Wilson, daughter of a Methodist minister, but he had wished for some time to build a house for himself. In his own account, George says that for several years he:

Castlestead soon after it was built.

... had frequently made overtures to Mr Burnaby, one of the partners with Sir Thomas and Mr Taylor White of the lead mines at Greenhow from whom J. & G. Metcalfe had been renting the rights for the weir for £20. Mr Burnaby had always replied that Sir Thomas had long before pledged to Mr Yorke of Bewerley Hall that if ever he sold Castlestead he should have the first offer of it. It had always been known that Mr Yorke was anxious to buy it.

George's chances seemed slight – he had to pursuade Mr Yorke to change his mind. But Mr Yorke was:

... most obdurate saying hard things to me for having a wish to buy it. Castlestead I have wanted all my life, Castlestead I must have. For Castlestead I will give any money, any money.

Mr Burnaby was much amused and discussed the matter with his partners. Bayne, the tenant farmer, paid £18 per annum, so they calculated that the asking price would be £900. Mr Burnaby offered it to Mr Yorke who refused, saying 'Too much, dear Mr Burnaby! Not that fair offer which one gentleman ought to make to another!'

When told Mr Yorke had declined, George was afraid that the price would be '4 ugly figures' but agreed the £900, plus £500 for the weir rights at the same time, on 5 May 1853.

Seven and a half years were to elapse, however, before the purchase was completed. Mr Burnaby

The weir near Castlestead, 1905.

evidently had reason to regret his sleight of hand, although he excused his dilatoriness to Mr Strother, the Metcalfe solicitor, by saying there were many problems with the mortgagees. He himself wished to get out of the contract and offered George £200 if he would relinquish his offer, but was refused. Eventually, on George's 34th birthday, 26 December 1860, the transaction was completed.

A year earlier, convinced that he would be the eventual owner, George had employed Messrs Major of Knowsthorpe, Leeds, to start laying out the gardens, making terraces and planting shrubs. To maintain them he engaged George Gray Watson who had been a gardener at Ripley Castle.

The building of the house started in April 1861, to plans drawn up by William Reid Corson, a member of the same firm of architects as employed for the mill. 'All the stone for grit purposes came from Mr Yorke's Wood under Crocodile Rock, and all the steps and landings from my own quarry at Scotgate.' Cowling and Barker, Glasshouses men who did much of the building work at the mill, did the mason's work at a cost of about £1,850 and George Grange the joiner's work for £1,550.

The Metcalfes moved in with their three children on 13 May 1862, a fortnight after the railway, which George had been instrumental in bringing into the dale, was opened.

Mr Hodgson, the engineer for the railway, drew up plans for an iron lattice bridge of 100-foot span across the river, by the weir. It was made in sections by Messrs Joice of Newcastle. Coming over a bridge at Gateshead, something happened to one of the railway trucks and one girder was hurled over, down into the street below, luckily without damage to passengers or traffic. However, there was a delay of about three weeks or so.

By the time the girders were delivered to the Glasshouse siding, the scaffolding and both piers were ready, and all was set for the erection of the bridge.

'John the Bridgeman' who was supervising:

... had got, as he thought, both girders planted. He turned away to say good-day to Young at the cottage when he heard a call and turning round had to his dismay to find that one of the girders had broken away from its binding chain and all lay broken and bent in the bed of the river.

However, after new castings it was eventually completed at a cost of £700.

The house was given a water-supply from the mill and in 1865 gas was also piped in. Between 1867 and 1877 outhouses were added – a vinery, stable extension, cowhouse, joiner's shop, archway and walls, iron gate and a billiard room over the coach-house. In 1876, the whole house was painted, papered, and decorated by Hummerstones of Leeds for £450, and the furniture and carpets were supplied by another Leeds firm, Constantines.

George and Isabella were very happy, with six sons and a daughter, until 1879, when she died suddenly from a stroke. Five years later George married the governess, Phoebe Annie Stranger, with whom he had another boy and girl, though he was too old and sick really to appreciate them. He died in 1898. Annie moved away, finding the house too big, and the two oldest sons, George (who also died suddenly, but in mysterious circumstances, in 1902) and John occupied the house in turn, the latter's wife managing it is an hotel.

In around 1906 an Indian cricket team is said to have lodged at Castlestead, presumably while playing at Headingley. In 1912 the family became bankrupt and the house was sold. During the First World War it was occupied by a girls' school for a while, then it became an hotel. During the Second World War children from the Hull Sailors' Orphanage were billeted here. The house was later split into several flats, although from across the river it still appears an imposing mansion, rivalling the long-gone Bewerley Hall, just as George had intended.

An advertisement for Castlestead Hotel, c.1920.

GLASSHOUSES SCHOOL

The photograph (top right) is of the railway crossing at Glasshouses, with the school in the background, taken around the turn of the twentieth century. Originally called Low Plain, the village was almost entirely built by the mill firm of J. & G. Metcalfe for its workers, adopting its present name from the Glasshouse Mill in about 1865.

George Metcalfe, son of the J. and nephew of the G. of the firm's title, was almost solely responsible for bringing the railway to Pateley Bridge in 1862. I was always puzzled as to why he had not made provision for a station or even a halt at Glasshouses, although there were goods sidings for the mill. The answer

The level crossing at Glasshouses, with the school in the background.

was, of course, that there was no village at the time. Only one row of houses, Guisecliffe View, had been built to augment the few cottages and farms scattered around. Passengers had to walk up to Pateley to board the train.

The school was built in 1860 to replace one inside the mill. The Factory Acts of 1833 and 1844 insisted that all child workers in textile factories had to receive part-time education, and the employers were responsible for ensuring that there was adequate provision locally. Where there was a school already established this could be used, but many firms preferred to provide their own because it meant that they had control of their employees throughout the week. As the mill had been enlarged in 1842, there was adequate space within the precincts, in an upper room just inside the gates. There was a wooden external staircase to the room, which can be recognised by its differently shaped windows. By 1859, however, the work was increasing rapidly, helped no doubt by a prestigious contract to spin the flax for the household linen to be woven by Waltons of Knaresborough for the Great Exhibition. The room was needed for other purposes and was no longer big enough to accommodate all the children, even in shifts.

The first schoolroom was on the upper floor, in the nearest building to the mill gate.

The new building, across the road, was designed by Corsons, who had planned Castlestead, and the school transferred across on 1 April 1860. There were two rooms, a large one for the part-time pupils, and a smaller one for younger brothers and sisters who were allowed to attend full-time until their eighth birthday, when they had to become half-timers in the mill or leave the school. There was also a house attached for the master. He was a fully trained teacher, having been to college after his pupilage, and had a woman assistant, who had been a pupil-teacher but was not college trained, for the little ones. There was also a pupil-teacher and a monitor, an older boy or girl. One of the master's duties was to instruct his pupil-teacher each day out of school hours. There are frequent complaints of understaffing and of the problems of teaching large numbers of children who had never been to school before, sometimes coming in for the first time at the age of 10 or 12. The children attended for either a morning or afternoon session one week, and then reversed the following week. The hours were 9a.m. to noon or 1 to 4p.m. with six hours in the mill each day. Homework was given and the pupils were expected to reach the same standards as those who were fortunate to be in full-time education. The basic instruction was the three Rs, of course, plus religion (Methodist) and singing, history and geography when they could be fitted in. The older boys were taught drawing, while the girls learnt needlework with the master's wife.

The firm kept strict control over the school. All supplies, such as textbooks and pens and ink for the older pupils (the younger ones had to provide their own slates) had to be ordered through, and justified to, the mill manager. Whenever there was a stoppage in any part of the factory, a broken machine for example, all the children from that section were sent over to the school out of the way, even though there was no room for them. There were complaints when the afternoon shift went into the mill noisily or took in mud from the unpaved playground. Most of the difficulties sprang from lack of understanding or imagination, rather than unpleasantness.

By 1867 numbers had increased considerably with the building of a new wing onto the mill, so it was decided to enlarge the school. On 11 July the pupils broke up for the summer holiday (determined each year by the onset of haymaking) and work started the following day to pull down the front and back gables of the large room and extend it by one bay at each end. The work was completed and the school was ready to be back in operation by 1 August.

The first master at the school was John Horner, a Glasshouses man who was also a Methodist local preacher. In 1870 he emigrated to the United States, where he became a minister of some distinction. We had never known what had happened to him until some years ago when I was head teacher at the school and two gentlemen came in just as the children left one day. The elder, a very frail 90-year-old, was the last surviving grandchild of John Horner. The family

Glasshouse Mill in the early-twentieth century.

Left: *John Horner, the first master in the new school building. He was a local preacher. After emigrating to the United States he became a prominent Methodist minister.*

Right: *William Hardcastle was the headmaster from 1893 to 1921. He was a Rural District Councillor and Justice of the Peace, as well as secretary of the Nidderdale Agricultural Society.*

had known very little about their antecedents, except that they were from Yorkshire, Glasshouses had been mentioned, and they had a picture. The younger gentleman had discovered the village on a map and brought his father to fulfil a lifetime's ambition. When he saw his grandfather's writing in the school log-books, the old man broke down in tears. On his return to the States he sent me a photograph of his grandfather. We corresponded for just over a year, but then, sadly, no more.

John Horner was succeeded by Thomas Chambers. By this time there were 77 boys and 67 girls on the roll. In addition to the difficulties with the mill, there were frequent epidemics which swept through the large families living in small cottages, resulting in closure of the school for weeks on end. When annual inspections were introduced, no allowance was made for this, or for the children being only part-time – they were expected to reach the same standards as full-time pupils. The 1870 Education Act allowed communities to set up their own school boards to ensure that all children in their area received primary education. A school was built in Pateley Bridge, the vice-chairman of the governors being George Metcalfe, and more children were able to take advantage of full-time education.

By 1892 standards had generally risen considerably, part-time education was being phased out, except for the oldest pupils, and the firm was beginning to have financial problems. It was decided to turn the school over to the Pateley Bridge School Board.

The staff was completely changed and William Hardcastle, who had been pupil and pupil-teacher at the school, was appointed as master. The Metcalfes had paid for his training at Westminster College and he had been at Greenhow School before coming down the hill. He stayed until his retirement in 1921 and became a very respected and active member of the community and a Justice of the Peace, serving as a local and district councillor until the late '30s. During his time the building was improved several times, particularly in 1912 when a cloakroom was added at the back for the girls and infants, and the gardens of the houses behind were taken for additional playground space.

In the photograph *(top picture, page 65)* Firgrove House can be seen behind the school, built in 1870 as the mill manager's residence. The first occupant was R.N. Somersgil who unfortunately collapsed and died only three years later at the age of 42. John H. Metcalfe and his sister, Elsie Hodgson, lived in it between about 1913 and 1923. For a time it became the residence of the junior Wesleyan Methodist minister, one of a team of three then serving the circuit.

The railway lines were taken up after the closure of the service in 1964. The crossing-keeper's cottage was extended in the 1970s, but the gates have long gone. There are houses on the left, built in the early 1980s, but superficially the scene is very similar at the time of writing as it was at the beginning of the twentieth century.

Billhead for Francis
Thorpe & Co.
from 1825–1883.

Haymaking in New York Mill field.
Male mill workers had to help.

A billhead of Thomas Gill & Sons Ltd from 1889–1980. Note the northern roof lights, provided to give better
light for working, in the main shed, rebuilt in 1889. The rope-walk at Low Laithe is in the distance.

Chapter 8

DACRE & SUMMERBRIDGE

Mary Barley

NEW YORK MILL – HEBDEN AND THORPE

When William Hebden, of Braisty Woods in Hartwith township, was looking for a site to build a flax-spinning mill, where better than on his field called Low Sun Dams alongside the River Nidd?

Unfortunately there was no through road between Summerbridge and Pateley but this did not deter William Hebden: he built the spinning mill at the bottom of the lane leading from Braisty Woods to the river, although we have no knowledge of its size. In 1825 Francis Thorpe, an employer of linen weavers in Knaresborough, leased the building, known at the time of writing as New York Mill, from William Hebden. The reason for this name is still a mystery. For some time there had been agitation locally to build a new line for the turnpike road line from Burnt Yates to Wilsill via Summerbridge and Francis Thorpe would have been aware of this. The road was built in 1827/8.

In 1834 he bought New York Mill and two years later added more land upstream and alongside the River Nidd. Here he built High Mill, an office and a warehouse. The weir which was built to power High Mill also fed a new watercourse across the field on the south side of the river.

Water-supply was vital and, to keep the water-wheels turning, a great deal of ingenuity was used in building new watercourses and reservoirs for storage. New York Mill had three water-wheels altogether but the site of the third is unknown. The original water race was started from the River Nidd below Crow Trees House, between New York Mill and Low Laithe. The race flowed under the mill and rejoined the river about 400 yards downstream. From here, and the later reservoir, water was piped across the Nidd to drive a new water-wheel for an extension to New York Mill. Similar to many mills at this time, the piping took the form of a wooden trough that carried the water – a study of mill watercourses in Nidderdale is worthwhile.

By the late 1830s Francis Thorpe began to make linen thread at New York Mill (a bobbin of which is held at Nidderdale Museum). The 1841 and 1851 Censuses show how the firm expanded. He also leased Folly Gill Mill and another at Low Laithe. The flax was mainly bought from Russia and the Low Countries via the port of Hull. This was a boom time for the flax mills. However, shortly after this there was a general slump in 1837/8 and 1841/2. Although the effect of the depression was less severe in Nidderdale, Francis Thorpe closed his lease on Folly Gill at this time.

New York Mill was working full time in 1841, for 69–72 hours per week. Francis Thorpe had built 40 cottages for his workers close to the mill and the population of the township rose from 449 to 943.

Women and children worked in the factory. The men employed were mechanics, overlookers, hecklers (a tough job of straightening the flax fibres) bleachers and dyers.

In 1832/3 information was collected by one of two Parliamentary Inquiries into factory conditions and a detailed picture of working conditions in the mills at this time is described. New York Mill employed 150 mill workers and about 50 flax dressers, bleachers and dyers. Life was hard, with children as young as eight being employed in the mill as doffers, taking full bobbins from the spinning frames and replacing them with empty ones. Average wages per week were from 1s.6d. to 2s.8d. for children under ten, and 6s. for adult women, with men earning an average of 17s. Francis Thorpe was no callous employer though. He was careful to point out to the commissioners that the tow-carding room at New York Mill had two large ventilators to extract the dust.

As a result of the enquiries the 1833 Factory Act was passed, prohibiting the employment of children aged under nine in the textile mills. Hours that children were allowed to work were stated and children had to go to school for two hours a day. For this Francis Thorpe established a school at the mill with a Mr Rawson as teacher.

A second Act was passed in 1844 limiting children under 13 to a six-and-a-half-hour day and requiring attendance at school for 15 hours per week, and the minimum age of employment was reduced to eight years of age. Throughout the nineteenth century boom times in flax spinning kept giving way to periods of depression – some firms failed, others, including that at New York Mill, survived.

The influx of Irish workers to Nidderdale after the

Irish potato famine of the 1840s is shown in the 1851 Census when 14 Irish teenage girls were lodging at one house at New York with a husband, wife and two children. We do not know which house but it was probably in High Row. By the l861 Census they had all disappeared.

Francis Thorpe built up an extensive welfare system for his employees. The factory inspector of 1848 published an impressive account of Francis Thorpe's system. He started by saying that a rule at the mill was that any girl having an illegitimate child would be discharged and if the reputed father worked in the mill, he would also be discharged unless the parties married. It was thought the rule worked well as they did not have to dismiss more than eight or ten during the 20 years previous to the inspection.

Wages were paid on a Saturday morning to allow the wives to shop for the weekend. Full wages were paid for such holidays as Christmas, Whitsuntide and Pateley Feast. No foremen or overlookers were allowed to keep a shop, so there could be no pressure on workers to trade with them. No overlookers were allowed to carry a strap or stick to beat the children. No retail beer shop was allowed on the premises and 150 of the staff were members of the Summerbridge Temperance Society.

A Mechanics' Institute was established in 1841 as well as a school. The Institute had 109 male and 39 female members by 1848. There was a library of 700 volumes and evening classes were run for both men and women for writing, spelling, music and chemistry (for the dyers).

A scheme for free medical treatment was started in 1834, the workers paying 2d. per month and the balance being paid by the firm. There was a clothing club for bed linens, blankets, counterpanes, ticks, shirting, checks, canvas, etc., where workers could buy items wholesale for cash.

A mutual burial society established in 1838 provided a death benefit of £5 and members were admitted from the age of one to 45 – 480 members paid a levy of 1s.3½d. per annum. Finally, a cow club was started in 1843 as a mutual insurance.

In Yorkshire we hear a lot about the industrialist Titus Salt of Saltaire and his model village, but Francis Thorpe seems to have been equally concerned for his workers. He was a Wesleyan Methodist and no doubt contributed to the chapel built at Summerbridge in 1827. He died in 1854.

New York Mill then passed into the proprietorship of two former employees – Richard Pullan, mechanic, and Robert Benson, clerk, who continued to trade under the name of Francis Thorpe & Co. Richard Pullan had joined New York Mill in 1832. He was an ardent Primitive Methodist and by his generosity Belle Vue Chapel, Low Laithe, was erected.

In 1883 there were disastrous floods in Nidderdale and at New York Mill large quantities of linen thread and flax which had been laid out to bleach on a green between the mill and the River Nidd were lost or damaged. Water in the spinning room was up to a depth of 4 feet 9 inches. A newspaper cutting of 3 May 1883 stated:

A catastrophe of more than unusual darkness has overshadowed the village of Summerbridge and New York. The hands will have received notice to leave before this is printed. For sometime the business has been running at a loss, but the masters have tried to beat off the danger that bad times was forcing upon them.

Francis Thorpe & Co, Hartwith with Winsley, Flax spinners and Linen Thread Manufacturers, Local Liquidation.

June 1883 – The stoppage of New York Mills is causing considerable distress in the locality.

In 1884 the Nidderdale estate was up for sale. A notice from the local papers advertised:

Sale by Auction at the Prospect Hotel, Harrogate, freehold estate, situated on the River Nidd and comprising the well known and old established New York Spinning Mills, with residency cottages, numerous factories, farms and store quarries, containing in all 162 acres of land.

The estate was offered in lots, but not one was sold and the mill was still unsold in 1889.

THE GILL FAMILY AT NEW YORK MILL

Thomas Gill, who was in partnership with Joseph Todd of Summerbridge between 1861 and 1868, moved in 1868 to Thruscross to set up a flax- and hemp-spinning business at Low Mill, West End. This mill stood alongside the River Washburn, from where it obtained water for the mill-wheel.

Thomas Gill had five sons and some daughters. Four of the sons followed him into the business, whilst the fifth and youngest son, Thomas, later became a corn miller at Dacre Banks corn-mill and then at Pateley Bridge. Thomas Gill senr had trained as a mechanic and had a record of early success in business, perhaps due to his inventive father, Charles Gill, who had died in 1851. Charles was a self-educated man who entered Dacre Banks flax-mill in 1793, at the age of 19 years, and who built new machinery, including the 'Tow Card' the 'Porcupine or Rotary Gill' and the 'Gill Box'. As he never patented any of the designs, he cannot be credited as the inventor. In 1879 Thomas bought Dacre Banks Mill (rebuilt by the Ingleson family in about 1800) which he used for hemp spinning and corn milling and patented an improvement to twisting frames for twisting heavy yarns like hemp. He died in 1880, leaving his sons to carry on the business.

After the closure in 1883 of New York Mill and the

estate, which subsequently stood empty for five years, the four sons of Thomas – Charles, John William, Joseph and Harry – decided to bid for the mill in 1888. In 1862 the railway had been built up the dale to Pateley Bridge and as New York Mill was nearer to Dacre Station than West End it was easier for the import of raw materials, as well as sending out the finished goods. They traded as Thomas Gill & Sons, for although Thomas had died, his widow Margaret still had a strong interest in the business.

Their architectural and business adviser was a cousin who lived in Rotherham, another Charles Gill. There are interesting family letters written by Thomas' son Charles to the Charles in Rotherham: 'March 1, 1889. We have got possession of New York

The rope-walk at Low Laithe, High Mill.
Pictured are young members of the Gill family.

at last. March 9, 1889. John William has started work on the machinery.' John William was the second son and the mechanic of the family. He too in time invented machinery, especially somethng known locally as the 'Teetotal Heckling Machine'.

In 1891 electric lighting was made and installed – the first in the dale – causing much excitement locally.

New York Mill had been built in stages as Francis Thorpe (the previous owner) had expanded and, because of the inconvenience of these additions, Gills rebuilt it on the shed principle (single storey) and added northern roof lights. The three water-wheels were replaced with a 100hp water turbine and later supplemented this with a gas engine.

There was a grand opening on Tuesday 18 March 1890 when a Wesleyan circuit gathering and public tea was held in the main shed in the newly restored New York Mill. At 3p.m. a sermon was preached by Revd Joseph Posnett and at 4.30p.m. a public tea was provided on the premises. Tickets cost 9d. for adults, and 6d. for children. At 7p.m. there was a public meeting which was addressed by Revd Posnett, Revd J.S. Lucas (vicar of Hartwith) and other 'friends'. There was a collection at the close of the afternoon and evening services, with proceeds going to the Summerbridge Chapel Improvement fund and the circuit funds. Singing was led by the Summerbridge String Band. A special train left Dacre Station at 9p.m., stopping at intermediate stations to Harrogate.

Charles Gill became the managing director and his brothers became directors. The firm later became a limited company.

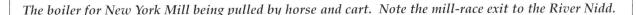

The boiler for New York Mill being pulled by horse and cart. Note the mill-race exit to the River Nidd.

In 1889 an iron aqueduct was erected across the River Nidd from the goit (mill race), replacing a wooden one, giving a higher fall of water for the turbine. There was a growing demand for string and cords including window-sash cording. Some flax was still being spun but hemp was the main yarn. This was purchased from the Baltic countries and Italy, and brought to the mill in bales. Many of the workers from West End came over to work at New York, living in some of the houses built by Francis Thorpe. As many had stood empty for five years, Gills had to refurbish them. As before, the majority of the employees were women and girls. When a mill house became empty, a family with a number of daughters had priority.

Comparatively few men were employed – those who were employed being the mechanics, a boiler man, lorry driver and estate workers. At the rope-walk at Low Laithe Mill, which was acquired later, there were only three or four men, the line for the ropes being spun at New York Mill. During the Second World War parachute cord was made at Low Laithe Mill. Like many other mills in the valley, it had good financial years and lean ones. As it was entirely dependent on water-power, frequently in summer the mill was on short time. Fire, too, was a great hazard, most men being pipe smokers and carrying loose matches in their waistcoat pockets – only one had to lean over a machine, a match fall out and a fire was quickly started. There was a huge fire at the rear of the clock tower in 1908, and another in 1936.

The fire at New York Mill, 1908, at the rear of the clock tower. Note the water pump.

The front of the clock tower at New York Mill during the fire of 1908. The ladies with hats (right) were Ethel and Maud, daughters of J.W. Gill, who were serving cups of tea to the firemen.

As each son of Thomas Gill retired a younger member of the family took over. After the Second World War New York Mill was re-equipped with improved carding and spinning machines. Spinning frames running at 500 to 800 revolutions a minute were replaced by machines running at 3,000 revs per minute. Overhead sprinkler systems were also installed. At one time a railway truck in Dacre siding was filled each week for customers in the London area. As this truck was occasionally delayed en route, Gills invested in a lorry and a long-distance driver.

In the 1950s, because of mechanisation, fewer ropes were needed for agriculture. Wooden scaffolding tied together with rope was replaced with metal held by bolts. Sash windows were superseded by casements and so fewer sash cords were required. Nylon and polypropolene took the place of hemp for ropes. The wide use of sellotapes for parcels and packaging made string obsolete. Something had to be done.

This was the time when New York Mill turned to spinning synthetic carpet yarns, tested first on the existing machinery. After many headaches and alterations it proved a viable proposition. New machinery was bought, mainly from Mackies of Belfast. The machines were considerably longer than the old spinning frames. As trade improved, the company expanded to a newly built factory at Hookstone Park, Harrogate. Times appeared to be good.

In 1968, at a luncheon given by the company to all the employees at the Granby Hotel in Harrogate to celebrate 100 years in business (1868–1968), the management had to announce they were to have a 'takeover' by Jute Industries of Dundee, later known as Sidlaw (after the Sidlaw Hills just west of the city). They continued trading as Thomas Gill & Sons under the same board of directors together with a chairman from Sidlaw. Trade continued successfully for number of years until the Americans (subsidised by their government) started to flood the English carpet-yarn market. In 1980 the Harrogate factory, known as

Left: *Low Laithe rope-walk, with G. Robinson tying single ends on to the twister after parting down the warp.*

Right: *Low Laithe rope-walk, with A. Ward cord laying.*

Left: *New York Mill from across the River Nidd, c.1940.*

Right: *New York Mill from the east, c.1960. The buildings were,* left to right: *mill shed, clock tower, mill offices with cottage at the east end, warehouse with large barn door, Victoria Terrace (houses for the foremen).*

Glynil Mill, was the first to close, then at the end of the year New York Mill was closed. The rope-walk had suffered the same fate a few years earlier. Fortunately, almost all the employees who were not near retirement found new jobs. The mill was bought by a local syndicate and was eventually turned into units for small industries. Ironically one was a carpet company.

TODD BROTHERS, SUMMERBRIDGE

Todd Bros Nidd Valley Foundry, Summerbridge, Mill-wrights, Iron Founders, Ironmongers, Plumbers, Glaziers, Tinsmiths, Whitesmiths, Iron and Steel Merchants, Agricultural Engineers, Cycle Agents, Mill Furnishers, Oil Merchants, Bolts, Nuts, Screws and Washers, Sanitary Wares and Cement always in stock.

*Todd Bros, ironmongers of Summerbridge, c.1904.
Pictured in the doorway is Alice, daughter of Joseph Todd. Outside is Jinnie, daughter of Michael Todd. It was taken from the row of cottages, opposite the school, which were used as workshops.*

Todds also made the black iron fireplaces which were found in so many dales farmhouses, and it was said that the best bread was baked in their ovens. One can be seen in the kitchen at Nidderdale Museum, Pateley Bridge.

When the reservoirs were being built at the top of Nidderdale for Bradford Corporation, Todds received regular orders for castings, brake blocks, plumbers' blocks and firebars for Angram and Scar House reservoirs.

Todds employed many workers and moulders in the foundry which was a large building built near the River Nidd below Summerbridge School. Three dams, two of which were to the east of the main road and one to the west, collected water from springs on the hillside above the village to turn two water-wheels in the foundry. The water was carried through a large-diameter pipe under the present school field to a pen trough for the water-wheels. The race emptied into the River Nidd.

Todds rented the foundry from the Robinson family who owned the water rights in the village. It seems there was a dispute about the rent, which Todds

This is the only known photograph of the large building of Todd's foundry (background). There were two water-wheels, one over the other. The moulders were Gordon Barley, Norman Barley, Bob Petty, Harry Petty and ?.

refused to pay, and the foundry was then allowed to go to ruin; it was eventually demolished in the 1930s because it was unsafe. Work was then carried out by Todds in the 'little mill' near the dams and the cottages by the river, one of which was used as a shop. Water-wheels were made, erected and serviced by Todds locally and as far away as Topcliffe and Hunsingore. One such can be seen running at Ponden Mill, Darley, although not turning any machinery.

The foundry was supposedly built in the seventeenth century, but was it built as a forge for local iron works which were in use in the township at this time?

There were five generations of Joseph Todds in the business over the years. The first Joseph was born in 1783, came from Pannal with his family and died in Glasshouses in 1840. The second Joseph was born in Pannal in 1819; he married Mary Weatherhead from Bewerley and became a mill-wright (mechanic), living at Low Plain, Glasshouses. They had a large family.

In 1861 Joseph II went into partnership with Thomas Gill at the foundry in Summerbridge. In 1861 Thomas had patented an improved yarn-twisting frame and joined with him to make textile machinery. The partnership was dissolved in 1868 when Thomas rented Low Mill, West End, to spin flax and hemp with his five sons, but not before many iron fireplaces had been made bearing the name Todd and Gill.

Joseph II then took two of his sons into the business – Michael, born in 1844, and Joseph III, six years younger. Joseph II died in 1890 and Michael and Joseph III then became known as Todd Bros.

Fireplaces of this era had Todd Bros cast on them. Michael died in 1917 with no son to follow in the business. Part of the assets were sold and Joseph III carried on, taking his son Joseph IV into the business. Fireplaces then had Todd & Son cast on them. Joseph III died in 1926.

Workers at Todd's foundry, taken below the village school, Summerbridge. Picture includes: Charles Todd, Joseph Todd (standing), young Joseph Todd (centre, sitting, in white coat), A. Bramley (behind him), Michael Todd (standing, extreme right).

Foster Beck water-wheel, one of several made by Todds.

Joseph IV built the shop on the main road at Summerbridge, the ironmonger's shop being half of the business. After the death of Joseph IV it was bought by Albert Dixon and then by the Newbould brothers who run a flourishing business at the time of writing, still in the Todd name.

Unfortunately, Joseph IV's son, Joseph, was tragically killed at Folly Gill Mill before his father died. He had been in the business only a few years, and so ended the long run of Joseph Todds.

In the family they were always known as 'Old Joe', 'Young Joe' and 'Joe Amongst Bairns', and are remembered in a rhyme: 'Old Joe, Young Joe, and Young Joe's son. There'll never be another Joe 'til Old Joe's done'. Joseph III was my grandfather.

DACRE & SUMMERBRIDGE REMEBERED
Thomas William Skaife, Tailor

Thomas William Skaife, who had lived all his life in Summerbridge, wrote the following notes in the early-twentieth century. He was a well-liked and highly respected gentleman, a very good tailor, a Sunday-school teacher and a great worker for the Summerbridge Methodist Chapel and the young people of the village.

His ancestors were the grange keepers at Braisty Woods for Fountains Abbey. His grandmother was a Todd and his mother a Bramley, both members of old Nidderdale families.

In 1751 there were six Church-ways from Summerbridge to Hartwith. From Butcher Pasture, Whinbush Farm, Dougill Hall, Manor Farm, Parsons Stoop, and Stripe Lane. At Dacre there was a man named Bradbury who when he had completed his piece of linen he would walk to Leeds carrying it on his shoulder and back again the same day leaving his horse in the stable.

In those days the track (or road) from Braisty came down Braisty Lane and on this side of the river and across where the houses have been renovated near the bridge. Another road or track up Carrington's wood (Woolich) through top of Steels wood. The Green Lane came into the bank at that time past the church down to Hardcastle Garth and there is an old lane at the bottom of Carringtons farm that used to come to White House which was one of the Bleach Houses. The last lot of Cottages were made into Farm Buildings when I was a small boy.

They used to go from Dacre to Smelthouses by Braisty Woods with Panir ponies.

Smelthouses was a very old village having got the name by the Romans smelting lead brought from Greenhow. Two pigs of Lead found on Hayshaw Moor bearing the Roman Stamp, one is at Ripley Castle and one in the British Museum.

All the lead used in Fountains Abbey was from Greenhow and the white Marble Pillars were from the bed of the river up the dale.

Braisty and Dacre were busy handloom places. I have

Advertisements for Summerbridge firms.

a sheet woven by Mr Hardisty or Mr Watson Dacre in the old days. We made Drab, Light Brown Smocks for farmers.

Kirbys had mills in Smelthouses.

I think the first mills would use the water-wheel in all probability for grinding corn. There was an old mill-stone quarry at Braisty where coming from it is a broken millstone. I have never been able to learn where it was worked. There were a lot of small mills in the district. Kirbys had three, one at Low Laithe and one at High Mill, then the large mill at New York, one up against the house above the chapel (Elmwood Farm). One composed most of T. Holdsworth's house (next to the fish shop). Dacre Banks Corn Mill and Linen Mill run by Grange and Bell.

What we call the Foundry was first a Linen Mill, then Mr James Atkinson had a mill where R. Light's garage is.

Some of the Bentley family had a Twine Walk on the side of Smelthouse Glen the motive power a pony or mule fixed to the arm of an upright post. I suppose they made halters and whipping strings for farmers, they used to attend Knaresboro market with these.

The old houses in the district are roofed with grey slate which was got from Guyscliffe.

The Corn Mill at Dacre banks was in full work in 1805 and how long before that I cannot make out. There was a wash wheel there. About this time many small mills sprung up in the district.

I have not been able to get to know when the New Line was made from Burnt Yates to Wilsill. In 1863 Grainge says the New Line was made a few years previous.

Most of the cottage houses in Summerbridge was built at from £60 to £80 each.

My mother used to say she remembered when there were no houses past Mr Reg Scaifes shop at that side of the road. A little wood stood where the Dutchman and Post Office are with a small dyke through some of us remember it being piped down the field where Mrs Wilkinsons houses are built.

I have good cause to remember the large house next to Mr Scaifes shop being built for I fell through the joists into the cellar (Melrose House).

Re small mills
Mr Wilkinson was the first I can remember working they used to cut a tremendous lot of clog soles and stack them to season. I have heard it said that Mr W. used to walk to Skipton and go into Lancashire to sell them.

Summerbridge crossroads, c.1880. Pictured are: Rose Cottage (facing); opposite, from left: *two cottages, Melrose House, cottage and village shop, paper shop, Melrose House, village shop and cottage, The Flying Dutchman (public house), Post Office and a private house.*

Summerbridge Chapel in 1894, with Elmwood Farm behind on the left.

Mill Cottage, Summerbridge, c.1915. It was a small mill run by water power from a dam. It was later used as the moulders' 'pattern shop' for Todd Bros foundry. The Scatchard family are pictured in the foreground.

Summerbridge crossroads, c.1940. Pictured are, from left: *Paper shop, Melrose House, village shop and cottage, The Flying Dutchman (public house), Post Office and a private house.*

Above: *Summerbridge Post Office.
Mr Smith Skaife the postmaster is
on the top step with his son,
Mr T.W. Skaife, below the sign.*

Left: *Summerbridge reading-room was
supported by Mr Skaife for young men.
It was almost opposite the Post Office.*

Right: *Nelson Ripley and his donkey.*

Left: *Dacre Mill in 1974. The corn-mill
was behind the flat-roofed building. The
large building behind is the sawmill at
the time of writing, but was originally
the flax-mill, operated by the Inglesons,
and then Grange and Bell.*

Then the mill against the top Dam at New York has never worked since I can tell there was a wash wheel in there.

Then there was the big mill with three wheels and an engine. I will say more about this later.

Then the Linen Mill which became the Foundry worked by Messrs Todd and Gill. I think we will come back to this later.

Then there was the Corn Mill and Linen Mill worked by Grange and Bell.

The greater part of T. Holdsworth's house was a mill worked by Mr Addamson he used to shop hay and straw for the farmers and turn bobbins for New York Mill. This had a large narrow wheel with wood pentrough on stone pillars and came from the corner of the top dam.

Mr Richard Bell who lived up at White House had a small mill behind Dobsons house (Elmwood Farm) above the chapel this was a large narrow wheel with a pentrough like the other on Stone Pillars. He used to make Peggy Sticks Stools Bread boards and all such things and they mostly went to Knaresboro market for sale.

Mr Rogerson had a twine walk in the Croft the full length of the field it was worked by an engine. He was considered the Gentleman of the village and he was certainly very gentlemanly when he was away dressed up in his best he was several times taken for the Prince of Wales whom he was much like.

I have said the foundry was a linen mill and over what became the moulding shop was a Beam Machine you could hear this working all over the village it was for stretching the woven pieces of Linen cloth. It made the fabric closer and narrower in width and longer in length I suppose this kind of machine is in use today.

This was afterwards worked by Todd and Gill. I think it was for 7 years when the Partnership was dissolved in 1868.

Thomas Gill and his family going to West End. The foundry was carried on by J. Todd with millwrights shop, blacksmiths shop. Here they cast all sorts of useful things. They would employ about 20 men and boys. At his death it became Todd Brothers who added the ironmongers Shop for Paints brushes Buckets etc until the death of Mr Michael Todd (Mrs Houseman's Father) when the firm sold out and Mr J. Todd just took over then he transferred the business to the old cottages and eventually sold to Albert Dixon.

I cannot leave these cottages without a few words about Local Character Nelson Ripley he used to take his donkey into the cottage with him.

The railway was opened in 1862. The most difficult place was the rock cutting above the station (Dacre). It was thought one goods a week would be enough. When they were making this the public house was the house next to R. Lights garage. It was kept by J. Dalby.

The new line was made from Burnt Yates to Wilsill in 1828. Reg Scaife's shop is the village shop at the time

Summerbridge from Dacre, before the council estate was built.

The bottom of Summerbridge village, with the Methodist Church spire in the background.

of writing. Wilkinson's house was on the east side of Dobson Bank.

DACRE GRANGE

The Dacre township boundary follows the River Nidd, Padside and Darley Beck for at least two-thirds of its length. During the twelfth century, Dacre was granted to Fountains Abbey by Bertram de Haget. The gift was confirmed by Roger de Mowbray who reserved the hunting rights.

The monks built a grange at Dacre together with outlying farms at Heyshaw, Banger House and New Houses and surrounded them with large enclosed fields. Pastoral stations were also built at Deer Ing, Monk Ing, Foldshaw and Oxen Close. A large flock of sheep was wintered at Heyshaw and then sent on, during the summer months, to the limestone fells in Wharfedale and the Lake District. Store cattle were grazed at Monk Ing and Deer Ing. In 1450, 3,000 stone slates were used in the re-roofing of Banger House and in 1448/9 new smoke houses were erected at Dacre Grange and Monk Ing for curing meat.

In the mid-fourteenth century a dispute arose about tithes and other church dues from Dacre, because it lay in the parish of Kirkby Malzeard and the church was some eight or nine miles distant. Most of the people used to attend the chapel of ease at Pateley Bridge within the Ripon parish without paying anything towards its support.

According to an edict issued by the Archbishop of York in 1351, they were:

... *living in a certaine Beastlie manner to the perill of their solles. Manie inhabitants with their wyves, children and families do dwell farre distant from any parish church, to which for the swelling of waters and other tempests greatlie in the winter season some men cannot passe without greate difficultie and corporall danger.*

The Archbishop ordered that tithes and dues should no longer be paid to Kirkby Malzeard and attached Dacre temporarily to Ripon parish.

In 1361 the arrangement was made permanent and Dacre was put under the care of the prebend of Studley, which ministered to the part of Ripon parish in which Pateley Bridge Chapelry was situated. The great tithes (tenths) of corn, hay, wool and lambs, plus the yields of iron and lead mines, were to go to Pateley. The remaining small tithes were to go to the common fund of Ripon Minster. Even in the nineteenth-century Census returns Dacre people were putting Ripon (parish) as their place of birth.

As early as 1309 iron was being forged at Dacre Grange by an agreement between Roger de Mowbray and Fountains Abbey, permitting one forge and two furnaces which might be moved from place to place, making iron where convenient. The monks were also allowed to burn charcoal on abbey lands between Michaelmas and Easter. Two Roman pigs of lead were unearthed in the Heyshaw area, probably 'lost' in transit from Greenhow. One was sent to the British Museum, the other kept by the Ingilby family at Ripley Castle until it was sold in the 1990s.

In 1552 Sir William Ingilby bought the township of Dacre from Sir Arthur D'Arcy. He had purchased it from Sir Richard Gresham who bought the Fountains' Nidderdale estates from the King at the time of the Dissolution of the Monasteries. By 1603 Sir William Ingilby had sold the security of 22 farms in Dacre to the tenants in the form of a lease for 1,300 years, receiving annual rents of 3s.4d.

The tenants were still obliged to attend the manor court twice yearly and to have their corn ground at the lord's mill. They also had to repair the mill-dam. In 1615 eight more farms were similarly sold. In the Ingilby papers these leases refer to Dacre in the township of Laverton. Also by this time the tenants were paying a fixed annual rent in lieu of church tithes.

Early in the seventeenth century Dacre Pasture was a stinted common with farms situated around the perimeter. The farms were occupied by such old dales families as Hardcastle, Atkinson, Wood, Benson and Yates. Encroaching on to the common were some very early enclosures near to Dacre Grange, and an isolated enclosure down the lane leading to Chapel Gate near Thornthwaite Church (built in 1402). The

other ways out of the township were Broad Gate to Menwith, Darley Gate, Summerbridge Gate, Harper Gate to Thruscross, and Dyke Gate into Bewerley. An early track up the valley ran from Dacre Banks to Bewerley via Harewell Hall.

In his will dated 1536, Robert Beckwith of Dacre left bequests for:

... *mending Summer Bridge 3s.4d., to William Sotheron, chaplain of Hampsthwaite to sing trental* [30] *masses for my soul, and all Christian souls, to Sir George Eles, chaplain of Brimham to pray likewise, to the church at Fuyston 3s.4d.*

Reading the court rolls is quite fascinating and time-consuming, for example:

We present Robert Wilkinson for graving sods on Dacre Pasture to thatch his house with; 3s.4d. We lay a pain that George Gill do sufficiently open and scour the ditch at the lower end of a pasture close called Bottoms betwixt certain dates upon a pain of 10s. We present Robert Benson Constable for Dacre for the next year ensuing. We present William Hardisty that he owes suit and service to the court and tho' summoned and solemnly called has made default, 10s.

One court roll gives an account of beating the bounds on June 7, 1698:

To John Ingilby Bart, I hope this will find you well and happy in your health which shall ever be most welcome news I can hear of. I thought it proper to send you a Rotation of our riding the bounds of your Manor of Dacre which was performed with that general satisfaction that the like has not been known in memory. We were near 80 mounted and ye infantries numerous. We met with no dispute but by John Beckwith of Bewerley and Seth Dickinson of the same place about the end of Guyscliffe Scarr towards Bewerley who came and told us when we were within an Intack that we were out of our boundary.

I demanded their reason and to show evidence they said they would produce it, so we sat down under a wall on the grass in pure air and a pleasant day...

It all came to nothing and they proceeded round the bounds to Dacre where Sir John had laid out a most generous treat and ale. Dacre Pasture Enclosure Award was in 1845. Heyshaw and Braithwaite Moors were enclosed in 1876.

The 1672 hearth-tax return for Dacre gives details of the houses and the number of hearths they each owned. There were 70 taxpayers, most of them owning one or two hearths, six with three hearths, and one with five (William Hardcastle). The largest number was Sir William Ingilby with nine hearths at Harewell Hall, rebuilt by him in 1652.

The initials W.I. are between two 'stars' on the

Above: *Low or Lacon Hall, Dacre, which was taxed on seven hearths in 1672.*

Right: *Harewell Hall, Dacre. Mary Ward took her secret first communion in the recusant chapel in the attic during the late-sixteenth century.*

Left: *Dacre Parish Church and Vicarage, which were built 1837. Note the wooden spire.*

Right: *Providence Independent Chapel, Dacre, built in 1827.*

coat of arms of the Ingilby family. In the 1590s Harewell was twice raided by the authorities who were looking for recusant priests. None were found. Mary Ward, a daughter of a recusant family who moved around the county to avoid persecution, made her first communion in the attic chapel at Harewell when, as a girl of 13, she was staying with her widowed cousin, Katherine Arthington. Mary became a nun and founded the Institute of the Blessed Virgin Mary, the first order of nuns in England after the Reformation, which eventually established the Bar Convent, York.

A second large house in Dacre is Low Hall, or Lacon Hall as it was originally known, paying tax on seven hearths when Matthew Wood was living there in 1672. Before 1787, Robert Benson lived at Low Hall. He was the son of Christopher Benson, lineal ancestor of the Right Revd Edward White Benson, Archbishop of Canterbury. His Lordship visited the old family home at Low Hall in the summer of 1892.

Most of the Nidderdale farmers of the seventeenth century were illiterate and signed their wills with a cross. Only one-third of those in Dacre and Hartwith who took long leases from Sir William Ingilby in the years 1604–16 were able to sign their names. In 1695 William Hardcastle, a farmer of Dacre Banks, gave a house for use as a school, together with an endowment of £200. This school continued until its closure after the First World War when the children from Dacre, Dacre Banks and Heyshaw had to walk to Summerbridge School.

A second school in Dacre was Braithwaite School on Braithwaite Moor to the south-west of the town. Under his will, Edward Yates of Dacre left a house and 23 acres of land at Deer Ing together with nine cattle gates on Dacre Pasture and £140 for provision of a schoolmaster who was required to remain single. Matthew Nelson, who had emigrated to America, left £787 to the school in 1869, £606 of which was spent on rebuilding the premises.

Dacre has two places of worship at the time of writing: the Providence Independent Chapel (United Reformed) at Dacre, built in 1827, and the Parish Church at Dacre Banks, built in 1837 on land given by Sir William Ingilby. Previously the Quakers had a chapel at Sand House (together with a burial-ground), built in 1682 which closed in about 1800. The building was demolished and some of the stone was used to erect the Quaker Chapel at Darley in 1802, now closed.

Whitehead, in his book on the *History of Congregational Chapels in Nidderdale*, tells some amusing stories of ministers and the congregation at Providence Chapel. One told by Mr Bryan, a minister, is as follows:

Matthew Hardisty, the caretaker was a unique character; he was one of the last of the handloom linen weavers. I have often stood by his loom, which practically filled his little cottage, and listened to his sage philosophy. He lived for the little chapel that was always spotless; we paid him one shilling a week. On Sunday mornings, just in the middle of the sermon and with unfailing regularity, Matthew would stalk down the aisle, open the stove door and shovel in more fuel, the congregation of farmers being quite undisturbed and their attention in no way distracted. Dear old Matthew! It killed him when, in the fourth year of my ministry, we gutted the place and re-seated it, modernised it, and built a vestry. He died shortly afterwards, in 1897, and we all felt he was broken-hearted. He was caretaker for 40 years.

The railway came to Dacre in the 1860s. Work began in 1860 on a line from Ripley to Pateley Bridge, with a station and goods yard at Dacre Banks. It opened to traffic on 1 May 1862 and was closed in 1962, lasting just 100 years. This had made a great difference to the dale, bringing in coal, slates and visitors, taking out stone from the quarries, finished goods from the mills, and milk to the rapidly rising industrial towns of Leeds and Bradford.

Dacre Station. The porter was Mr Poucher.

Chapter 9

IT'S AN ILL WIND

Mary Barley

One late afternoon in August 1983 a disastrous fire ravaged one of the oldest houses in Nidderdale, Holme Hall (also known as The Holme), an early timber-framed yeoman house in Darley. Fire had completely burnt the thatched roof and many interior timbers. Fortunately it has been restored and has lost none of its happy atmosphere. The following information was provided by an eyewitness to the fire.

Left: The bedroom floors after the house fire at The Holme, Darley, in the 1980s.

Holme Hall had for generations been owned by the Pullan (Pulleyn) family, one of whom took in washing in the great kitchen and so started Pullans' Darley Laundry, which operated from before the First World War until just after the Second. The house was a stone building as seen at the time of writing, facing south with a thatched roof, stone-mullioned windows and a front-door lintel engraved 'WLl667EL' for William and Ellen Luty, who were both buried at Hampsthwaite, which was then their Parish Church. Originally it was a farm of 200 acres, but when it changed hands in 1983 it had only a couple of acres.

The house is of two storeys at the front with three chambers over, and to the rear is a long cat-slide roof covering the later service areas of the

The south-west end of The Holme. Built in the fifteenth century, it was encased in stone by William and Ellen Luty in 1667.

Right: 'Dairy' was carved on an inner door to avoid paying the window tax (1696–1851) on that room at The Holme.

Left: The east end of The Holme, where the successful laundry was started before 1914.

Above: Pullans' Darley Laundry workers, pre-1914. The laundry was started by the Pullan family of The Holme in their kitchen at the east end of the house.

Right: Darley village.

house. It has four bays, kitchen, fire bay, hall and parlour, it being very rare to have a kitchen in so early a house in the dale. It was originally built as a single-aisled house with the hall open to the roof. The front and back doors were opposite each other across the kitchen fireplace.

Although built of stone, there was evidence of timber posts hidden behind layers of wallpaper, as was the way with our Victorian ancestors, to keep the draughts out! It was noted that the stone house was about 3 feet longer than the timber-framing at the west end. As well as the initials and date on the door lintel the Lutys had also carved their initials and date on a beam in the hall. It was the custom of the yeomen of the dale to put these date lintels on houses they were proud to have built. Below this beam was some attractive oak panelling and on one of the doors leading from the hall was carved the word 'Dairy'. This was to avoid paying window tax on that particular room. Windows were taxed from 1696 to around 1851, the price on each window varying greatly over the years.

The stairs were within the aisle and there was an eternal cry of 'watch your head' as we went up the low staircase; a semi-cellar dairy, a bathroom and a small sink were also along the aisle. Upstairs were two four-poster beds of a mellow mahogany which must have been built in situ. Unfortunately there was no way into the roof.

In 1981, after the deaths of Mr and Mrs Pullan, the house was put up for sale and Mr Pullan jnr pulled some plasterboard down in the rear service area and I was privileged to see into the roof space. As was expected, here were some extremely large timbers and posts and the remains of a fire hood from the days before the hall was floored over. This all had to be seen with a torch in very cramped conditions. At some time a second layer of rafters and purlins had been placed over earlier thatch. All this confirmed our first thoughts that there had been a timber-framed house on this site long before it was encased in stone by William and Ellen.

When the house was put up for sale it was bought by Mr Foster. He was very interested in its history and its previous owners and planned to put it back to its former glory as a yeoman's house. Much hard work was put in during the spring and summer of 1983, although the Fosters were not actually in residence. Paper and plaster were stripped off the walls, the panelling temporarily taken down and modern fireplaces were removed. The new owners were delighted to find a large arched fireplace in the parlour at the west end of the house, within the exterior chimney. This accounted for the extra 3 feet added to the house when it was encased in stone. Originally the

parlour would have been unheated.

I received a phone call to view this fireplace and was just standing admiring it when the door was opened by a stranger, a passing motorist, who had seen a wisp of smoke rising from the thatch near to this fireplace. We all rushed outside, the fire brigade were called and we hurriedly moved our cars onto the road. By this time the whole of the ridge was alight and burning fast.

The local fire-engine and crew arrived in about eight minutes. Considering that the part-time crew was made up of the local butcher, the baker, a farmer, and others it was a magnificent effort. Later on they were joined by the regular firemen from Harrogate. My husband, seeing the fire brigade rushing out, enquired from the local policeman where the fire was. On being told it was the Holme at Darley, he remarked: 'My wife has just gone down there. I hope she wasn't in the roof with a candle.' So much for confidence in the study of vernacular architecture!

It was very sad to sit on the wall with the owners and watch the house burn. Fortunately the firemen were able to save the panelling.

The official explanation for the fire was a spark from the small wood fire in the dog grate which had caught on to the extremely dry thatch. When the Fosters had found the arched fireplace they had the chimney swept and some plaster must have dropped out, leaving a hole through to the thatch. However, this gave our group a chance to see the roof timbers without the thatch.

One particular scarfing gave us a clue as to the date of the original house from a similar one on the Bolton Percy Gatehouse of the mid-fifteenth century. So here we had a timber-framed house of the fifteenth century, later encased in stone in 1667. This and the fourteenth-century Kettlesing Manor are the two oldest houses still standing in Nidderdale.

Happily the house has had a great rebuild and so has been returned to a beautiful home again. The owners were fortunate to find more great oak timbers to replace the ones burned or charred. And so for the owners and local historians this lovely thatched house in Nidderdale will be there for future generations to enjoy and perhaps puzzle over as we did.

The beautiful four-poster beds had been sold prior to the house sale and so did not burn in the fire, but yes, it was an ill wind that did not blow anybody any good on that August day in 1983.

The house was re-surveyed by the North Yorks and Cleveland Vernacular Buildings Study Group members K. and B. Hutton, H. Voakes and K.M. Barley (survey No. 43), in late 1983, and timber framing was revealed.

Above: *Weavers' cottages at Clint.*

Above left: *Clint stocks and cross.*
Palliser was a Knaresbrough draper.

Left: *Hardgate cottages.*

Below: *Map of the Bishop Thornton area.*

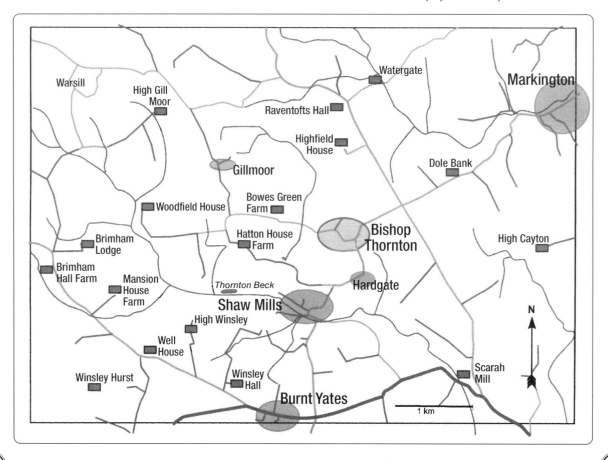

Chapter 10

DOWN THE DALE

Elsy Moss

CLINT

Clint township lies to the south of Bishop Thornton parish, with Thornton Beck as the boundary. It is an area of small hamlets and farms, and in the past the inhabitants' main occupation, along with agriculture, seems to have been spinning and weaving. There are several small lanes between the fields and Spinner Lane and Low (or Law) Lane were very important as they led to a footbridge over Thornton Beck, which brought workers to the fulling-mill in Walk Mill Close.

The adjoining fields, Tenter Gate or Garth, and Pond Close were a part of this medieval industry, where the webs of woollen fabric would be finished, stretched and dried, and in 1531 the annual rent for the Walk Mill was 15s. In the nineteenth century the same site was in use as a 'Book House' or 'Bauk Mill', where linen was bleached. These fields were also valuable as they had the rights of 'Beast Gates' on Bishop Thornton stinted common.

The footbridge is still known as Joye Bridge, the Joye family of Hardgate being responsible for its upkeep, and in title deeds it was passed from father to son for several generations. The present version is relatively new and has two handrails but originally there was only one, and an elderly resident of Shaw Mills recalled that on returning home from her first communion at St Joseph's she had the misfortune to fall from the bridge and ruin her new white dress.

In medieval times the footbridge served another important role in the textile trade – the broggers, who brought the raw wool on horseback and took away the finished webs of fabric from the cottages and farms, made good use of it, their horses wading across. They used the footpath which comes down from Burnt Yates through the fields past some of the spinners' cottages on the right and crosses Law Lane, with access at the time of writing via stone stiles. The path then crosses one of Beckside's fields down to the bridge, continues up hill to Hardgate, and again crosses the main road from Shaw Mills to Bishop Thornton and re-enters the fields through a kissing-gate and up to West Hill Cottages and Colber Lane. All the properties housed spinners and weavers.

Law Lane was also most important for access to the 'Poor Land' called Hop Bank, containing four to five acres. In the 'Endowed Charities of the West Riding of Yorkshire' is a lease for 21 years from 1808, with an annual rent of £6.6s.0d., the rent to be received half yearly and distributed by the overseer among poor persons in the township not receiving parochial relief in sums of 2s. to 5s. There was also access to 'Nelson's Land' near Shaw Mills, the annual rent from which being distributed in the same way. Full use was made of the wide verges, which were auctioned each year at the Nelson Arms to the highest bidder, and the lane was gated at intervals to prevent stock from straying.

Rights of way were often a cause for dispute and in 1454 the verdict of the jury was that:

John Pannal to have a common way with carriage and beasts, 14 feet wide, from his tenement in Clint, as far as two acres of land called Ellerschawe, lying within the north field of Clint, namely by one moor called Whiplamor, as far as a certain close of the said John Pannal containing two acres of land beyond the same close, as far as a close in the tenure of William Hoggeson, and beyond the said close as far as the middle part of a fence between the two closes.

William Hoggeson farmed Beckside on Law Lane, so perhaps the law suit gave rise to the name 'Law Lane', and in the same court in 1471 his son Richard Hoggeson surrendered 6.5 acres of land in the hamlet of Clint called Arkhillfield to William Ellisworth.

The Hoggeson family farmed this land for many generations and their secondary occupation was tanning. When the area which is the front garden and drive of Beckside was cleared, very large stone troughs were unearthed. They are used for floral displays but originally these were tanners' vats. Many tanners were called 'Barker' and several came from Ripon and as far away as Otley, to obtain the various barks required to produce different colours in tanning. Volla Woods in Bishop Thornton provided much of this valuable commodity. The Hodgson family would have plenty of opportunity to sell their leather, for Sir Thomas Ingilby obtained a charter, granted by Edward III, for a weekly market in Ripley to be held every Monday.

In the sixteenth century, the spelling of the family's name changed, as revealed in the 1558 will and probate of another William Hodgson of Beckside, who is buried in Ripley churchyard, showed that he owned stock and goods to the value of £11.l0s.8d., which would not include the heirlooms of best beast, best furniture, etc. His inventory shows the enormous change in values over 430 years:

... four cows, £4; three calves, 22s; one mare and one filly, 33s. 4d; two wethers, four ewes, four tups, four hogs, 29s.; two swine of a quarter old, 4s., three coverlets, one pair blankets, three pairs linen sheets, one pair samcran sheets, two pairs worn sheets, 15s., two board cloths and two towels, 4s., four brass pots, 20s., one cauldron, 13s.4d, ten pieces of pewter, two candlesticks, one salt, one reckon and a rack 2s., two arks and one chest, 3s., one maskfatt, one tub with other hustlement, 2s.

The house has changed dramatically over the years. In the hearth-tax returns of 1666 Laurence Hodgson had only one hearth. Most houses at this period were thatched. In 1946 the original well at the back of the house was still used for domestic purposes, and a small stream from the hill in front provided water for the animals; a large midden occupied most of the area which is the front garden and drive at the time of writing. Although the front porch and kitchen wing at the back of the house date back to around 1946, and the wing to the right of the porch is Victorian, the stone is well matched and not obtrusive.

The original hall house is still visible and the chimney-stack above the modern porch indicates the gable-end of the house. The original inglenook is still intact but the space to the left, known as 'the Priest's hole', is now a lobby with a glass door into the back garden. During the alterations, interior walls of wattle and daub were revealed, but were very badly decayed and sadly had to be removed, but the beautiful spinal beam with pyramid stops is intact.

The original entry to 'the house' or living area is now a window, matching the mullions on either side, and the date stone above, JT 1686, possibly indicates when the thatch was removed, the walls raised by seven courses, bedrooms created from lofts, and mullion windows, made to match those downstairs, were created under the eaves of the new roof of Yorkshire flagstones. The ground-floor rooms may appear to be rather low, the reason for this being the seventeeth-century fashion of having two steps down inside; most of the Ripley houses were built to this design. Even in 1946 the old doorway was the entrance to a 'through passage' to the well at the back door; the room to the left had a packed-earth floor and stalls for cattle. It is difficult for us to realise that the room to the right of the door was the only living area.

One of the old cottages in Shaw Mills had a platform over the inglenook with a 'stee' for access, where the children slept. The room at Beckside is quite large and perhaps, as only bedding is mentioned in the inventory – the parents' bed may well have been in a cupboard.

SHAW MILLS

Shaw Mills is a hamlet, one of four within the parish of Bishop Thornton. The area has always consisted of dispersed settlements and its natural boundaries are streams. Shaw Mills lies to the south, beside Thornton Beck.

During the Saxon period the quern was used for grinding the family corn, as had been the custom for centuries. The Norman occupation from 1066 brought strict government, with water-mills replacing the use of querns for grinding corn; this was compulsory and extremely unpopular, as it entailed long journeys to the mill, where the first moulture (or share) of the flour went to the miller for the manorial lord, the second moulture to his assistant and what was left to the customer and, as no preservatives were added, this meant a fortnightly journey for small returns. Like many children's rhymes, that which follows was political in origin:

There was a jolly miller and he lived by himself, as the wheel went round he made his wealth. One hand in the hopper and one in the bag, as the wheel went round, he made his grab.

The western boundary of Shaw Mills is Colber Beck, which divides the parish from north to south and is the source of water for the corn-mill, and later the flax-mills. In the Claro Wapentake Hearth Tax 1672 (Claro Wapentake was the medieval equivalent of Liberty of Ripon and Nidderdale District), Thomas and William Shaw paid for two and three hearths at the corn-mill, and it is thought this is the source of the hamlet's name.

Shaw Mills, with the village pump on the extreme right.

An early view of Shaw Mills.

As the land is generally of poor quality it was necessary to have another occupation alongside farming, and textiles were the usual choice. To the east and lying on the Nidderdale Way to High and Low Kettlespring Farms and Ripley are the field names Pond Close, Tenter Garth and Water Mills Close, which indicate the site of a medieval fulling-mill, woollen textiles being the first cottage industry, and the surnames Slinger and Webster are still in the parish. In the seventeenth century the Joye family at Hardgate who were responsible for the upkeep of the wooden footbridge across Thornton Beck grew two fields of flax. The change from wool to flax had begun.

With the Industrial Revolution, Shaw Mills expanded rapidly. The manorial rights of Colber and later Thornton Beck were purchased by the Metcalfe brothers of Pateley Bridge. High Mill was built for 'scutching' and 'heckling' of flax, very arduous work carried out by men and older boys. Little Mill House, the original corn-mill, was kept for its customary purpose, and Low Mill was run by the Shutt brothers, the workforce being women and children. The goits and clews of sandstone were created to harness the water power, and are, with the mill-ponds, still intact at the time of writing.

Cottages in Town Street, Pump Row and High Mill Square were built using local sandstone (as were the mills) to house the workers. Four small shops appeared and, in 1808, a Methodist Chapel was opened in the upstairs rooms of three cottages in Pump Row and the downstairs rooms became a dame-school for children whose parents both worked in the mills.

The Nelson Arms, with its date stone of 1791, was

The Nelson Arms.

opened and milk was sold at the hatch at the entrance. This practice continued until the advent of bottled milk after the Second World War. The landlord supplemented his income as a cordwainer for the village, making and repairing the clogs worn in the mills and on farms. Later a cobbler worked in the village until the 1930s.

By 1850 the flax industry was also in decline and, with commendable enterprise, the Atkinson brothers switched to rope making. Hemp requires similar machinery to flax and no doubt the demand for rope increased with the advent of sash windows. Ironically, when a bridge was at last built to accommodate the heavy carts, the coming of the railway in 1863 caused this industry also to become unprofitable, since the mill was too far from the stations at Hampsthwaite and Birstwith to compete.

manufacture of food products, and here began the production of the world's first instant coffee, 'Bantam', packaged appropriately enough in minute tins with a miniscule spoon. It never became popular, due to its unfortunate habit of solidifying in the tin.

G.L. Murphy of Leeds came and produced paints and PVC fabrics, black for blackout material, and in the 1950s coloured lissom fabric for library-book backs, and silver and gold for cheap evening shoes. Later he introduced suede for industrial gloves and skin rugs at Low Mills. At High Mills art suedes were produced in many beautiful shades; this continues, but Low Mills is a housing complex at the time of writing.

Left: *The village pump, c.1960.*

Below: *The village store and Post Office, now closed.*

Maria Briggs, a widow of some standing, changed over to silk spinning and in 1871 employed Robert Threlfall and his three sons as her managers. They later became the owners and lived at Sunny Lea, near High Mill. The Threlfall family did much to create the village we know today, re-housing the workforce in better-designed and built cottages and bringing Robert Stead from Kirkstall to open a general store, later building the High Dam for increased water power. John Threlfall was largely responsible for building the Methodist Chapel. No doubt the family's influence helped in gaining permission for a sub-Post Office to be opened in the general store, where telegrams were dispatched and received.

The village pump provided drinking-water for the inhabitants, but Thornton Beck was the source of supply for all other domestic purposes. After two epidemics of typhoid fever the parish, at last, at the request of the Ripon Union of Parish Councils, provided 'earth closets', shared by two or more families. These were emptied twice yearly by the villagers themselves and later by the 'Night Soil men', who made their last rounds in 1965.

Shaw Mills was noted for its fine spinning and the firm boasted that the silk of Kaiser Bill's underwear was spun in their mill, but the supply of raw silk from Japan became scarcer and more expensive, the First World War took its toll on manpower, and in 1921 the mills closed.

Ten years later, in 1931, John Threlfall leased both mills to Mr Randall Gibson of Farnley, Leeds, for the

Farming is still the main industry, though mechanisation has reduced the numbers employed, and farmers' wives often cater for tourists. In 1960, Sunny Bank replaced Pump Row on a new site next to Mill Bank Terrace. With the advent of piped water the hamlet was extended with Grange Close. The village pump became a sentimental reminder of the past. The General Store and Post Office closed in the 1980s.

In 2000 The Nelson Arms also closed, but there remains a welcoming seat in the youth club garden for travellers on the Nidderdale Way.

HIGH MILLS

The approach to High Mills is only suitable for walkers, as the narrow road beside the goit, which supplied Low Mill with water power, is for access only and was made as a carriage drive to the Threlfall home, Sunny Lea. It was originally gated at both ends and closed one day each year to denote its private status.

The walk from Low Mill by the side of the goit must have been well used by 1851 when the Census

High Mill House.

showed that 95 people worked in the three mills. The worker responsible for opening the clews, the gate which controlled the water flow, to create the extra water force which started the mill-wheels, began at 6a.m. each morning, followed by the workforce at 7a.m. The doors were then locked and reopened an hour later for a breakfast break and latecomers.

On the right at the time of writing is the house, Park View, once occupied by the knackerman who cured hides, his view across Thornton Beck being the old deer park of the Abbot of Fountains which ended at Monks' Wall. On the left a small weir controls the height of the mill-pond and on the right is a row of mill cottages, much altered, which was built in the 1890s by Robert Threlfall to house the workforce and replace High Mill Square and Retting Row.

High Mill Square, 'The Lighthoose'. According to the 1851 Census, a mother, her niece and 19 lodgers were living in this house.

These were a vast improvement, being model cottages with a living-room, kitchen and three separate bedrooms, one earth closet and one coal-hole to each house. Behind these are the ruins of four earlier houses containing a stone-floored living-room with stone sink and a stone staircase to one bedroom. In one of these an Irish woman and her niece had 19 lodgers. All came after the Irish famine of 1846. When they arrived in Liverpool they believed their destination to be Shaw near Manchester, not too far for them to return home. What a shock it must have been, but there was consolation in finding work, a home and a Catholic community.

These houses, which originally had open hearths, were improved in 1870 by iron ranges with side ovens from Todds of Summerbridge. One of these can be seen in Nidderdale Museum's Victorian kitchen, presented by the mill manager at the time of writing in memory of his father, Ronald Steer.

In 1812 the Metcalfe brothers of Pateley Bridge purchased the manorial water rights of Colber Beck from William Brown who owned considerable property in the parish. At the beginning the mill had just five windows and was two storeys high, with a water-wheel on the outside of the end wall which was later enclosed. Extensions were made by subsequent owners. There is a small quarry behind, which was used by the parish for road repairs, but some of the stone may have been quarried for the building of the mill.

By 1812 flax had been established as a cottage industry for at least two centuries. It was processed and spun in the home and then woven by specialists, as shown by George Linton's inventory of 1687. He was a linen weaver and farmer of Hardgate, Bishop Thornton, and the total value of his possessions was £64.14s.2d., a considerable sum for the period. The Hardgate area had many small fields and these were apparently well suited to growing flax. As the business expanded more flax was required and imports from the Baltic came up the Ouse on barges to Boroughbridge and then by carts to Shaw Mills.

Whilst the Metcalfe brothers were there the business was more or less static, and in 1828 they transferred their business to Glasshouse Mill. The

Above: *John Threlfall's cottage at High Mill.*

Left: *Hope Cottage.*

Atkinson brothers took over, James living at Low Mill House and his brother at Woodfield. The boom year of 1845 increased the population figures to 396.

However, by 1851 the industry was in decline and the brothers moved first to hemp and rope making and then, when this also became unprofitable, to silk. The machinery could be adapted to the changes of fibre. Their mother, Elizabeth Atkinson, is shown on the 1871 Census as the widow a of silk spinner, and Maria Briggs, aged 60, is shown as a silk spinner employing 70 hands, with Robert Threlfall and his three sons as managers. This family came from West End and were skilled spinners.

Robert expanded the business, the mill was enlarged and a third storey added. With the need for extra power, using turbines, Thornton Beck was harnessed and the High Dam, goits and clews created. The small building across the road, which is the mill offices and garage at the time of writing, was built as two cottages for hand-loom weavers, space below being living quarters and upstairs housing the looms. This mill is still working in 2003, producing leather and suede for the fashion industry.

The access for carts and farm traffic to High Mill was at the top of Shaw Bank and along Cut Throat Lane, not the site of a murder but the local butchers' slaughterhouse, and is only suitable for walkers and local traffic. Although paved for a short distance it quickly reverts to its early origins as the road to the Corn Mill at Little Mill or Bog House Farm, and

Colber Beck crosses the road at this point. There is a footbridge and in the group of trees on the hill the remains of the mill-dam are visible. The lane turns sharply left and is gated, with the beck now a mill goit, complete with clew, still in working order for the High Mill.

The hump in the front field of the farm is all that remains of the corn-mill. Further along to the right is Sunny Lea, the Threlfall home which has been much altered, and further goits taking water to High Dam, on private land. To the left is Hope Cottage, with half of the last grindstone from the corn-mill in use as a step. This house is two of the remaining cottages of Rotten Row, probably a corruption of Retting Row, this being the first process of the flax industry. The stalks were tied in bundles, weighted with stones and stuck into the water for three weeks. The next process, scutching or beating off the outer slimy coating, was carried out by men and older boys. The ruined buildings in front of Sunny Lea housed the third process of heckling, also an arduous task carried out by men. The green on the right where some of these activities occurred is fenced off at the time of writing. The back of the mill is visible and the Atkinson rope-walk building lay parallel to the long wall behind Hope Cottage.

THORNTON GRANGE

Thornton Grange farmhouse stands on Cut Throat Lane, the spring line at the top of Shaw Bank in Bishop Thornton. It faces due south and has had many alterations, additions and changes of name in its long history.

When William Woodward (whose initials are carved on a blocked door lintel along with a date) made his first improvement in 1726 the house was known as Normanstone, Mill Bank. On the large stone plinth of the existing cottage he more or less

Thornton Grange.

rebuilt a two-roomed house with stout walls, 2 feet thick, with a steep stair to the upper chamber and an end chimney-stack to serve the large inglenook in the living-room or 'house'.

The lintelled and initialled doorway led straight into this room and there was a stone link (or sink without an outlet) by the steep stair. The roof was thatched, the pitch being 40 degrees. A scarfed spinal beam carried the whole weight, the interior walls being wooden panels, and the water-supply came from a substantial stone pump in the front garden, which has lavender beds and low clipped box edgings at the time of writing.

The windows all had double-splayed stone mullions and leaded window-panes, one of which is still visible over the blocked doorway. Downstairs the floors were of flagstones and upstairs 11-inch-wide floorboards, some of which were probably removable to enable this area to be used for the storage of large implements which were not in regular use. The upper floor would not have been very suitable as a living space, the windows being at floor level and the roof rising steeply immediately above with the thatch no doubt visible through the purlins and spars.

At the back of the house was a barrel-vaulted dairy cellar, running into the hillside and entered from inside the house through an iron-barred door, an eighteenth-century fashion. It kept an even temperature throughout the year because a layer of clay ran between the outer and inner walls.

In the 1827 land survey William Woodward's son-in-law, James Shutt, was the owner-occupier, farming 38 acres. He also ran Low Mill, spinning flax and employing women and children. The footpath down to Shaw Mills lies across the lane, directly opposite the farm and through some of the fields, and would have had, at that time, Mill Cottages to the right. His interest in the mill must have been long-standing, for in 1801, at the age of 31, he ran a Wesleyan Methodist class in the mill, which had 30 members. In 1808 he converted the first three cottages of Pump Row to become the first Methodist

Chapel upstairs and a small dame-school downstairs. When these were demolished in 1965 the long chapel hat pegs were still in place.

It is not known whether he was responsible for the next alterations to Thornton Grange, but it is much more likely to have been his son-in-law, John Johnson, as the new roof is of Welsh slates which were not easily available before the coming of the railway. At some point the property, plus the next farm, was purchased by the Thorber, Atkinson and Dearlove families.

The Atkinsons ran the Shaw Mills flax industry and the Dearloves weaving mills in Knaresborough, where the spun yarn from Shaw Mills was made into linen cloth, the speciality being damask for hotels and the railway.

In the 1851 Census, John Johnson of High Mill, Normanstone, farmed 130 acres and his father, William Johnson, and his father-in-law, James Shutt, also lived there; both were shown as retired farmers. As there were also two house servants, they would certainly need the extra extension at the west end of the house, abutting the original chimney-stack.

The old house walls were raised, larger Victorian sash windows were installed and a new front door with entrance porch replaced the hall-house door. The new cottage extension had a separate door and the new lower-pitched roof had gutters and fall pipes, which had not been needed with thatch. Hidden behind a large shrub in the garden was a substantial earth closet.

The barns were also extended, one section with windows, the proposal being to make this into a horse-powered grinding-mill, possibly to replace the existing medieval corn-mill in the adjoining field or to relieve the water power of Colber Beck for the exclusive use of the Top Mill, where the men dealt with the early processing, scutching and heckling of flax. This change was never completed, the windows were infilled with stone and the building once more became a barn for storing hay and corn.

As the mills changed to silk spinning in the 1860s it is not surprising that in the 1871 Census the house was simply called 'The Grange', where Samuel Morrell and his family lived. The room to the east of the front door became a grocer's shop until the 1920s; perhaps this was when the double sash window was installed and a concrete lintel inserted, the only artificial material in the whole building and, unlike all the other windows, without jambs.

Samuel was also a Methodist and along with the new mill owners, Robert and John Threlfall, was largely responsible for the Wesleyan Chapel which was opened in 1904.

In 1936 Francis Stott and his sister came to the farm which was once again called 'Thornton Grange'. His family had for many years been the parish joiners. They provided for the needs of the area, including furniture making.

All the people mentioned in this article are buried in the old churchyard in Bishop Thornton.

DOLE BANK FARM

It is surprising how many interesting features are hidden from view in old buildings – Dole Bank is a good example. One of the largest farms in the parish of Bishop Thornton, it lies on the border of Markington and the east–west road, created when the stinted common was enclosed, passes the entrance.

The present building is mainly of Victorian origin, with date stones and carvings from earlier buildings. One is used as a lintel for the front door and also serves as a sill for the large landing window above. Another is over the large sitting-room window and bears the date 1670 with the holy symbol 'HHX' above.

William de Dal, who farmed here in 1230, established a chantry chapel with priests; the large barn in the farmyard behind is of cruciform design. This was badly damaged in a fire and the authorities demanded that the shape was not altered, so the burnt, rose-coloured stones still remain.

In 1297, Nicholas de Dal was assessed for the tax known as a Lay Subsidy at £4.8s.8d. for two horses, five oxen, four cows, four bullocks, six pigs, eight hoggets, six quarters of wheat, a half quarter of barley, a half quarter of peas, twelve quarters of oats and hay. As wheat could only be grown on good land he was obviously an enterprising man who had made good use of his 200 acres. However, in 1362 Dall Bank passed from the de Dal family to William de Markyngton. This may simply have been land ownership, for Johannes de Dal paid poll tax of 8d. in 1379 and the chantry chapel and priests remained. Although these chantries were disestablished in Edward VI's reign, little notice seems to have been taken of the law, and things continued as usual.

When Edward Ledom farmed Dole Bank in 1586 his name appeared in the Tythe Evaluation but no amount was stated. However, in 1649 when Thomas Berney, gent., leased Dole Bank from Sir William Ingilby for 21 years at an annual rental of 13s.4d., with tithes, he pointed out that he ploughed out all his own land and grazed his sheep on the other side, being Fountains' land, which is land of less value. Times were growing harder, for in 1652 he paid a recusant fine of £156.11s. for his adherence to the old faith.

Marriage between influential families in the area often changed people's lives. In 1602 Sir John Gascoigne married an Ingilby of Lawkland and became heir to the estate. He and John Ingilby, who were both recusants, had to sign and swear in 1606 to a 'New Oath of Allegiance', which caused even heavier fines to be paid, although neither of them regarded themselves as 'renegade' or 'apostate', in other words false or traitor. Even the extra fines did not deter the Gascoigne family, for in 1677 they

purchased Dole Bank with the firm intention of creating a nunnery there. These plans must have been far advanced, as the Gascoigne coat of arms is carved over the back door; and this part of the house both inside and out is seventeenth century.

Although mention is made of Mary Ward, a cousin of the Ingilby family who was certainly in York in the building which became Bar Convent, there is no evidence that she actually came here; she may have assisted with the plans, for certainly some of the interior of the house has a rather strange design for a private dwelling.

These plans received a heavy blow in 1678 with the State Trial of Recusants, and it seems that although Frances Bedingfield had led a small group of Mary's women here, the nunnery was never really established. Their pastor, Thomas Thwing, a priest and nephew of Sir Thomas Gascoigne, certainly lived at Dole Bank. Both were arrested and although Gascoigne was acquitted Thwing was executed at York.

In Ewan Messenger's will of 1700 he is described as 'of Dole Bank in ye Constabulary of Bishop Thornton, Gentleman'. Years later, John Messenger, priest, left a set of Breviaries dated 1758, as well as a handwritten book on the Mass, dated 1756. These were held in St Joseph's Presbytery. Ideas were changing and life was easing for recusants.

In the 1827 Parish Evaluation, Richard Darnborough farmed 105 acres at Dole Bank, with John Greenwood, of Birstwith, the proprietor. In 1835 Richard certainly had a vote when, in common with the majority of Thornton township, he voted for the Liberal candidate, Lord Morpeth. In 1841 he does not appear to have used his vote, although the candidates were the same and his rent was over the required £50 threshold. In the 1851 Census Dall Bank (the name still used by local people) was occupied by Thomas Atkinson with Nancy, his wife, and four children. The family were still there in 1868 when Joseph Atkinson also voted Liberal, but as Isaac Holden was the candidate favoured by the Ingilby family, did this influence his choice?

Many changes occurred in the twentieth century and mechanisation has totally changed the farming pattern. At the time of writing Dole Bank still sits peacefully by the roadside, but the land is worked by adjacent farmers; 100 acres is no longer a large farm.

WATERGATE

Watergate is one of the oldest farms in Bishop Thornton parish, being mentioned as a 'detached holding' in the fifteenth and sixteenth centuries. It is well named, for until the 1960s the road from Thornton to Fountains Abbey, which passes the buildings, was indeed a ford across Hebden Beck on the boundary with Markington to the east, curving westward to form the boundary between Sawley and Bishop Thornton.

Watergate, built in 1665.

Almost all the freehold tenant farms in the parish surrounded the stinted common which allowed them to use their rights to the appropriate number of cattle gates allotted. In the case of Watergate, their fields on the lower ground near the beck were much richer and included crops such as grain, the common being used mainly for grazing.

At the time of writing the main entrance faces south, for this is the new wing, possibly the third rebuild, created from outbuildings when Naylor Warwick gentrified the property by raising the roof, probably adding the upstairs storey to both sections and placing a new date stone over the door for his 1880 transformation. He faithfully reproduced the windows with dripstones, a pedimented doorway, kneelers at the gables and no doubt the very handsome farm buildings; the very large staircase window does not quite match the rest of the property.

The 1665 hall house was in fact placed east to west and also appears to have been a rebuild, for the bottom courses of stone are much larger. This would make the possibility of an earlier building much more probable, because it was common practice in medieval times to build houses facing these directions where the doors and windows opened, as they believed that the Black Death could be 'carried on the South Wind'. Nidderdale had many victims of this devastating plague which came in waves, beginning 1348 and continuing spasmodically until 1664, usually starting in Knaresborough and spreading up the dale. It claimed 54 per cent of the population so we can see the need to take precautions.

The blocked front entrance can still be seen in 2003, although shadowed by Naylor Warwick's imposing porch. The date stone is worn and not easy to identify. The axial stack is in this wing and still serves the kitchen. There is a household pump at the back and Hebden Beck is only the width of the

garden away. This is the only farm with a mounting-block still in its original place.

As a consequence of the close proximity of Hebden Beck, and the inconvenience of a ford on the doorstep, it is not surprising that the farm had its own small cattle bridge. Whether this was used exclusively by the family and animals is not known – perhaps when the beck was in full spate pedestrians were allowed to use the very stout edifice.

It is often difficult to discover the names of tenants on farms, but in the valuation of 1827 Thomas Ridsdale was both proprietor and owner of Watergate, farming 51 acres, his assessment being £15.10s. per annum. Although William Lupton from a nearby farm was the enumerator in the 1851 Census, there was apparently no return for Watergate. However, in the 1871 Census James Ridsdale aged 54, retired farmer, his wife Margaret aged 40, and four children from 17-year-old Jane, to one-year-old Richard Burton, are listed.

Census returns can sometimes be inaccurate, as in the 1881 Census where Richard Burton Ridsdale is given as 'widower, retired yeoman, aged 69', living in a cottage with his 19-year-old daughter as housekeeper and his son James aged 16 as the farmer's son – a real mix-up of names. Watergate farmhouse was occupied by William Haxby, hind, and his wife and family, obviously in charge until James reached manhood.

The last Census in 1891 is the more accurate because Miss Stead, the niece of Richard Burton Ridsdale, gave a wonderfully descriptive picture of her uncle and his age. He owned greyhounds which he fed on legs of mutton, and started a fish farm for trout by stone-lining the banks of Hebden Beck by the farm, placing metal grids at each end and importing round, dressed-stone troughs from Leeds for breeding. The enterprise does not seem to have been very successful but his outings with his friends to the inns in the area were a topic of conversation for many years.

In 1835 and 1841 Thomas Ridsdale voted Liberal, but in 1848 his son Richard voted Tory – whether this was due to the change of candidates, or whether his relatives, the Steeds who voted Tory, had persuaded him to change, we can only surmise. When the voting pattern in Nidderdale is studied it becomes apparent that when farmers improved their status by moving to more profitable farms they often changed from being Liberal Nonconformists to voting Tory and becoming Anglicans or Roman Catholics.

Certainly the pace of life was speeding up, with mechanical aids to lighten the drudgery of many farming tasks becoming available and the realisation that the ability to read about new methods made local schooling a priority. The mills in the area had begun to meet these needs and both St Joseph's and St John's Churches had schools in Bishop Thornton.

At the time of writing Watergate is still a working farm, incorporating Raventofts Farm, and has been run successfully for many years by the Baul family.

RAVENTOFTS HALL

Raventofts Hall was the home of the Archbishop of York's forester and before the Stinted Common Enclosure Act in 1758 it would have been very secluded with the access a bridle-way. Information from before the fifteenth century is scarce, but 'toft' was often the Saxon name for an isolated farm, which would fit this dwelling very well.

The house has been enlarged with a wing added, and some of the stonework, which has ogee moulding around the windows, is very similar to that at Fountains Abbey. There must, however, have been a much older forester's house on this site as the forester's job was to collect the rents for the Archbishop and generally oversee the parish. By 1456, although the farmers were technically 'free men', he also collected the corn and hay tithes for the Dean and Chapter of Ripon, so perhaps a more appropriate title would be that of steward.

The Walworth family came early in the fifteenth century to this important position and in 1460 John Walworth built a parochial chapel dedicated to St John the Baptist, referred to as the 'Capella Foresica'. It stood on a hill in the centre of the parish and by the side of the Bridle Way or Coffin Road, which skirted the stinted common. Some of the paving-stones for walkers are still in place, but the tower of the 1826–8 rebuilding is all that remains as a landmark. Parishioners were still required to make their four main communions each year in the Church of St Wilfred in Ripon, where they also had to go for baptisms, marriages and funerals. Some exceptions were made, as in 1470 authority was given to Robert Castilforde, perpetual vicar of the Prebend of Studley, to marry John Wittes of Thornton and Margaret, daughter of John Walworth, in the Chapel of Thornton, on the Feast of the Holy Trinity.

After the Reformation many people in Bishop Thornton did not obey the law and attend the new Anglican services, although the penalties for recusancy were high, being 1s. for each service missed and for the gentry £5 per week. The Rising of the North in 1569, when Catholic gentry tried to revive the old religion, was well supported by Nidderdale families. After its collapse John Walworth was convicted, but not executed. Between 1500 and 1604, 56 people from Bishop Thornton were presented as recusants and of these 31 were repeat offenders. Nearly half the Catholic population of the West Riding lived in the Ripon and Claro districts. In 1584 the numbers were 422, when the tax on recusant gentry was £240 per annum, and in 1600 the number had risen to 1,013. By 1614 fines had increased to £1,200, to be paid in instalments, and shortly after this the Walworth family were ruined and Raventofts Hall and land were purchased by Sir William Ingilby.

Most of the building dates from the seventeenth century and it is interesting to note that to the right of the relatively modern porch there is no fire window, although the axial chimney-stack serves back-to-back fireplaces in the entrance hall and main room; one of the bedrooms and other rooms with fireplaces do possess small fire windows. When both of the downstairs fireplaces, which had been blocked for many years, were reopened in the 1970s, it was discovered that the main room had an inglenook with stone hobs and smoking chambers with iron bars for hanging hams and bacon above, and on each side of the fire basket was log storage space.

However, the distance between the back-to-backs is 9 feet and, even allowing for all the walls to be 24 inches thick, this leaves a space where the fire window should be of 30 inches by 24 inches, just large enough for a priest to shelter in if the authorities paid a visit, the access being from above, most probably at the top of the staircase. All of the downstairs rooms have stone interior walls but upstairs some of the traditional wood panelling for room division still remains, where unobtrusive openings would be easier to conceal.

A kitchen wing was built at right angles to the main block. This had a large fireplace for cooking with plenty of light and space for spit roasting, so food preparation would have been transferred from the main room. Although the bressumer beam and stonework has smoke and heat marks, they may have been caused by a deeper inglenook and larger fire from an earlier period.

Many people who had lived in the area, including a previous occupant, believed that the room over the kitchen was used for the Mass, and certainly Raventofts always had a resident priest. Many families, including the Ingilbys, sent their sons to Douai in France to be educated, some eventually training as priests. Newton Hall near Ripley was a starting point for the priests, and they then made their way up the dale, travelling by night. Nidderdale fortunately has many small groups of trees and by careful planning the journey could be made under cover. Raventofts also had the traditional ghost, a headless nun who walked in the orchard at midnight, no doubt giving the priest a relatively safe time for exercise.

There was also a cockpit in the orchard, the remains of which are still visible, and it was certainly used long after the official abolition of this sport. As it was not unusual for farmers to arrive at Raventofts to pay their rent, perhaps this and cock-fighting were good excuses for attending Mass. From 1741 all missionaries in the West Riding were under lay patrons with the exception of Raventofts, which was under the vicar as it was 'an ordinary house with a Chapel contained in a room'.

Father James Skelton and Henry Maire were imprisoned in Ripon gaol in 1743, under suspicion of corresponding with Prince Charles, the Young Pretender, and at this time, of the 54 families in

Right:
*Raventofts
Hall.*

Left: *St John's mortuary chapel.
Only the tower remains at the
time of writing.*

Right: *A close view of
Raventofts Hall,
which has no fire
window downstairs.*

Left: *The new kitchen wing
at Raventofts Hall with the
Mass room above.*

Bishop Thornton, 23 were Papists. Henry Maire retired to Cliffe in 1777 and was succeeded by Fr Jeremiah Wilson and Fr Gart. They soon left and an émigré priest, Fr Pier Roucheron, is then recorded.

By the middle of the eighteenth century the Hall became the main centre for Nidderdale Catholics and on 6 October 1785 Bishop Mathew Gibson is recorded as confirming 48 people, Richard Talbot being the priest, having succeeded when Fr Skelton died in 1760. The Relief Act of 1791 was passed, allowing licensed Catholic chapels, and Raventofts Hall returned to being a farmhouse.

Perhaps the fact that the east half of the parish, beyond Colber Beck, was farmed by the lay brothers of Fountains influenced the yeomen to retain their old faith. 'It was the Mass that Mattered.'

RAVENTOFTS MILL & FARM

In Bishop Thornton there are only two straight roads, created when the stinted common was enclosed in 1758. The north–south road, from Sawley to Ripley, and the east–west road, from Markington to Shaw Mills, cross at right angles at the Drovers Inn. They gave easier access to the farms and fields newly created by the enclosure, as the original paths and bridle tracks had skirted the common through the old farms, the church and the mills.

One of the original bridle-ways led from the Sawley road down to Raventofts Mill in the eastern half of the township, easily accessible for Sawley and Warsill parishes also. It was probably the earliest in the area as the Archbishop of York's Forester, the lord of the manor's representative, lived at Raventofts Hall. The income from tithes and the dues imposed for the compulsory grinding of corn at the lord's mill were an important part of the landowner's income.

The Boddy family were the millers for a number of years. They also operated a sawmill. As with many families in Bishop Thornton, they were staunch recusants and would have welcomed the opening of St Joseph's Roman Catholic Church in 1809. They lived at Raventofts Farm, about a mile up the hill from the mill, where they worked 115 acres. The earlier house had stone slates and Yorkshire slide windows, but was considerably enlarged with the impressive Queen Anne façade with its sash windows by John Boddy in 1827. His family eventually moved away, some to America, in the mid-nineteenth century.

In 1871, Joshua Jackson was the corn miller and was joined by his son some time before 1881.

The bridle-path beyond the farm enters woodland and on the right the few remaining walls become visible amongst the trees. The bridge over the beck is a substantial stone structure, strong enough to bear laden wagons of grain and wood. It is gated, as the fields on the Sawley side are open. The bridle-path passes Ashfield House and eventually rejoins the Sawley–Ripley road.

GILMOOR

Colber Beck in Bishop Thornton divides the free farms of the eastern half of the parish from the lands of the monks of Fountains Abbey in the west.

Gilmoor, or Gillamora, was the sheep grange sited along Colber Lane and from there, on a clear day, the towers of York Minster are clearly visible. The many hilly fields are suitable for pasture rather than arable farming. Over the centuries the size has varied slightly; in the 1827 survey, when Thomas Kay was the occupier, he farmed 146 acres, but by 1871 Robert Stubbs, his wife and children farmed 130 acres.

The fields have interesting and informative names. 'High Bouse' and 'Low Bouse' are pastures. 'Homestead and Mill', which has a good supply of water, is the stack-yard and was possibly the site of the monks' grange. Whether the mill was for grinding their own grain, mainly oats, or just for grinding holly leaves for winter feed is not known. There is a 'Stripe', which lies parallel to the lane, as do the other long narrow fields in the parish, and is not in any way connected to open-field farming.

Another field, called 'Isaacs', was a medieval coal pit where the lay brothers extracted coal for Fountains Abbey. There is considerable evidence of this, including fossil impressions.

The Gilmoor farmhouse, which is seventeeth-century in origin, was originally thatched. The Victorian sash windows and the lower-pitched Welsh-slate roof were added after the railway came to Nidderdale. During roof repairs it was easy to see from the inside that the walls had been raised and the upper crucks reused for the slate roof. They were not in their original pairs and the third pair was new timber. The original ones had been used in the open cart shed to the right of the house, which serves as a sifting-out area, because they were twisted and not suitable for a slate roof.

The modern glass-panelled entrance door is the only light in the baffle entry and the axial stack above serves the back-to-back inglenooks in the main rooms. To the right of the door in the sitting-room the inglenook has a fire window to the rear. As the bedroom contains a fire-

Gilmoor in the summer.

place an end chimney-stack was needed.

In the room to the left of the door the inglenook is equally impressive and makes this a very gracious dining-room, accommodating the enclosed steep stairs. A door on the left leads to the kitchen, which originally would have been the parlour bedroom. Children sometimes slept upstairs but in most inven-

Left:
Gilmoor
Farm,
showing
details of
alter-
ations.

Below:
The
details of
Gilmoor.

Bowes Green.

tories the upper rooms were for storing farming equipment, plus apples and pears for winter use, and hams.

A new entrance has been made directly into the kitchen area and a door at the back leads down into the eighteenth-century dairy, which is almost underground with barrel-vaulted ceiling. There was a layer of clay between the inner and outer walls which absorbed ground water to keep the temperature even for storing dairy produce.

Many Yorkshire Cistercian houses sold their wool at Boston Fair in Lincolnshire, but as Ripon also had a wool market in the fourteenth century they may have used this outlet, although there was a strong trade in wool with the Continent. The Cistercian order, which desired simplicity and therefore wore a white woollen habit, developed granges and had lay brothers, 'Conversi', to work the land. Through their various activities, however, they must have had to deal with outside forces. Did they in fact lose good beasts from their fields in the early-fourteenth century, after the Battle of Bannockburn, when the Scots certainly raided Fountains, Killinghall and Hampsthwaite? There is a Scotsman's Close in Bishop Thornton, but this lies near the Drovers Inn used when Scottish beasts were brought down to sell in England in the eighteenth century.

Bowes or Booze Green on Colber Lane was a dairy grange for Fountains, and we know that the name is of very early origin because Roger de Mowbray gave this farm to the monks, resulting in a lawsuit as the land belonged to the Archbishop of York. The farm there at the time of writing was built in 1659. This date stone is over the back door with the owners' initials in between, '16 TB FB 59', and, like Gilmoor it was originally thatched. As it was much altered in the nineteenth century it is difficult to realistically work out the original plan, but it certainly replaced the monks' grange, for in the 1827 survey this is called 'New Homestead' and again the stack-yard is called 'Old Homestead'.

At that time Mark Hutchinson was the occupier and Thomas Bunn the proprietor, with 201 acres. By 1871 Joshua Dickenson, his wife and nine children farmed 198 acres. In the 1851 Census four families of farm labourers are also listed; there is no indication of where these families lived, but there are numerous outbuildings which have changed their use many times over the years. At the time of writing the Sowray family farms both Bowes Green and Gilmoor and has done so for many years.

This farm also has many strange field names: 'Old Frank', 'Sorrow Sykes', 'Zealand', 'Rape Close', 'Tinkler Stripe' and 'Mucky Lane'. As the bridge over Colber Beck is relatively new, and Colber Lane a road maintained by the farmers, 'Mucky Lane' would be very apt. 'Sorrow Sykes' is still very appropriate, and several farms had 'Rape Closes', so this was even then presumably a successful crop. 'Tinkler Stripe' was one of the wide verges, supposedly used by gypsies and itinerant workers who helped at harvest time.

From the front of the farm the new Victorian wing and windows are visible, as are the outbuildings which were erected at this time. However, the back view reveals the external chimney-stack, the altered height of the roof, the original kitchen and arched fire window. The date stone and the large cornerstones indicate the desire for a substantial building. Both these farms had the right of 'turbary', the collection of peat from the moor, which was the usual fuel for cooking before the arrival of the railway and the availability of cheap coal.

Footpaths across many of these fields were used when neighbours helped one another and provided access to the church and to the two schools of St Joseph and St John's in Bishop Thornton. Most of the lanes originally had very wide verges, which were annually auctioned for cattle grazing. Many lanes were gated at intervals to contain grazing beasts.

As the land in the parish is not highly productive, most households had dual occupations – in the past this was the spinning and weaving of wool, and later flax, for the Ripon market. In the twenty-first century holiday visitors enjoy the peace and farm food at Bowes Green.

WOODFIELD MILL

This corn-mill, now an elegant country house, still functioned until the 1950s and was known locally as 'Whopping Mill' because of its 40-foot wheel, the largest in the area. It lies on the western boundary of Bishop Thornton parish and Thornton Beck was its source of power. A small weir and clew on Thornton Beck, which runs beside the house, forms the mill-race with the mill-pond lying immediately behind the mill to power the large wheel.

Although always a corn-mill, from the end of the eighteenth century Woodfield was jointly used for flax bleaching and possibly retting. In the 1851 Census Robert Ingle was the miller and James Atkinson, who lived at Woodfield Mill House, was a flax spinner employing 20 people. His cousin, Thomas Atkinson, was an overlooker.

Woodfield Mill.

Four cottages were occupied by bleachers, flax spinners and card feeders. This would be an ideal area for bleaching as water-mills needed no chimney, the fallout from which would otherwise soil the yarn. The Atkinson brothers proved to be very versatile, improving their methods of spinning and building a bauking (bleaching) mill on the site of the medieval fulling-mill at Walk Mill Close. They also used chemicals to bleach the yarn, which took weeks rather than the months taken when it was left out in the sun and rain.

A rough track lay directly in front of the mill and crossed Thornton Beck by a footbridge, proceeding to Mansion House Farm and the road to Brimham Rocks and Burnt Yates. This was the nearest mill for farmers to use in the surrounding area, which includes Warsill. Transport was always a great problem. One elderly farmer remembered making four journeys with his father on foot, with a sack of grain tied to each side of the horse's saddle, although each return journey with the flour would be lighter.

As the century wore on, the mounting cost of importing flax from the Continent by boat, barge and flat cart was pricing out linen yarn. A further cost was taking the spun yarn to Knaresborough for weaving. It is not surprising that all sections of industry in Nidderdale welcomed the coming of the railway in the 1860s and in many cases were instrumental in hastening its arrival.

By the 1871 Census Woodfield Mill had reverted to its main use as a corn-mill, the cottages were empty and Abraham Dobby was the miller. His house dated from 1782 and is exactly the same design as Mill House in Shaw Mills, which has no date stone but, when this was altered some years ago, coins of 1788–90 were found, carefully placed in the spinal beam.

After the First World War farming methods were changing, more transport was used and machinery for harvesting became available, although the custom of farmers helping each other through these busy periods still prevailed. The footpaths, which today are used for pleasure, were then for workers, schoolchildren and churchgoers.

In the 1930s a building was constructed beside the road leading to the mill, using stone from some of the disused cottages; it became a collection station for milk. Mixed farming was still practised and each farmer brought his milk in large cans with a brass plate to denote ownership. The lorry collecting them returned empty cans and when reloaded crossed the bridge and went up the steep hill to Mansion House Farm on to the paved main road to Birstwith Station. The destination was the Co-operative Dairies in Leeds.

Country people were always prepared to walk quite long distances for enjoyment. Their destination on Saturday evenings in the 1920s would have been Woodfield Mill. The upper floor became a dancehall and the music was that of the local fiddler.

Chapter 11

CHURCH & CHAPEL

Hampsthwaite Church.

HAMPSTHWAITE CHURCH
Muriel Swires

Hampsthwaite is the earliest recorded church in the dale, founded by William de Stuteville of Knaresborough in 1175. The church registers only date from 1603. It is almost certain that an earlier church existed here because early-Norman grave slabs and one possible Anglo-Saxon one can be seen in the building. The church is dedicated to St Thomas à Becket. William de Stuteville's brother-in-law was one of the four knights involved in the murder of Becket and after the foul deed fled to Knaresborough. Maybe William wished to clear himself of any participation since Becket had been canonised in 1173 as St Thomas the Martyr.

William de Stuteville died in 1203 and was buried in Fountains Abbey. In 1257, Richard, Duke of Cornwall, who was William's successor, granted the church to the friars of the House of St Robert of Knaresborough, which accounts for the number of early incumbents listed as friars. It remained in

the patronage of St Robert's until 1538.

No doubt this first church would have been a simple building with nave and chancel – no aisles or tower. The services would have been mostly in Latin and conducted behind the rood-screen between nave and chancel. There would have been no hymns and only occasional sermons and before the fifteenth century few seats except stone benches near the wall – hence the expression 'weakest to the wall'. The floors would have been strewn with rushes or straw and there was no heating. Aisles were added when processions became popular – on Ash Wednesday, Palm Sunday, at Candlemas, at Corpus Christi, etc. The tower was added at the beginning of the sixteenth century. Towers were primarily built to house the bells.

Much damage was done to the church in the Scottish raids following the Battle of Bannockburn, but restoration seems to have taken place quickly.

An interesting brass, one of the few from the period 1340–70, shows a long-haired and bearded man in typical dress of the time. He was probably a member

101

Above: *The interior of Hampsthwaite Church.*

Right: *White marble memorial to Amy Woodforde-Finden in Hampsthwaite Church.*

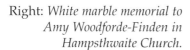

Left: *Early grave slabs inserted in the wall of the church porch at Hampsthwaite.*

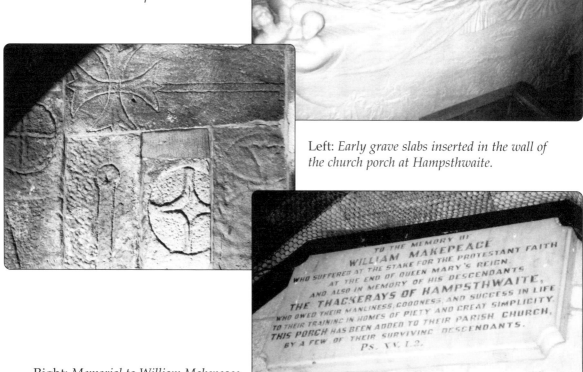

Right: *Memorial to William Makepeace Thackeray in Hampsthwaite Church.*

Hampsthwaite village with the vicarage on the right, 1930s.

Above: *Church Street, Hampsthwaite.*

of the Beckwith family of Clint. In 1347 there are references in Grainge's *History of Harrogate and the Forest of Knaresborough* (1871) to John, William and Adam Bekwyth. Some vandal in 1570 tried to make it do duty for another person by roughly cutting an inscription on the figure: 'PRAYSE GOD FOR YE SOULE OF AD DYXON, UNCLE TO VYCAR DYXON, AUG 15 1570.' Thomas Dixon was the vicar between 1558 and 1587.

In 1349 the incumbent died from the effects of the Black Death and in 1361 another vicar died from a later outbreak of the plague.

A chantry was dedicated to the Virgin Mary and St Anne in 1510. Chantry priests said Masses for the repose of the souls in purgatory where they went to purge their guilt before going to heaven. In his will in 1536 Robert Beckwith left several spiritual bequests:

I give to the house of St Robert to pray for my soul, 3s.4d. Also I give to Sir William Sotheron, chaplain of Hampsthwaite, to sing a trental of masses for my soul and all Christian souls 5s.

'Sir' here is not for a knight but a title used for priests who were not university graduates (who were described as Master). There were several other bequests and among the witnesses to the will was Sir Thomas Dacre, vicar of Hampsthwaite.

With the Dissolution of the Monasteries in 1538 the church became the property of the Crown. All chantries were closed in 1547 because it was decreed in England that there was no such thing as purgatory.

Samuel Sugden, vicar from 1670–86, was frequently in trouble. In 1682 he was accused of tavern haunting, brawling and immorality. At the back of the church is an oak panel with the carved names of Samuel Sugden, 'Vicar 1671', and his four churchwardens. Other fine woodwork in oak, including the pulpit, is of this period. A gallery was built at the west end in 1725 with the inscription: 'MR THOMAS LEUTY BUILT THIS LOFT AT HIS OWN CHARGE 1725.'

An entry in the Parish Register on 6 August 1785 tells of Matthew Mason who was executed at York for breaking into Hampsthwaite Church and stealing 17s. and some copper and silver cups. Peter Barker's name is also mentioned – he was totally blind but a joiner whose work was much sought after, and who rang the bell every night at eight o'clock.

The church, except the tower, was rebuilt in 1820. When it was pulled down evidence was found in the nave which suggested that it had previously been enlarged or altered on three different occasions.

The parish of Hampsthwaite was very large and included Felliscliffe, Birstwith, Menwith with Darley and extended as far west as Padside. During the nineteenth century three daughter churches were built at Darley, Birstwith and Felliscliffe, so a smaller church was needed, and the alterations were carried out in 1900.

Robert Thompson of Kilburn constructed the lych-gate. John Haxby, the village joiner, restored and used the old oak pews and panelling and repaired the pulpit. John's brother, William, was the sexton and parish clerk and on Sundays he rang three bells single handedly with a bell rope in each hand and one attached to his foot by a loop.

The font is a simple Norman tub font. Near it is a memorial to the composer Amy Woodforde-Finden. The white marble effigy has scenes from her songs and was given by her sister, Mrs Sinclair MacLeay. It is the work of George Wade of London and was unveiled in 1923. She is buried in the churchyard with her husband Col Woodforde-Finden.

The porch was constructed by the Thackeray family of Hampsthwaite, descendants of the famous novelist, William Makepeace Thackeray, and over its door is an inscription in his memory.

Over the door, inside, is the royal coat of arms. In the south aisle is a portrait of Jane Ridsdale whose memorial is outside in the graveyard – she was only 31 inches tall. The tower screen is also the work of Thompson of Kilburn. The east window, known as the 'Peace Window', was given by the Aykroyd family to celebrate the signing of the Treaty of Versailles in 1919. A new organ was installed in 1949.

The Rogationtide service of 1951 was the first to be broadcast from a Nidderdale church.

In the graveyard surrounding the church are many more interesting memorials.

RIPLEY CHURCH
Muriel Swires

The earliest settlement and church we know of in Ripley was by the river, about half a mile south of the present village. When the river changed its course the church on the bank became unsafe, so it was decided, in the mid-fourteenth century, to move it stone by stone. Farmers from Killinghall, then part of Ripley parish, and Ripley transported all the stones and fittings from the 'Sinking Chapel' to the present site.

As early as AD705 Bede, in his *Ecclesiastical History of the English Nation*, mentions a synod held near the river Nidd. Bones were moved from the early chapel burial-ground when the new church was built, but 600 years later, in the late 1980s, when Yorkshire Water workmen were installing a new pipeline, bones were disturbed in a second burial-ground. An archaeological investigation of the site in Chapel Flats Field uncovered 124 skeletons laid out in graves in the Christian manner.

Ripley Castle, the home of the Ingilby family for nearly 700 years.

Other objects were found, including an eighth-century bronze buckle and a fragment of some page-turning tweezers of the kind used by ecclesiastical scholars. This revived the interest in the theory of the synod site being near Ripley. In the Knight's Chamber in Ripley Castle is a small seventh-century bronze fragment with scroll decoration excavated from the site.

Thomas Ingilby, grandson of Sir Thomas the Judge whose tomb is in the church, had the present church built in around 1390. He died in 1393 and both he and his wife were buried in the new church. However, there are records of two chantries and two chantry priests in 1289. One was dedicated to St John the Baptist and the other to Our Lady. Rectors are listed from around 1300 and the rector in 1369 died from the plague.

In the church are materials and features from the old chapel, with part of the old oak rood-screen inserted in the south aisle, the double piscina in the chancel, and the twelfth-century columns in the north aisle but, in the nineteenth century, the capitals of these were replaced in concrete. The Parish Registers date from 1552.

The altar tomb of Sir Thomas Ingilby and his wife is in the south aisle. He was a judge who died in 1369 and is dressed as a knight in armour. She is in the dress of the day. Around the sides of the tomb are images representing their children. This same Ingilby was granted a weekly market for Ripley in 1357.

The church was dedicated to All Saints and its earliest-known rector was Richard Kendall who died in 1429. He was buried at Ripley and a brass in the church commemorates this.

In the churchyard on the north side of the building is the so-called Weeping Cross. Arthur Gaunt, FRGS, wrote in 1950 that it was probably a Death Cross similar to those marking the way on corpse roads. The track from Clint to Ripley can still be traced. He thought that the 'knee holes' were possibly receptacles for votive offerings and not for mourners to kneel in. This, however, is just

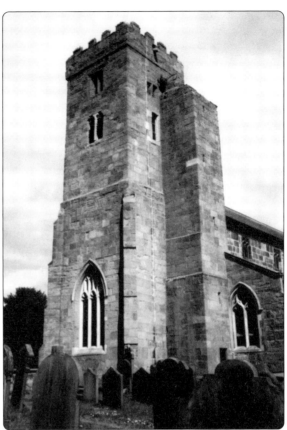

Above: *The Death or Weeping Cross, with eight niches. In the centre of the upper stone is a deep rectangular hole to hold the shaft of a large cross.*

Ripley Church tower was raised in 1567 with the staircase enclosed in a huge buttress.

Below: *Ripley fair, 1908.*

conjecture, as the very early date and use still remain a mystery.

Much alteration has been done over the years. From the Valor Ecclesiasticus of 1535 we know it was a wealthy church. In his will of 1542 Thomas Wescow of Killinghall left 1s.8d. for 'the building of Ripley Steple'. It was 25 years before the tower was raised, with a staircase encased in a huge buttress. At the same time the nave walls were raised and the clerestory added with five windows in each side to give more light in the church.

Where the vicar's vestry is at the time of writing was a chantry with a piscina. The hagioscope, an opening through which the priest could be seen officiating at the high altar, is still there but hidden behind an Ingilby monument. When chantries closed in 1548 the two priests were Henry Shaw and William Thompson. Nineteen years later Henry Shawe, curate of Ripley, was persecuted for not having communicated for one or two years – he was probably the last incumbent of the chantry chapel of St John the Baptist.

Ripley was well endowed – indeed we find the rector in 1544 leaving the parish for Peter Knaresborough of Killinghall to find a priest to take the services. The tithes and glebe land were leased to the rector for £33.6s.8d. per annum, and he undertook to find an able priest and pay his wages.

An Act of Parliament in 1581 made recusancy (being a Roman Catholic) punishable by a fine of £5 a week. The Ingilby family were recusants. Francis, son of Sir William and Lady Ingilby, was ordained a Catholic seminary priest in Rheims in 1583 and returned to England a few months later. In 1585 Elizabeth I passed an act making it treason for a Catholic priest to be found in England, or to harbour one – an innkeeper was put to death for sheltering a priest's horse. Francis secretly held services in Yorkshire, and particularly Nidderdale, for two years. Margaret Clitheroe of York sheltered him. He was finally captured in 1586 and imprisoned in York Castle, from where he was taken to the Knavesmire to be hung, drawn and quartered on 3 June 1586. In 1987 the Sir Thomas at the time of writing travelled to Rome to attend a service in which Pope John Paul beatified Francis, the first step to canonisation. In St Joseph's Church, Bishop Thornton, is a shrine to him with a portrait in oils copied from the one in Ripley Castle, painted by Barbara Bruce with permission from Sir Thomas.

Much destruction was done to churches in the seventeenth century by Cromwell's men. Amongst other damage the troops defaced and smashed part of the 1369 Ingilby tomb. Sir William Ingilby and his sister Jane joined the King's Army at Marston Moor in 1644 and after the battle they escaped back to Ripley. He took refuge in the Knight's Chamber, but trooper Jane met Sir William Waller at the castle gatehouse, brandishing two pistols, one in each hand,

stating that her brother was not there. Cromwell was informed and so he confronted Jane himself. He billeted his soldiers in the church where they damaged the Ingilby monuments, but he spent the night in the library facing the indomitable Jane holding the pistols. His soldiers shot loyalist prisoners outside the east wall of the church, where the bullet holes remain. Other prisoners were shot outside the castle gatehouse. Most of the Anglican clergy had supported the King, with the result that many were ejected and replaced by Puritan priests. Nathaniel Rathband was a Puritan rector in Ripley in 1656, but was thrown out in 1660 at the Restoration of the monarchy.

Pews were bought and sold in the seventeenth century, the rents being an important source of income. The poor who couldn't afford to pay were uncomfortably crowded into seats at the back of the church. The Ingilby family had larger pews in a family chapel, now hung with hatchments with their coats of arms painted on.

In 1667 the aisle walls were embattled and in the mid-eighteenth century the floor was raised and square pews of oak installed. The nineteenth century saw many alterations. The organ of 1846 was replaced 14 years later. In 1862 new roofs were installed, pillars and arches were stripped of plaster and refaced, the porches were rebuilt, the floor lowered to its original level and pews were replaced by open seats, as well as the installation of new windows. The clock in the tower was presented to the church in 1879. Six years later the chancel screen was decorated with shields of the passion symbols and the choir stalls were put in.

Flood lighting was introduced and a new organ installed in 1938. After restoration the old bells, dated 1640, 1701 and 1717, rang out to celebrate the new millennium – they had not been rung for 30 years.

There are other interesting features in the church, among them a very old stone with an ancient flagon engraved on it, stained-glass windows and an Ingilby monument of 1617 with an effusive epitaph which someone in 1623 obviously took exception to and added underneath: 'NO POMP NOR PRIDE, LET GOD BE HONOURED.'

THE QUAKERS IN NIDDERDALE
Mary Barley

The Quaker movement was established in Nidderdale in the mid-seventeenth century. It particularly appealed to farmers and weavers who lived some distance from the Parish Churches of Ripon, Kirkby Malzeard and Hampsthwaite and who had become disillusioned by the Anglican clergy. These people were attracted by the teachings of George Fox, who placed great importance on a simple religion and the inner light. There was to be no Mass or communion and no altar, just a group of people gathered together to praise God silently and to speak only when divine guidance moved them, and who became known as Friends.

Thomas Taylor from Preston Patrick in Westmorland was the first person to preach the Quaker message in Nidderdale. His brother also preached in Hartwith, Dacre and Felliscliffe and sowed the Quaker seed in the dale. According to the chronicle of pioneering days of Quakerism, 'The First Publishers of the Truth', William Settle of Harefield, Pateley Bridge, received him. William Settle died in 1661.

Among the earliest converts were Miles Oddy of Bent House, Dacre, and Peter Hardcastle of Hardcastle Garth, Hartwith. The Hardcastles were formerly grange keepers for Fountains Abbey and were at Hardcastle Garth for over 200 years. A plot of land was enclosed in the field behind Hardcastle Garth House for Quaker burials in 1658. The first burials recorded were those of John Hardcastle on 16 May 1661 and Peter Hardcastle on 17 January 1661/2.

Early Quakers were great evangelists in the 1650s and their refusal to pay tithes to the parish priest and to take oaths or bear arms made the government fear they were revolutionaries. 'Swear not at all' and 'Let your yea be yea' were commands not to be broken. Quakers were severely persecuted after the Restoration of 1660. Acts were passed in 1662 and 1664 forbidding the gathering of more than five people, other than the inhabitants of the house concerned, for worship not authorised by law. The 1664 Act fined Quakers £20 for such gatherings and £40 subsequently; some people were even transported. The years 1660–77 were the worst for the Quakers. The law entitled informers to receive one-third of the fine – no wonder the spies were busy. It was not until the Toleration Act of 1689, under the rule of William of Orange (1689–1702), that houses could be registered for dissenters' meetings.

When this act came into force the house of Peter Hardcastle of Hardcastle Garth was registered as a Quaker meeting-house, together with the houses of Miles Oddy of Bent House, Dacre, and Peter Moore of Bewerley. In 1696 a new meeting-house was built at Sand House, Dacre, although burials had taken place there in an enclosure from 1688, including the burial of Alice Oddy, wife of Miles. By the end of the seventeenth century Quakers were found to be living within a few miles of these meeting-houses at Longscales, Ripley, Killinghall, Padside and Menwith. In the upper dale seven Quakers were presented for non-attendance at the established church. Before the Toleration Act, Quakers frequently interrupted Church of England services and had to be forcibly removed. They called these churches 'Steeple Houses' and would not doff their hats in deference to any man, not even the magistrates.

Life was hard for the Quakers, the rules were severe, the dress very simple and manner and deportment considered important attributes – a

The lintel and doorway of Hardcastle Garth where the Quaker meetings were held in 1666.

woman would be reprimanded for wearing ribbons on her bonnet. No mourning apparel was to be worn for a funeral, no gloves, scarves, or cakes taken on the death of a neighbour.

If a Quaker married a person 'out of the faith' they would be disowned and occasionally the mother of a daughter marrying out would also be disowned for indulging her daughter. Young folk wishing to marry had the ordeal of appearing before the Women's Meeting, the Men's Meeting, and the Joint Meeting to be examined about 'being clear of all others'. In 1827 Thomas Walker of Darley was reported for marrying out of the faith, but continued to attend together with his wife and children. After five years they were allowed back into the faith.

Captain John Levens, a Parliamentary leader during the Civil War, joined the newly founded body of Quakers and suffered imprisonment in York Castle for refusing to take the oath of allegiance. He died in 1688 and was buried in his own orchard at Levens Hall, Killinghall, as were his two sons. Peter Hardcastle was another who spent a long time in York Castle, and he wrote an article called 'The Quaker Plea'. He said Quakers would not swear an oath or swear on the Bible:

The more we are suppressed by rigor and violence, imprisonment, persecution and banishment, the more people will incline towards us, for it is common in all ages that whatsoever people have been persecuted for conscience sake, the more will people be favoured towards us.

In a paper of 1705 entitled 'Quaker Sufferings for the Tythes', we read:

1: Taken from Thomas Hardcastle of Hardcastle Garth by John Scaife, Constable of Hartwith and Samuel Midgely churchwarden (so called) by virtue of a Justice's warrant for church dues, two pewter dishes worth 11s.8d., one warming pan, one tankard, in all 17s.8d. Demanded at first 2s.6d.

2: Taken from Robert Hardcastle of Ripley and Thomas Gill of Hampsthwaite by John Midgely, Constable of Birstwith for that called a church lay charged upon Wreaks Mill and by virtue of a Justice's warrant, one mare worth £1.10s.0d. Their first demand being 5s.

After the Toleration Act, the Quakers became less aggressive and settled down to a more sober and gentle life. They were mainly farmers who, judging by their wills and inventories, were reasonably prosperous but not wealthy. Quaker women needed to be of strong character to keep the home and farm going while their men folk were in prison.

The pagan Roman names for the months were not recognised by Quakers. The first day of the week was Sunday, so they wrote 'the first day of the third month, 1688'. In a book written by W.H. Sessions, *More Quaker Laughter*, instead of people saying '30 days hath September', etc., they had their own rhyme:

The fourth, eleventh, ninth and sixth,
Have thirty days to each affixed,
And every other, thirty-one,
Except the second month alone,
Which has but twenty-eight in fine,
Till leap year gives it twenty- nine.

Quakers looked after their poor well and many wills left money to charities. Thomas Hardcastle of Hardcastle Garth, yeoman, signed his in 1724; he left a total of £245.6s. to charities, of which £180 was owing to him. Robert Spence, butcher of Hartwith, also signed his in 1793 leaving £217.14s.6d.

Education was also very important to them – Quaker schools were founded at a very early date at Ackworth and York and several local children attended them. Many Friends signed their own wills in the early-eighteenth century, showing that they were literate.

A surprising number of Quakers travelled to North America to visit Friends – some made the hazardous journey several times in the eighteenth century.

Gateway into Dacre's Quaker burial-ground, which dates from 1685. John Skaif paid £21 for the meeting-house in 1802.

In 1721 one meeting at Darley on the 28th day of the 8th month reports: 'Nothing to present to the meeting except love.'

However, by the late-eighteenth century, after visits to the dale by John Wesley, Methodism took root in Nidderdale. Methodist rules were not so harsh as the early Quakers' and so, by the end of the eighteenth century, Dacre meeting-house fell out of use. The stone was sold to build a more convenient meeting-house at Darley in 1802.

The two previous burial-grounds at Hardcastle Garth and Dacre had no headstones but by the nineteenth century headstones were allowed. Many of those around the Darley meeting-house are of the Walker family. The last burial at Darley was in 1896 and in 1950 the meeting-house closed and was sold. The Friends meeting-house for Nidderdale at the time of writing is in Harrogate – it was built in 1854 for the use of visitors to Harrogate Spa.

METHODISM IN NIDDERDALE
Eileen Burgess

One of the features of the dale in several of our villages and hamlets is that of houses which have obviously been converted from another use. Barns, mills and chapels, redundant from past centuries, are now homes.

Above:
Bouthwaite Chapel. William Snell, who defended Thomas Mitchell with his clogger's knife, may have lived in the cottage next door.

Above right:
Low Lofthouse, home of the Rayner family and one of the earliest meeting-houses.

Right: *Lupton Fold, Pateley Bridge. The Lupton family was prominent in early Methodism.*

What is striking is the size and position of many of the former places of worship – tucked away in remote farms, like Newhouses and Woodmanwray, or standing proudly like the Playhouse in Pateley Bridge. They bear witness to the great fervour of the Methodists in the dale during the nineteenth century, although they were probably seldom filled to capacity, except on celebratory occasions.

Methodism was brought to Nidderdale in the middle of the eighteenth century by preachers from the industrial West Riding. They found ready ears in places where the Anglican ministry was of poor quality, although strong enough to organise a fearsome resistance to men like Thomas Lee. He was a quiet, softly spoken man, not the ranter we might imagine, but very courageous. Several times he was attacked by a large mob that had been incited by the Pateley Bridge curate, and on at least one occasion was nearly killed. His first visit took him to Hartwith and drew listeners from far and wide. One of these was Francis Darnbrook of Greenhow who invited him to preach to the lead miners. As a result, Darnbrook lost his job and was thrown off his land.

Small groups of these people, men and women who were affected by the preacher, came together for mutual support. They met in houses and barns for prayer, Bible readings and discussion of their faith. One elderly man, who had heard Wesley preach, described the scene to his grandson, John Swales:

On meeting night the house was lit by tallow candles and had a peat fire, the floor had been washed with buttermilk and sanded, extra chairs and forms brought in. The Leader had a little round table in the corner. The hymns were repeated line by line.

By the time John Wesley came for the first time in 1766 there was already a firm basis on which his movement could operate. Although he was an Anglican minister and insisted that his sect was intended to supplement the work of the Church, not supplant it, he was refused permission to preach in the church at Pateley (then St Mary's at the top of the hill). Instead he was taken to Thomas Green's orchard nearby, where the men stood in the rain with their heads uncovered. He said that he had not seen such a congregation since Newcastle.

Green was a churchwarden and Thomas Pullan was a church official. Matthew Rayner led the orchestra in Middlesmoor Church as well as leading three Methodist classes, and others maintained their regular church attendance. Wesley insisted that prayer meetings must be held outside the normal service times.

The great strength of the movement was that it involved ordinary men and women. They were actively encouraged to take part in all aspects of the life of the group, in contrast with the Anglican Church where services were essentially performed by the parson with the laity making laid-down responses, but with little participation otherwise. In Methodism the congregation played an integral part, giving testimony and joining lustily in the hymns. By 1765 the Pateley Chapel paid 3s. for a copy of the words of Charles Wesley's hymns, which were used with local tunes.

Ordinary men and women used their organisational skills to administer their class meetings. These were groups of about 12 members paying 1d. at each weekly gathering. One of the more educated would read from the Bible and from Wesley's commentaries, which was followed by a discussion. Members were free to speak of their own faith, giving testimony of the goodness of the Lord. They were helped with purchasing and reading their own Bibles – the great emphasis coming from personal salvation. They were taught to read, but not necessarily to write. The most fervent members organised themselves into 'bands' whose proceedings were completely confidential and demanded high levels of commitment.

As the movement grew, some of the more prominent class leaders attracted more members than they could cope with in one class – Jonathan Lupton had 42 in his. There were five classes at Lofthouse, two under William Rayner. Members who were noted as having particularly strong testimony were invited to become local preachers. They had a trial period when they were exhorters, accompanying a trained man and gradually taking services, then a probationary period when they were observed for the quality of their preaching. After a final examination on their knowledge of scripture they were admitted to 'Full Plan'. This demanded a high degree of commitment – walking vast distances in all weathers to take Sunday services after a week of hard manual work. They had to have a high standard of moral behaviour; in the early days they had to ask permission of their fellow local preachers if they wished to marry and could be expelled if the woman was not a Methodist – in 1843, Brothers Lee and Cowling were both dismissed. Improper behaviour, including drunkenness, led to expulsion; as ale was the only drink available until the mid-nineteenth century this

North Pasture, Fellbeck.

Newhouses Chapel.

was a very real temptation. 'Brother Taylor never attended a place of worship except when he had to preach' and Brother Gill was expelled for 'heterodoxy and contempt of this ecclesiastical court'.

Some of the local preachers were real characters, particularly those of Greenhow whom Harald Bruff described. As he could not write, 'Ly' repeated his sermons to himself for several hours in order to learn them. 'Eli', another, would pray 'Git thee gone, Satan! Pick up thi trapsticks an away wi' thee. Aye, that's reet. Now us can praise t'Lord wi contrite hearts.' Another, renowned for his fiery preaching, was standing on planks across a water tub, addressing an outdoor gathering. 'A little while and ye shall see me no more' was emphasised by a heavy stamp – the plank snapped and he descended into the water!

Mary Barritt, an itinerant preacher from Lancashire, wrote:

We had a good time at Braisty Woods... in Dallowgill in one night 36 souls found peace with God... I visited Greenhowhill but a Local Preacher lived there that had proved a hindrance to the work. However, lasting good was done.

After speaking one Sunday morning at 9 o'clock, a young man in the crowd laughed at her. She cried out three times, 'O God, bring down that laughing sinner', whereupon 'his face gathered paleness and in an instant he fell down in distress until Tuesday morning'. He converted in Pateley Bridge Chapel and became a local preacher. Mary's work led to women preachers being banned in 1803 – she married a minister, Revd Zachariah Taft, and presumably worked through him for the rest of her life.

The work of the classes and preachers was supervised by the travelling minister, based first at Haworth and then at Otley in the early days, who visited each area once a fortnight and each society once a quarter, more often in cases of sickness, to keep the books and take a list of members each year. He had to administer the Lord's Supper as often as possible (after the schism from the Anglican Church) and conduct quarterly Love Feasts. He was paid a small stipend and provided with accommodation,

The first Wesleyan Chapel in Pateley Bridge was opened on 22 September 1776. In this chapel, where John Wesley himself preached, men and women sat on different sides and entered by separate doors.

Longscales, Kettlesing, was the site of the first Wesleyan Chapel in the lower dale.

although when the Pateley Bridge circuit was formed in 1811 he complained about the standard of furnishing – members had presumably offered their redundant equipment.

Members originally met in cottages or barns, but as the movement grew, dedicated buildings became necessary. Thomas Green converted two or three cottages into a meeting-house, but the first purpose-built chapel in the dale was at Pateley Bridge, on land given by Sarah Ragg, née Gouthwaite, in 1776.

Harvest festival. The chapel is possibly Fellbeck.

Summerbridge Wesleyan outing. The picture includes: Harry Gill, Michael Todd, Charles Gill, Annie Todd, Smith Skaife, Arnold Bonner, Mrs J.W. Gill, Maud Gill, Smith Skaife junr, Harry Petty, J.A. Gill, Maggie Todd, Raymond Gill, Alice Skaife (by the railings).

It was followed shortly after by Lofthouse, given by Moses Rayner, and Longscales at Kettlesing. In contrast with the Anglican churches these were preaching houses, with the seating grouped around the pulpit. Men and women were separated and had their own entrances. Until Methodism broke away from the Anglican Church after Wesley's death there was no need for a communion table.

Wesley came to the area four more times. In 1770 he preached at Tadcaster at noon and Pateley Bridge in the evening, when it rained on the congregation in Thomas Green's orchard. Two years later he preached in the evening, and on the way to Otley with his wife stayed at the Moorcock Inn above Darley; 'Perhaps Providence sent us to this house for the sake of these two poor souls.' On the third occasion in 1780 he was finally allowed to preach in the church. His final visit was in 1788 at the age of 85, when he left Pateley Bridge at 4a.m. and reached Kendal that evening, travelling in a little yellow painted chaise with two cropped horses – 'little black uns they were'.

Wesley's pulpit in the first chapel, where the minister was Revd Holman. Also pictured are: *Mrs Todd, Annie Busfield, Misses Shann, Mr Shann, G. Pudsey, J. Richmond, R. Bowes, W. Marshall, ? Dawson.*

In the early years of the nineteenth century the Industrial Revolution brought new problems and opportunities. The Methodist tenets of fair play, industry and high moral code helped to bring a strong work ethic. Many of the textile-mill owners had risen from the ranks because of these ideals and as employers found that their support led to a stable, industrious workforce. The Metcalfes at Glasshouses, Francis Thorpe of New York Mill and Shutts at Shaw Mills were all prominent members and gave liberally to support the chapels, expecting in return high levels of behaviour but not tolerating improvidence, ignorance or licentiousness. They tended to clamp down on many of the traditional amusements and concentrated on 'improving' recreations.

One of these was the establishment of Sunday schools, which were very important locally as the established schools were nearly all Anglican. Many of the children were employed full time in the mills in the early-nineteenth century and, until half-time education became compulsory in 1833, it was the only schooling they had. Although there had been an earlier attempt, Pateley Bridge and Bewerley Sunday schools were established in 1818, meeting in the George Inn and the old monastic chapel respectively.

In one session they read the Bible and learnt simple arithmetic, and in the second recited texts and Bible passages and learnt hymns. They were able to buy Bibles, prayer and hymn books at cost price – these were also awarded as prizes for good attendance and progress. Special anniversary services, when the children took an active part, increased their confidence, and each year they were rewarded with a treat – in later years this was walking to the mill-owner's house, playing in the gardens and having tea.

Wesley's form of Methodism had never been the only one – there were several running parallel, although only one had any impact in the dale. A small group of followers of Benjamin Ingham met in the King's Arms, Pateley Bridge, for a while. However, in the 1820s the Primitives, led by Hugh Bourne and William Clowes, gained a considerable foothold. They tended to be more fundamental and appealed to the lower working class, whereas the Wesleyans had been popular amongst skilled workers and the middle class. The Primitives had chapels in most of the larger villages, although they had only a quarter of the number of Wesleyan adherents. In Pateley their first chapel was behind the Post Office, but was replaced in 1859 by the building which is used as the Playhouse at the time of writing. The Low Laithe Chapel in the centre of the village was replaced by Belle Vue, endowed by Richard Pullan of New York Mill, the only Primitive mill owner. In Lofthouse almost all the Wesleyans seceded to the Primitives, but later many returned.

To reinforce their faith, both branches of Methodism had regular revival meetings. Love Feasts had been established by Wesley himself – special preachers were engaged for lengthy services when testimony could be given by any of the members present. To sustain them, and probably to remind them of the Last Supper, Love Feast Bread was passed round, together with a large, two-handled cup of ale (later water).

The Primitives had camp meetings. A description of one at Glasshouses in 1869 recorded that:

Friends mustered at the chapel at 10a.m. and from thence marched through the village and sang several hymns and tunes that were popular among Primitives of former days. Then they walked to the Camp ground where short sermons were preached by the Minister and

Laying a foundation-stone for the new Wesleyan Chapel in Pateley Bridge, 1908.

Summerbridge Wesleyans at Birchwood. Included in the picture are: *Alice Gill of Dacre Banks, Nellie Dunn, Bessie Eccles, Miss Redshaw, F. Nelson, F.M. Gill, Minnie Gill, Mary Gill and Alice Skaife.*

four other preachers. The audience was very attentive and remained to the end of the service.

Even more ambitious was a Wesleyan rally at Brimham Rocks in 1887, when special trains brought people from as far away as Leeds and Ripon, with transport by carts from Dacre Station. A choir of 100 from local chapels led the worship and the catering was done by the women of Pateley Bridge, Glasshouses and Wilsill who baked 60 stones (about 1,000kg) of bread amongst other things. As always there was criticism that not everyone supported the event as they should have done, and the load was carried by just a few. Nothing changes!

Finance was always a problem, especially for the Primitives. The mill owners put in a great deal of money and when mills got into difficulties the chapels suffered. The construction of buildings, and having them rebuilt, was always costly. The debt of £300 for the first Pateley Chapel was not cleared for 70 years. However, the involvement of the mill owners could bring its own problems. Up to 1846, John Greenwood of Birstwith gave £2.10s. a quarter to the Methodists at Wreaks, and in 1835 built a chapel, but never conveyed it to them. He said he wished his heirs to continue the provision if they so desired but, being Anglicans, they didn't.

They pulled the chapel down and built the school in its place. It was not until 1858 that a replacement was erected outside the village at Clapham Green.

Throughout the nineteenth century the social life in the villages revolved around the chapels. As well as the Sunday schools there were many other organisations. Improvement societies were established for the further education of the men, although some of the lectures must have been beyond the knowledge and interest of the members. Women had their 'Bright Hour'. Once teetotalism took hold in the 1870s the Band of Hope became an important feature, encouraging young people to sign the Pledge. Revd Hosea Hewitt, the Independent minister, declared in the local paper that Pateley Bridge was 'a very pandemonium of drunkenness and vice.'

The YMCA had its influence on older teenagers. One minister drew up a list of amusements which were acceptable and those which were not: bagatelle, circus, chess and fishing were allowed, but billiards, pantomime, whist and shooting were not. The theatre was the most difficult because, although many people said it could be a force for good, there was an association with immorality. He must be turning in his grave now that his chapel has become the Playhouse!

A children's tea party at Dacre's Wesleyan manse.
The two little boys on the left are believed to be Harry and Fred Summersgill.

By 1892 attitudes became more relaxed, for the Primitives agreed to have a magic-lantern show, providing all youngsters were kept out of the gallery. Presumably the slides were of a religious or improving nature.

Concerts were excellent ways of raising money. A variation was the Fruit Banquet when hymns, songs, and recitations were interspersed with trays of sliced fruits, tarts and pies which were passed around for refreshment. Sunday-school and chapel anniversaries brought special preachers, concerts and public teas. There were two classes – high (with ham) at 9d. or 1s. and plain tea (bread and butter and cake) at 3d. Tickets were sold beforehand and free ones slipped to regular members who could not afford the cost for their large families. They attracted large numbers – the tiny hamlet of Heathfield catered for 300 at its June gathering.

Christmas Day tea was a feature of the chapels – Pateley Primitives, not having a Sunday-school building, used the Oddfellows' Hall next door for 300 in several sittings, followed by a concert which was 'not overly religious'. The ladies each hosted a table whilst the men stoked the boiler, carved the ham and waited on the guests. The celebrations concluded with a concert by members.

Music was always important in Methodism. Even tiny chapels had choirs, whose members were taught to sight-read music. The standard of music was very high, in fact Nidderdale was known as the most musical of the dales. Some of the villages could manage to perform the *Messiah*.

Methodism continued strongly throughout the dale during the nineteenth and early-twentieth centuries, but began to decline as the industries closed. Greenhow struggled once the lead mines failed in the 1880s. In 1933 the Methodist connexions united nationally. In each village the membership was transferred to the largest or best chapel, and the others closed. Since then several more of the smaller hamlets have lost their place of worship, although Wath, one of the smallest in the country, remains open.

Warsill Chapel.

Chapter 12

TRANSPORT

Eileen Burgess

BRIDGES

Nidderdale has some interesting bridges, ranging from the miniature Thornthwaite packhorse to the strong practical Hampsthwaite. Although none can be counted as ancient in their present form, they have had many predecessors over the centuries.

We find it hard to imagine just how difficult it must have been to cross the rivers and becks in winter before there were bridges. Stepping-stones were an aid in fine summers, but no use in wet seasons. Even so they continued for centuries in some places – Glasshouses Hippings (stepping-stones) across the river were not replaced until the middle of the nineteenth century and a few streams still have them, as well as across the river from Low Hall, Dacre, to Manor Farm, Hartwith.

The earliest bridges were just planks of wood set across supports. The oldest version of Fellbeck's name, Fellabrigabec, meant 'the plank bridge across the stream'. The original site of the bridge was not where it is at the time of writing, but was downstream near Fellbeck Old Hall, where the beck joins a tributary: the present bridge dates from the creation of the turnpike road in 1756. In some places the wooden plank was replaced with stone flags to make a clapper bridge, such as the one on Colber Beck in Bishop Thornton. There was one on Tang Beck where Randall Lane, the packhorse route from Otley to Ripon, crossed it. Unfortunately, it was washed away in a storm. Was this Wham Bridge, which was maintained jointly by Birstwith and Felliscliffe, but in 1759 was out of repair, Felliscliffe refusing to continue repairing it because all the damaged stonework was at Birstwith's end?

Packhorse bridges were just wide enough for a laden animal to pass over – the parapets were low, so the packs could ride over them. Thornthwaite Bridge is a delightful miniature, a single tiny arch, almost a semicircle. Although known as a packhorse bridge, it doesn't appear to be on any direct trade route and was probably intended for people going to the nearby Thornthwaite Church, established as a chantry chapel of ease in 1402 to save the long journey to Hampsthwaite Parish Church.

Randall Bridge, Tang. The clapper bridge on Randall Lane, over Tang Beck, was washed away some years ago. This photograph, taken in 1945, shows the large flat bridging stones supported by a central pier. It was on the same route from Otley to Ripon as Haxby Bridge. The man on the extreme right may be Frank Pepper, who lived nearby at the time.

Left: *The packhorse bridge at Thornthwaite. This very tiny bridge was probably erected for worshippers going to the chapel of ease nearby, which was established in 1402. The priest was maintained by parishioners keeping the 'chapel stock' of sheep along with their own, and paying 1s. for each ewe.*

Right: *New Bridge, Wath. The predecessor to this bridge was erected in the sixteenth century. When this structure replaced it, the orginal bridge was only wide enough for a horse, the packs having to extend out over the sides. Carts had to have one wheel removed. In 1890 a second bridge was built alongside and the centre wall removed.*

Left: *New Bridge at Birstwith is a beautiful bridge which was built in the 1820s to replace an earlier one, known as Haxby Bridge. It is on the packhorse route from Otley to Ripon, and is wide enough for carts.*

Wath or New Bridge, dating from at least the sixteenth century and included in Cary's map of 1787, was a single-width packhorse bridge until 1890. Carts, which were going over to take corn to the mill, had one wheel removed, the axle sliding along the parapet whilst it was propelled by the remaining wheel.

There is another 'New' bridge at Birstwith – so called because in 1820 it was a replacement for the old Haxby Bridge on the packhorse route from Otley to Ripon 'Up Swincliffe, Down Swarcliffe And ower t'New Brig into Hartwith.' The earlier one was the subject of a penance in 1594 when Francis Ellis and his concubine had to appear at Kirkby Malzeard (the Parish Church for Hartwith) and do penance there and then bestow 20s. on the bridge.

The earliest mention of a bridge at Pateley is in 1320 when the Archbishop of York was granted the right to hold a market and fair at Pateley Bridge. It was a wooden footbridge with an animal and vehicle ford alongside, which can still be seen just upstream. Leland said it was a wooden bridge in the sixteenth century. It was probably rebuilt in stone in the eighteenth century and widened in the early-nineteenth, though the dates are not certain. Underneath on the town side are the masons' marks, where each man registered his work. In 1833 it was repaired at a cost

Above: *Pateley Bridge. The ford was upstream and can be seen when the river is low. Under the arches, the original eighteenth-century bridge and its nineteenth-century widening can be distinguished – the original section is ribbed. Masons' marks were visible in the right-hand arch until flood-prevention work was carried out in 2000.*

Above: *Hampsthwaite Bridge. The Roman road crossed slightly higher upstream. Before the turnpike road (A59) was built, the bridge was on the important cross-country route from York to Lancaster. The walls are of much finer dressed stone than the arches, suggesting they are of a later date.*

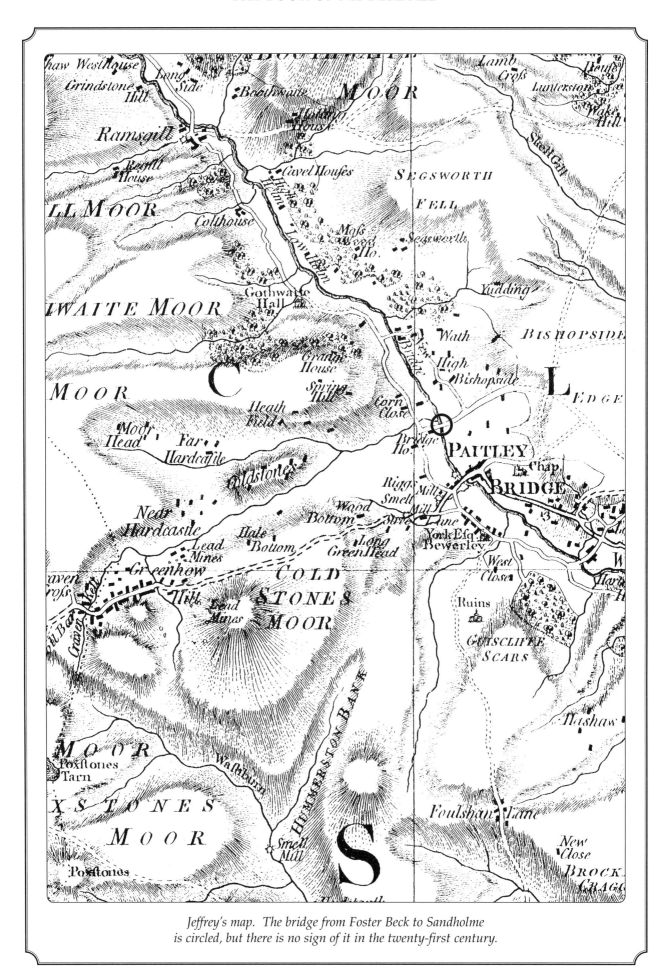

*Jeffrey's map. The bridge from Foster Beck to Sandholme
is circled, but there is no sign of it in the twenty-first century.*

Whitley Bridge, Darley, provided access to Hartwith Church. It was here that James Atkinson met his sweetheart. Notice the stepping-stones in the foreground. This bridge was washed away and not replaced for several years.

of £76.3s.2d. by the contractor John Allason.

Making or repairing a bridge counted as a pious act in medieval times – leaving a bequest was said to aid in the transition to heaven, a practice which continued at least until the end of the sixteenth century among the Roman Catholics of the dale. John Bayne of Riggs left 3s.0d. for the 'widing' of Lofthouse Bridge in 1595. Hampsthwaite Bridge was the subject of several bequests – one from Maud Beckwith of Clint Hall who gave 3s.4d. in her will of 1544. It was on the main route from York to Lancaster, but strangely it was never a county bridge, much to the dismay of the local inhabitants, who resented having to keep it in repair for strangers to use. Eventually, in 1638, they persuaded the Wapentake of Claro (the medieval equivalent of the Harrogate District) to take it over. Even so, it was done on the cheap – two surveyors said it couldn't be built of stone for less than £400 and wood was too scarce locally. In the end it was patched up with wood for £25. Later it was built in stone and afterwards repaired by William Holmes in 1832 at a cost of £434.5s.2d.

Darley Bridge over the Nidd has always been a footbridge and was probably first built in the early-eighteenth century. In 1747 there was a dispute about Darley being a parish bridge – it was ordered that each township had to repair six yards from the spring side for the safety of the bridge and highway, at a cost of £2.10s.0d. This bridge has a tragic tale to tell. One summer evening in 1858, as Mary Jane Skaife was walking home from Hartwith Church, she was met at the bridge by her former sweetheart, James Atkinson.

They quarrelled, she tried to escape from him but, overcome with jealousy, he stabbed her and left her body in Stumps Lane. Grainge, writing a few years later, says that a stone marked the spot. Atkinson was sent for trial but was judged unfit to plead and was detained at Her Majesty's Pleasure.

One bridge has completely disappeared. A bridge at Sandholme, where Foster Beck joins the Nidd about three quarters of a mile above Pateley, was agreed by Fountains and Byland Abbeys in the late-twelfth century. The nearby farm on the Bewerley side was Bridge House grange, an offshoot of the Bewerley one, giving its name to Bridgehousegate ('the way to Bridge House') and so pre-dating the bridge at Pateley first mentioned in 1320. It was shown on Jeffrey's map of 1772 and was copied onto several others, but does not appear in Greenwoods' of 1818. Many floods and the construction of retaining banks have eradicated any traces of the foundations.

Bracken Bridge at Hampsthwaite was important because it was on the direct route to the Parish Church which served the south side of the valley up to the top of Thornthwaite. It was, therefore, maintained by the whole parish. In 1563 the inhabitants of Hampsthwaite and Rowden had to mend the highway from Bracken Bridge to Hampsthwaite mylne (mill) by midsummer. In 1821 it had to be repaired because it was the corpse or hearse way, but not a general carriageway 'except for the lower end of Birstwith'.

Summerbridge was first mentioned in the Fountains Abbey Bursar's Books in the middle of the fifteenth century. In 1536 Robert Beckwith of Dacre

Glasshouses Bridge. The first bridge was erected in the 1850s but was washed away soon after. There were several replacements. The wooden bridge in the photograph was destroyed by a flood in 1927. There have been two others since. One of the children may be Herena Wilkinson (better known as Rena Lonsdale).

Summerbridge, on the way from Fountains Abbey to its grange at Dacre.

left 2s.0d. for the repair of Summerbridge. It was on the route from Dacre Grange to the abbey and after the Dissolution of the Monasteries in 1547 it became a county bridge. In 1757–97 new wing walls and battlements were added at a cost of £300 by Richard Allanson. It was widened in 1904, following the improvement of Dobson Lane a few years before.

Wreaks Bridge, known at the time of writing as Birstwith, was built in 1812–14 at a cost of £3,791.12s.8d. and consisted of two arches of 28 feet each and one of 33 feet. Before the bridge was built there had been a ford for horses and carriages, with stepping-stones for ped-estrians. Hiram Craven of Dockroyd was the mason and Samuel Whitaker of Blackburn was pavior.

These bridges were built in times of horse-drawn traffic when the greatest strain on them came from the rivers. Today, heavy vehicles pound across subjecting them to pressures that the original builders could not have foreseen. It is a tribute to their workman-ship that the structures continue to serve us well.

THE RAILWAY

Darley Station, on the LNER line from Harrogate to Pateley Bridge, opened in 1862. It was not, however, the first attempt to bring a railway up the dale. In 1818 a group of manufacturers and gentlemen commissioned the great Thomas Telford to survey a line from Pateley Bridge to Bolton Percy on the Ouse. This would transport the stone and lead from the quarries and mines and bring in flax for spinning and

Darley Station, on the LNER line from Harrogate to Pateley Bridge, which opened in 1862. The single-track line ran alongside the river, looking down the dale.

123

corn for grinding, as well as coal and many other domestic supplies. The report published by Telford gives a fascinating picture of the dale of the time and its potential, as the Industrial Revolution was just arriving in Nidderdale. Interestingly, the proposed line took a route almost completely on the opposing bank to that eventually used.

The possibility of using the new steam engines to pull the trucks was left in abeyance – horses would be used at first. A great innovation was the suggestion that passengers might supplement the commercial revenue; had the railway been built, it could have been the first passenger service in the country, pre-dating the Liverpool and Manchester Railway by a decade.

But it was not to be – the scheme failed and for 30 years the idea was shelved. The new railway companies had far more profitable enterprises to interest them throughout the north. John Metcalfe, of Glasshouses Mill, whose family also had interests in the lead mines, coal mines and brewery and later Scotgate Ash Quarry, bought shares in the Leeds–Thirsk Railway. He eventually became a director and persuaded the company to draw up plans for a line linking Pateley to the Leeds–Thirsk line at Nidd in 1848. He was not the only person on the board pushing local interests and more powerful lobbies pressed harder. Time and time again the Pateley line was postponed in favour of other routes.

His son George, later of Castlestead, became a shareholder and took up the cause, speaking at every meeting. In August 1851 he condemned the directors so vehemently for their 'want of faith' in sacrificing the branch that he was forced to apologise for speaking with undue warmth. He was appeased by a promise that the company would proceed as soon as the Teesside extension was completed. However, a year later the promise was retracted, with caustic comments that if George would 'anticipate the directors and persuade the shareholders to agree', the chairman would not stand in the way.

In 1854, when the new North Eastern Railway Company was established, John and his son began to lobby again, this time with a deputation from Nidderdale, but still with little hope of success. George was determined to force the board of directors to carry out its promise. At every meeting he stood up and asked: 'When are we going to get our railway to Pateley Bridge?' In the end the directors became so tired of him that the chairman replied that he could have his railway, providing he could raise half the £80,000 capital, thinking, of course, that this would be the end of the matter. He should have known George better.

George brought together a committee consisting of local gentlemen and industrialists, with himself as secretary. Within six months they had raised over

half of the funding needed and the promise of all the land required. The only landowner to be difficult was Revd Henry J. Ingilby of Ripley Castle. However, he was soon persuaded when he was promised the honour of cutting the first sod. On the day the news came through that the work was to start, George was met with great celebration in Pateley Bridge.

On 20 September 1860, only 14 months after he had received permission to go ahead, there was a procession from Ripley Castle, through the village which was decorated with flags, towards Killinghall. It turned left into the field, through a floral archway bedecked with chrysanthemums proclaiming 'Success to the Nidd Valley Railway'. The line, almost 12 miles long and costing £8,000 per mile, took only 18 months to build, quite a feat even by modern standards, but with only muscle power for much of the work, it must have been prodigious.

There must have been a great army of navvies employed, who had to live somewhere, but where is not known. The original stations were Ripley Valley, Birstwith, Dacre Banks and Pateley Bridge. Hampsthwaite and Darley were added in the next few months.

When the day of the opening arrived, 1 May 1862, George Metcalfe was carried shoulder-high on a gaily-trimmed armchair through Pateley Bridge, with the brass band and a procession of local people in attendance, to a celebration dinner at the George Hotel (the Pateley Club at the time of writing), which belonged to his family. The *Leeds Intelligencer* said:

He bore his honours with all the affability of a newly elected Member of Parliament as the band played 'See the Conquering Hero Comes' and the ladies in the windows waved their handkerchiefs and made other demonstrations of applause. At the railway station he briefly addressed the people assembled. He expressed gratification at the success of a work in which they had been engaged for ten years.

Left: *The staff at Pateley Station, with Fred Faulkner standing.*

In the next few weeks special trains were put on to take local people to Harrogate. It is said that many had never been so far afield before, and when they reached the terminus they stayed on the train, not daring to alight in case they couldn't get home again! Imagine the excitement of those who took advantage of Metcalfes' offer to the railway employees of half fare on a day-trip to Scarborough on Feast Tuesday – to see the sea for the first time.

Pateley Feast in September was the time of year when the railway proved to be a tremendous boon. Families who had emigrated to the towns in search of

Left: *Pateley Bridge Station coal yard, 1924.*

Below: *Bewerley Bridgehousegate School, Marxh 1964, arriving for the special school trip prior to the railway closure. Pictured are teacher Miss Mabel Millard and headteacher Mr Geoffrey Townley with ?, Christine Foxton and Susan Bailey leading the procession of pupils.*

work were able to return for the weekend. By the 1880s the trains into Pateley were packed on Feast Saturday. One year the railway company, seeking to capitalise on this holiday, laid on a special trip out of the dale on the Saturday, again to Scarborough. It proved to be one of their biggest flops ever, since only a dozen people from the entire dale took up the offer.

The coming of the railway brought prosperity to the dale for about 40 years. The quarries in particular could be developed, since transporting stone out of the dale took only hours instead of days and much larger loads could be moved. Flax and hemp for the mills came directly from Hull or Leeds without using the firm's manpower and taking a tedious route via Ripon by canal and river, or over hill and dale. Agriculture benefited too, since farmers could supply fresh milk by the early-morning train to Leeds and Bradford without the hard work of processing it into butter and cheese, crafts which eventually died out.

During the first half of the twentieth century, older pupils travelled by train for secondary education in Harrogate. At the start of the twenty-first century, many stories are told by the older generation of the pranks (and sometimes wilful damage) they performed on the journey.

Once the bus services started, demand for the railway lessened. Indeed there was a deliberate policy to attract passengers from the trains. Since the bus service was more frequent and went directly through the village centres, it naturally attracted more custom.

Passenger train services were discontinued on 2 April 1952 at very short notice, but goods services continued until November 1964. Just before the final closure, two special trains were run: the last one for railway enthusiasts, but the penultimate one for all the schoolchildren in the dale, organised by the head teachers. The train left Pateley, picking up schoolchildren at each station. At Harrogate the stationmaster and Mayor in regalia formally greeted the train. On the return trip there was a stop at Hampsthwaite for a picnic lunch. When the train arrived back at Pateley, the up-dale children all left and the train continued down the line, dropping off the pupils as they reached their home station. It was a glorious spring day and the dale has seldom looked lovelier. BBC North was in attendance and interviewed one girl who was celebrating her tenth birthday that day. It really was a day to remember for all of us who were lucky enough to have been there.

What a tourist attraction the line would have been in 2003 had there been enthusiasts to work it! As it was the lines were torn up within a few weeks and our railway became just a memory.

The old workhouse, now Valley View Farm.

Old Church Lane, Pateley Bridge. The cottages down the left-hand side of the lane were known as Bedlam, indicating that the poorhouse for lunatics had been here. They were pulled down in 1963.

Chapter 13

POVERTY

Eileen Burgess

Being poor has never been comfortable, but in the days when there was no state assistance, it was often a humiliating and desperate search for the means of survival. The only assistance provided was local provision at the disposal of the other inhabitants who were always conscious of the cost.

In medieval times the church was usually responsible, often through the monastic orders, although it is unlikely that the abbeys of Fountains and Byland would have helped the inhabitants of Upper Nidderdale, as the Cistercians were essentially a closed order, keeping their vast wealth for themselves. Some private donations were made in wills as pious acts, but they were not sufficient to deal with the destitute, who roamed around the country as vagabonds. As these beggars often went around in large groups they could be a real threat – 'Hark, hark, the dogs do bark, the beggars are coming to town', as the old nursery rhyme remembers them. Forest of Knaresborough inhabitants were told in 1517 that they were not to harbour or rent lands to any Scottish strangers or vagabonds, on pain of a fine of 20s.

In spite of severe penalties – cutting off ears and hanging for persistent offenders – the problems grew. In 1601 the government decided to allow townships to levy a rate on their households and distribute the income among the deserving old and sick whilst ensuring that the idle should work for their assistance. This poor rate formed the basis of all local taxation until the mid-twentieth century; the time and money spent on poor matters was equal to the rest of the administration put together.

Each township had to appoint at least two overseers to manage the business, usually being chosen in rotation. They served for a year and were responsible for collecting the rate and distributing it. As they were often illiterate they sometimes had a clerk appointed to keep the accounts, though the overseers were responsible for their accuracy. In 1778 William Hebden, the Lofthouse schoolmaster, was appointed clerk for Fountains Earth township at a salary of half a guinea (55p) a year and a sack of coal. The accounts were presented at the Annual Parish Assembly, where those present were mellowed in a local hostelry with copious refreshments of ale, bread and cheese. In 1792 the inhabitants of Fountains Earth spent 2s.6d. on bread, 5s.9d. for 15½lb of cheese and £1.3s.0d. on

ale for the meeting, when the dole for a widow was £2.2s.0d. a year.

The rates were assessed on the previous year's accounts and were collected in two instalments, with a larger sum in the first payment. Credits and deficits were carried over into the next year. The sums paid out were usually small but could be augmented when there was a particular need, such as fuel, rents or midwife's fees.

In 1807 Major (his given name) Snell fell on hard times so he received 28d. weekly for 45 weeks, 1s.6d. extra when sick, and was given a gill of brandy at 10½d., and S. Longster was paid 5s.0d. for looking after his wife for six days. In Bewerley, old and infirm couples received between 3s. and 5s. a month, a widow with three children had 4s. and a sick couple 12s., when agricultural wages were 6s. a week.

One of the great problems was deciding who was eligible, since the township was only responsible for those who had settlement, having been born there. Anyone who went away to work was expected to take with him a certificate to say that his home area would be responsible for him. A great deal of administrative time was spent in chasing up doubtful settlements when people fell into the system. In order to minimise the problem in 1682 it was ordered that 'no inhabitant of Bewerley shall entertain anyone that is likely to become chargeable to the said town, pain £2.' About the same time a law was passed that all paupers and their families should wear a large 'P' with the first letter of the name of the parish in red or blue cloth on the right shoulder, so they could be identified – a rule not repealed until 1810. Birstwith introduced badging in 1752, but we have no record of it elsewhere in the dale.

Illegitimate children had settlement in the place of their birth and, until 1794, pregnant women were often moved at the last moment; after that date they were allowed to stay, although the cost was recovered from their own settlement parish. The fathers were committed to gaol if they did not undertake to marry the mother or maintain the child: in Stonebeck Down the father had to pay £2 for the labour and 2s. a week for the child. Sometimes it could be difficult to find him. In 1779 Margaret Greenwood had to be supported by Fountains Earth for a year, plus rent, fuel and the child's christening fee, a total of £5, whilst chasing the father, Ninian Proctor of Wath, cost 17s.8d., although there is no evidence that he ever paid up. In Dacre and Bewerley, some women were sent to the House of Correction on the birth of the second or third child, but this was not done in Bishopside. In Fountains Earth several women were given spinning-wheels to maintain themselves – in 1807 Esther Whitaker was given one with two smocks and a set of child's clothes.

In contrast, the very old and the feeble-minded were treated with compassion and lived in their own homes for as along as possible. Old Jane Whitaker had 8 yards of cloth for new sheets and Mary Chambers was paid 5s. for cleansing her. Old William Longster was boarded out at 3s.6d. a week, and was also supplied with 16s.3d. worth of tobacco during the year. Widow Holmes, a pauper, had a daughter Hannah, born in 1798, who was classed as an idiot. By 1803 she was being supported by the township. They were boarded out for a year in 1809, but then returned to their own home. Hannah was taken to the flax-mill at Bishop Thornton in June 1810, but after 18 months was brought back to Pateley. After six months she was in a filthy condition and had to be cleaned up. She continued to be a problem and was presumably later taken to the poorhouse.

The homes of the poor were kept in reasonable repair. In the autumn of 1804 three of the paupers' houses needed repairs to the cost of 5s. each. Furniture was also replaced when necessary and fuel was supplied regularly. Sarah Dovener received 30 loads of peat in June in 1790, and Elizabeth Atkinson was provided with fire elding (small wood to supplement peat) in 1772. Oatmeal was given out on several occasions, as were sacks of potatoes. New clothes were supplied as required. Joseph Wilkinson must have been in dire straits when he was given a pair of new shoes, two pairs of stockings, two new shirts, his clogs were repaired twice and a pair of breeches mended, at a cost of £1.2s.7d.

Pauper and orphaned children presented a problem. They were boarded out at the township's expense and at seven years old put out to apprentice – the hosts being allotted in rotation. They were fully kitted out and subsidised by the community. In 1762 Robert Atkinson was paid £4.14s.0d. for boarding and clothing Francis Herring, a poor child. In 1832 Margaret, daughter of Andrew and Jane Norris, was to serve as an apprentice to George Watson of Covill House for four years; he received £1.10s.4½d. for clothing her.

Each township had its own poorhouse, usually one or two cottages where the paupers looked after each other. Bishopside built its workhouse at Blazefield in 1746 at a cost of £170. In 1832 it had only eight or nine inhabitants plus a few children and old people, at a cost of 2s.7d. per head per week, under the direction of a master who himself was a pauper. Bewerley had a workhouse in 1804 which received

William Craven, a 50-year-old idiot from Fountains Earth, but by 1832 was sending its inmates to Scriven. Birstwith and Darley sent their paupers to Pannal for nearly 50 years, but from 1783 shared a primitive poorhouse with Hampsthwaite. The name Bedlam, in Pateley Bridge and Clint, probably indicates the site of the local madhouse at some time, again supported by the township with a pauper looking after the inmates.

Alongside all this public disbursement there was private charity, but until 1622 it provided money in a one-off payment only. In 1598 Nicholas Parker of Clapham Green gave 20s. for the poor of Hampsthwaite, the same year as Katherine Beckwith left 1s. to every poor householder in Clint. In 1622 Anthony Craven of Darley established a fund of £5 for Hampsthwaite parish, the interest to be paid to the poor, and others followed in a similar fashion. Lawrence Danson gave £2 from a farm at Leadhill, Mary Midgeley gave 10s. similarly from one at Winsley, and Thomasine Hardisty's charity added £10 a year in 1745. But charity was not always appreciated: Margaret Lupton in Bishopside left money for two sermons to be preached in May and November with 5s. to be distributed in bread. A week's notice had to be given so the poor knew to come – except that they didn't, so eventually the money was distributed to five widows. Four widows not on parish relief were more fortunate – they shared £36 a year from the Byril rents, distributed at Lady Day and Michaelmas. These private charities were administered by the overseers, but they were open to abuse and were often used to subsidise the ratepayers.

By the early-nineteenth century the system was breaking down throughout the country, due to the Industrial Revolution which caused a massive influx into the towns, so the Charity Commission was set up to enquire into all charities throughout England. It was followed in 1832 by the Poor Law Commission and two years later by the Poor Law Amendment Act. This made it almost impossible for able-bodied people to be aided except in workhouses. Instead of townships acting on their own, they were to group together in a union with elected guardians to administer a large mixed workhouse, within which the paupers were to be segregated according to type and sex.

The Pateley Bridge Union extended from the head of the dale down to Birstwith and Clint. Hampsthwaite was in the Pannal Union, Ripley and Killinghall in Knaresborough. Each township elected one or two guardians. They were naturally under pressure from their constituents to keep the rates down and were also under strict rules from the government as to what they could and could not do. The chairman of the Pateley Bridge Union, set up in 1837, was John Yorke, Esq., with John Metcalfe as vice-chairman. Yorke was very active, exercising direct control over the tenant-farmer guardians, whose landlords could on their behalf exert pressure

The 'new' workhouse. Pictured is the Board of Guardians, with the master, matron and nurse on the right.

and who filled half the places on the board. A clerk, relieving officer and workhouse master were appointed on modest salaries. As one workhouse was to be shared, the old Bishopside poorhouse at Blazefield was enlarged and improved to comply with the Act. Townships still had their own overseers until 1869, presumably to look after their local interests.

Although the rules were much more stringent, it was never expected that the old or sick should be treated harshly – it was not the original intention that they should be put in the workhouse, but cared for in their own homes. The rules were often stretched by the overseers: if there was sickness in the family, the rest could be dealt with as though they were all sick, or allowances paid from the highway or church rate, which were not subject to such scrutiny, although as time went on these fiddles became harder. Settlements still operated and could cause distress. In 1857 Rutherford's family had become chargeable to the parish, but his daughter had been more than five years in Bradford, so could not come back. Thomas Wright, aged 80 and living at Bishop Thornton, was to be returned to his native Great Ouseburn.

Paupers had the right of interview with the guardians if they felt they were being unfairly treated. In 1857 Ellen Walker, who was in the workhouse with her two illegitimate boys, complained about another inmate, Sarah Hall, whom she accused of striking and abusing her. As Ellen was taken to the house of correction in Ripon six months later the trouble was probably provoked.

Accounts had to be made up quarterly and audited,

and a considerable amount of time was taken up in having this done at Knaresborough. John Ingleby was the local treasurer with John Bradford, John Yorke's steward, as auditor until 1845, when John Mainwaring took over. They, too, were under continuous scrutiny from a government inspector. The county auditor said that the rent of a room, heating and lighting could be claimed, providing it was not a public house. On Mr Bradford's second inspection of the Fountains Earth overseer's account he rapped his knuckles, because it wasn't complete. He wouldn't allow the expenses incurred by a journey to the magistrate to be claimed, as it had been for 60 years, nor for a journey to Pateley to have the books signed. Such travel expenses had to come out of the overseer's pocket; it was most unfair on those who lived in the remote townships. In 1846 the Fountains Earth clerk's fee was also disallowed. One wonders whether the auditors paid their own expenses.

A quarterly rate had to be paid by each township to the union, but not all did so promptly. In 1856 five townships owed a total of £305. Bewerley with Dacre was especially difficult, since the commission said they should be assessed separately, which John Yorke resisted as Bewerley's rate would be higher. Both villages refused to contribute to the union and naturally the rest objected to paying more, so the union was at the point of bankruptcy. The matter was not resolved until after John Yorke's death in 1857.

The effect of all this was naturally felt by the most vulnerable – relief was discontinued to several paupers in Bewerley and Dacre. Bills were not paid, and the clerk said that he had unsettled accounts with 35 unions, but the guardians deserted him when he asked for money. One workhouse master absconded with funds and others took liberties with female inmates. The diet in the workhouse failed to meet minimum standards; the guardians retorted that it was superior, but as the suppliers were not paid, they were not likely to be generous with quality or quantity.

Revaluation of the district took place after John Yorke's death. Several of the larger landowners objected, but as there had been an expansion of the textile industry the load was spread amongst many more properties. The balance of power within the board changed when Charles Carr of Dacre, who had led the opposition to Yorke, was appointed chairman.

By 1860, there was more emphasis on the needs of the poor and improvements in provision were demanded. The Poor Law Commission threatened to close the Pateley Bridge workhouse, but this would have meant greater cost to the union in sending paupers to other workhouses outside the district, so a new building was sanctioned in 1862. It was much more conveniently situated, in the town rather than on the moor edge. The severe architecture of the building was to emphasise the dignity of the guardians and Poor Law, but the rooms were adequately furnished for 80 inmates and fires were to be kept in each room. Tenders for food stressed good-quality beef, best spirits and sugar. Coats were to be of best Etherley cloth and elm coffins had to be 12 inches thick. If the tenders were fulfilled then the inmates were better off than the poorest outside, but there was always the stigma of being in the workhouse.

Vagrants had their own quarters in the basement. They were admitted at 5p.m., given food and a rough box bed with straw and a blanket. The following day the men had to do hard manual work, such as breaking road stone, then they were fed and given another night's lodging. On the third day they were on their way to the next workhouse – Ripon, Knaresborough, Otley or Skipton.

After 1855 pauper children went to school and were put out to apprentice when they left. When Charles Gains, an apprentice, needed his hand operated on, the guardians paid for the treatment. His father, 14 years before, had absconded when it was found that he had fathered an illegitimate child – the overseer had spent many days unsuccessfully chasing him.

The guardians had to be more discriminating about their choice of officials; the medical officers were also subject to scrutiny and paid a regular £10 per annum, providing they visited paupers in their homes instead of expecting them to walk seven or eight miles for medicine.

The guardians also took responsibility for ensuring that standards generally were improved. In 1873 some very attractive cottages at Wreaks were actually 'some of the most vile and filthy places in the dale' – although John Greenwood did deal with them quickly when the matter was pointed out to him.

Towards the end of the nineteenth century attitudes changed again. The insane were sent to Menston Asylum and children to orphanages. Public assistance took over in the 1920s from the boards of guardians. The Pateley workhouse closed in 1914, apart from the vagrants' ward which continued until 1939. The Rural District Council kept part of the premises, which housed German prisoners of war and then navvies working on the reservoirs. When the Ripon and Pateley Bridge Rural District Councils amalgamated it became their main office, until 1974. Since reorganisation of local government there have been several tenants, the principal one being Nidderdale Museum.

Chapter 14

MY EARLY SCHOOLDAYS

Muriel Swires

When I was five years old, in 1926, I attended Fellbeck village school in the building adjoining the chapel. It had two rooms and an outside earth closet but no playground. We used the lane which ran alongside for play – it was covered with ashes.

Children walked miles to school from Eavestone, Warsill, North Pasture, North Oaks and Fellbeck Mill. The teacher walked daily from Blazefield, a distance of two miles.

In the main schoolroom was a stove with a huge pipe, some dual desks and a teacher's high desk in one corner. Along the length of the back wall was a large cut-out coffee jug and a teapot, both with legs running away from a cow and a bunch of cocoa beans. Underneath, written in big letters was 'RUN AWAY COFFEE, RUN AWAY TEA, MILK AND COCOA STAY WITH ME.' In the smaller classroom was an open fire and tiny chairs for the five and six year olds. In the afternoons one of the older children read stories to the little ones, and I well remember one big boy

putting the poker in the fire and touching Annie's knee with it. The smell of scorched black woollen stocking and the screams were most frightening.

Another day my friend Edith and I had the same answers to our sums. When asked who had copied, we were both silent and so had our heads banged together – at the time we were five years old! Each year on Ash Wednesday, mother made a pile of fritters and after school all the children called for one to eat on the way home.

We had regular visits from the school attendance officer, the nurse, dentist and doctor, as well as frequent visits from drill teachers.

There was accommodation for 24 pupils, but in 1928 numbers had risen to 29, so the school was closed and in August we were transferred to the board school at Pateley Bridge. Longsters must have run the earliest school buses in the dale. My brother and I were picked up at Bailles Lane End every day at precisely 8.34a.m., clutching our sandwiches. Most of the children had taken sandwiches and eaten

Fellbeck School, adjoining the chapel, c.1912.

them in the classroom at Fellbeck, but the master at Pateley wouldn't allow this. Fortunately, the lady at the workhouse (now the museum) took pity on us and opened one of the large kitchens. Not only was there a warm fire but she also made us a drink of hot cocoa. Sometimes on Fridays, for a special treat, mother would give us each a penny to buy chips from Garnett's chip shop in the High Street. How we enjoyed sitting on the long bench inside eating the chips, usually with scraps.

The cane worked overtime at the board school in those days, and the girls suffered as well as the boys, as I know from experience. Every time my brother

was caned he cut a notch in his pencil box and there were so many he couldn't find a space to cut any more. Most of the boys did this. Usually, it was because their hands were dirty or their work not up to standard, or they were chattering in class. I remember one boy who was made to lie face downwards on the desk and caned on the backs of his legs until the flesh broke and he bled. What wrong he had committed I can't remember, but no one dared say a word.

When the time came for me to leave, I had no regrets and few happy memories. Fortunately this all changed when I travelled by train to Harrogate to attend the grammar school.

Above: *Children of Fellbeck School, 1927.*
Left to right, back row: *Connie Learoyd, Doris Scott, Olive Scott, Peter Fawcett, Arthur Tuley, Frank Kirkley, Maisie Houseman, Jessie Kirkley, Annie Bell, Richard Tuley;* middle row: *Annie Kirkley, Marion Houseman, Tommy Houseman, Isabel Kirkley, Nellie Houseman, Eric Hawkesworth, Mary Pickard, Mary Hawkesworth;* front row: *Jim Swires, Kenneth Ingram, Charles Ingram, Mary Kirkley, Edith Jackson, Margaret Skaife, Muriel Swires, Alan Ingram, Robbie Kirkley.*

Right: *Knollside, Fellbeck, in 1912. Pictured are five members of the Jackson family with John Thomas Swires* (right): *Fred, Joe, Arthur, Christopher (who emigrated to Australia in 1913), and Willie.*

Chapter 15

MUSIC

Eileen Burgess

In the past, music was an outstanding feature of Nidderdale life. In the middle of the nineteenth century a London magazine reported that it was the most musical of the dales and had been well known since Handel's day.

Part of the reason for this was that Methodism encouraged hymn singing as it reinforced the spiritual message and strengthened the bond between worshippers in an enjoyable way. Each chapel had its own choir, which could reach a high standard – some were capable of performing the *Messiah*. It also added to the social life of the chapel, with outings and concerts. Particularly when combined with a tea, or an interesting speaker, the concerts could be an important source of revenue, bringing in much-needed funds for repairs or rebuilding.

Other denominations followed suit. In the 1830s Pateley Bridge Independent Chapel had an exceptionally keen group of men who walked to Masham on Saturday afternoons to take singing lessons from William Jackson. He was the organist there who wrote a handbook on festival singing and became conductor of the large Bradford Choral Society – he had belonged to the chapel choir when a schoolboy.

The choir members also combined outside the churches to form secular societies. The Nidderdale Harmonic Union was formed in 1855 from several groups and was superseded in 1882 by the Pateley Bridge Choral Union and later by the Pateley Bridge Choral Society. The Choral Union rehearsed in the Cocoa House – its conductor was John Wilson whose father had taught William Jackson. He was living in Harrogate, so had to come on the train and be accommodated each rehearsal night. Each successive society was proud of the tradition it had inherited. Summerbridge had a Singing Class in 1867, although the only clue to its existence is a piece of music in the museum collection.

One of the great problems was the weather. Before motorised transport most members walked to rehearsals, which demanded real dedication on winter nights, and several concerts were badly hit.

Brass bands were flourishing by the middle of the nineteenth century. They were encouraged and supported by the mill owners, who saw in them an innocent form of recreation for their workpeople, and who provided rehearsal rooms and lawns for summer Sunday-afternoon concerts. As teetotalism spread, several of them became Temperance bands – Darley and Summerbridge having the name in their titles. One of the earliest references was in 1855, when a report in the *Ripon Chronicle* told of a shameful incident when the Pateley Bridge and New York bands met, both presumably in full voice, and came to blows.

Summerbridge Band, 1903, soon after its formation.
Note the word 'Temperance' is inserted – obviously important!

They were bound over to avoid such incidents in future. The following summer, when George and Isabella Metcalfe, later of Castlestead, had their wedding celebration on their return from honeymoon, the Pateley Bridge Brass Band played throughout the Feast and the sports and then again the following evening for the firework display. The latter took place on Glasshouses Mill dam, with the band floating along in a boat. The band flourished throughout the rest of the nineteenth century, playing at every possible event – galas, feast days, weddings, the opening of the Cocoa House – and some of the members were long-standing, George

133

Hawkin being a founder and still playing 50 years later. George Metcalfe was its president, helping financially on many occasions. The band may have suffered during the First World War, for it seems to have died out soon after. One of the last recorded engagements was to head the procession of returned servicemen for a celebration to mark their homecoming in July 1919.

Nothing further is known about the New York Mill band, but its place was taken in 1902 by the Summerbridge and Dacre Temperance Band – all members were total abstainers. The Gills of New York Mill and Peter Wilkinson of the Dacre Banks sawmill lent money to purchase instruments. The band rehearsed in a variety of venues and took part successfully in competitions in the 1920s, but decided that membership in the bands demanded too much time and commitment from the players. John Brown was conductor for many years until his death in 1980. In the 1950s several members of the defunct Harrogate Band joined. Bill Jewitt was the oldest bandsman in the country when he appeared with his colleagues on 'Jim'll Fix It' in 1993 and he continued for several more years after that.

Darley Temperance Band was formed in 1901. Seven of its members were of the Skaife family and five others were Housemans. It played for agricultural shows and Hospital Sunday. When it was in a low period in 1936 Walter Aldon bought new uniforms to boost the morale. As with all the other bands it ceased to function during the war but re-formed in time to play for the opening of the Memorial Hall in 1947. It disbanded 12 years later and several members transferred to Summerbridge.

Middlesmoor had a band in the 1850s, but it had been defunct for half a century when, in 1914, Tom Bradley, landlord of the Crown at Lofthouse, decided to teach the up-dale men and they persuaded local

gentry to provide funds. When the instruments arrived they were carried in procession from the station to the pub. Although not one of them had ever touched an instrument, within six months they were playing hymns. Tom Bradley was succeeded by Tom Whitfield as conductor of Lofthouse and Middlesmoor Silver Prize Band. He was a player for 35 years until his retirement in 1986.

Nearly all the other villages had bands at some time. The band at Burnt Yates had a brief history – it played on the green to mark the end of the Crimean War in 1856 and, in March 1863, went to Harrogate to celebrate the wedding of the Prince of Wales to Alexandra by playing on the Stray, although the performance was stopped by a snowstorm. It was replaced in 1885 by the Shaw Mills Band, which disbanded 15 years later.

The Greenhow Victoria Band was mentioned by Thomas Blackah in his poem of 1865 about the Feast: 'The Nidderdale Rant', 'And Victoria Band maks under t'tree/ A bonny racket.' He, along with others of his talented relatives, was probably one of them, as a photograph shows him holding a violin. It was still going strong in 1883, but ceased shortly after when the mining industry collapsed.

Birstwith had two bands – a string one which played in church and a brass band. They both performed around the village on Christmas morning. The brass band had good players, but they couldn't all agree – on one occasion they began to 'fratch' among themselves and went home without making a single call.

Ripley was the only village without a brass band, although Sir William Ingilby sometimes conducted massed bands, presumably when they played at Ripley Castle. For most of the bands playing in the grounds of mansions such as Bewerley Hall and Swarcliffe Hall was part of the summer programme.

Lofthouse and Middlesmoor Brass Band, 1919. Tom Bradley, founder and bandmaster, is pictured on the far left.

There were also string bands in most of the villages. John Scaife, the organist and choirmaster of the Independent Chapel, was conducting the Pateley String Band when it changed its name to the String Orchestra in 1885. A few years later the seven brothers in the Skaife family of Darley combined with others to form the Darley String Orchestra – when some of them emigrated it folded and some of its remaining members joined the Darley Temperance Brass Band.

There have been several other enthusiastic families who provided the core of the musical tradition including the Eglins of Middlesmoor Church, the Scaifes of Pateley Bridge Independent Chapel choir which had the father as conductor, daughter as organist and others as singers, and the Abbotts of Dacre. In addition there were many talented individuals such as Minnie Green of Pateley, who became a professional singer by the age of 19 and Peter Barker, the blind Hampsthwaite joiner who could earn half a week's wages in one evening playing his violin.

During the twentieth century, church and chapel choirs continued. Felliscliffe Glee Singers gave a concert at Warsill in 1912 and a year later a cantata at West End, entitled 'The Promise of Jesus', which suggests that the members were mostly drawn from religious choirs, although their strength declined with two world wars taking many young men.

The Pateley Bridge Musical and Dramatic Society (the 'Operatics') flourished in the 1920s and early '30s. It produced Gilbert and Sullivan operas annually. The principals were invariably the same people – Dr Flintoff, Kitty Thorpe, Revd Early Ayre and Peggy Summersall. The chorus was large and its members took the smaller principal roles. Marion Harrison was the pianist and there was also a small orchestra to accompany. The group performed in the Oddfellows' Hall and took its shows to Scar village on several occasions.

Ballroom dancing was a passion for young people up to the 1970s and music was provided by a variety of combinations. Eddie Flowers, the Pateley Bridge postmaster, had his own orchestra in the 1920s, and there were the 'Revellers' of Pateley Bridge and the 'Merry Imps' – though these may have been different combinations of the same people. Billie Coates' 'Midnight Follies' with their crooner, John Nelson, were in great demand throughout the area. During the 1960s and '70s Arthur Layfield and his friends formed a succession of groups playing for dances including 'Trad Dads Jazz Band', Darley Dance Band and a Hawaiian Music Group. John Breckon led his group with a Hammond organ.

From 1970 Pateley Bridge had one of the best folk clubs in the UK, started by Zeke Deighton and Don Ward at the water-mill. Anyone could get up and sing and many visiting artistes of national renown such as Julie Felix, Mike Harding and Jasper Carrott also played there. Soon every pub in the dale was having its own folk night.

In the 1960s Graham Burgess and his mother, Elaine, formed the Dalesgate Singers, who had between 20 and 40 members and gave two concerts a year for charity in St Cuthbert's Church at Christmas and in May. Unfortunately, one year there was only one snowfall in the entire winter – the night of the *Messiah* performance.

Birstwith Band. This picture was taken in the field in front of Hardcastle Garth. Brothers William and George Houseman of Hardcastle Garth are on the left.
The note on the back says 'early 1900s', but the uniforms would suggest it was taken at least ten years before that.

Evening classes were the beginnings of several choirs. The Nidderdale Singers, conducted by Harry Gibson, came from a 'Singing for Pleasure' course in 1975. The Pateley Bridge Singers, which are still successful at the time of writing, came from a similar class for ladies. 'Nidd Chorale', formed in 2001, is re-establishing the 150-year-old tradition of religious music to supplement the choirs.

The Summerbridge and Dacre Band, and the Lofthouse and Middlesmoor Band, are very active, performing at functions up and down the dale, as well as in the handsome bandstand given in memory of Mr and Mrs Joe Longster by their daughter, Christine Svendsen. The Nidderdale Festival demonstrates the surviving interest by the audiences it draws for its musical events. Long may they continue.

Soldiers on parade in Bewerley Park, 1939.

A Christmas card sent to servicemen from the people of Bewerley and Pateley Bridge.

Chapter 16

WARTIME

Muriel Swires & Eileen Burgess

Although we read and see a great deal about life during the Second World War in the cities and on the battlefields, we rarely hear much about how people in the relatively safe areas fared.

Civilian life was much more drab than today. Although a small number of council-houses had been built before the war, there was much substandard housing in the dale. Where the Pateley car parks are at the time of writing, there were small cottages in yards which were very poor – one cold tap and a privy out in the yard, sometimes shared. Most of these, and the old brewery buildings, belonged to an eccentric old man, Freddy Campbell, who would not do repairs. He also owned other property in Lofthouse and Dacre. The brewery was filled with furniture which he had bought at sales, but would not release to young couples desperate to buy for their homes. The cottages owned by the mills were substantial but uniform, with none of the individual home improvements of today. The scarcity of paint and other materials made everything appear tatty. Many homes and public buildings had had iron railings, probably made by Todds, which were compulsorily removed to provide metal for weapon production, although subsequently they were found to be totally unsuitable and most merely rusted away in dumps.

The dreariness extended to the gardens. People were not encouraged to grow flowers; allotments were everywhere and people were expected to turn as much of their gardens over to vegetable plots as possible. At Bridgehousegate School, as well as many other schools, gardening became a compulsory subject for boys – the area between the school and cricket pitch was dug up by the children and planted. During the autumn children collected rosehips for syrup, an excellent source of vitamin C, instead of the imported orange juice. Householders were also encouraged to keep hens, for which they received a corn allowance, but in return they had to give up their egg ration.

The Ministry of Agriculture ordered all land not in production, including public parks, to be ploughed. Some pasture was kept but much was turned over to arable, often unsuitably. Most of Bewerley Park was ploughed. Potatoes, sugar beet, and other root crops were grown. Although some of the directives were stupid when applied to poor pasture, the regulations did make farmers learn new techniques and advance their methods. Records had to be kept of all animals, but in reality farmers often had an extra beast or pig which wasn't registered, or was destined for home consumption. A blind eye was turned unless there was real evidence of wholesale black marketeering. It did go on, to the advantage of some, but not to the detriment of everyone else. In any case, the police were often unofficial beneficiaries! Butter made on the farms became an extra weekly ration.

Nidderdale was still a working dale. Glasshouses, Summerbridge and Birstwith communities centred on the mills which worked right around the clock, making camouflage netting and ropes for all purposes, from heavy shipping ropes to the parachute cord which was made at Foster Beck. The raw materials were still imported but some were grown in this country. There were great manpower shortages in every walk of life, so in every job people worked long hours and helped out. Muriel Swires' father was a cobbler and, although she was a teacher by day, she and her aunt, who came up from Dacre on the bus, had to work every evening using the finishing machine, polishing, brushing, waxing and applying the heelball to the shoes he had repaired. Muriel also drove Wilkinson's bread van.

Olive Dougill drove the ambulance. Most people had first aid and air-raid precautions lectures. Muriel's father was provided with a stirrup pump and the family were shown how to use it. There were lookout posts manned by the Royal Observer Corps, one at Crossgates, Fellbeck; Muriel often gave lifts to the servicemen. The Home Guard walked up to the edge of the moor to their post which had originally been the bathing hut. Protecting the water-supply was essential, so the reservoirs were guarded. Buildings remaining after Scar House was completed were utilised as accommodation for the troops. The Home Guard had responsibility for some duties, although they were still vulnerable to attack from the air.

Any military information was regarded as secret, so it was not officially published in case it got into enemy hands, so not much is known about the aircraft which crashed on the moors, and the people directly involved are no longer with us. Enemy planes bombing Leeds or Teesside that had passed their targets could lose their bearings because there were no lights and they only had primitive navigational aids. Also our own planes returning damaged from raids or merely lost due to similar reasons could become casualties. Several crashed on the high moors, including at Heathfield and Pockstones. The rescue team included Stanley Light.

On 31 August 1940, incendiary bombs were dropped at North Oaks, Fellbeck, but fortunately no animals were hurt. Mr and Mrs Shepherd were in bed at the time and were awakened by explosions as other bombs were dropped on the surrounding moor. Two bombs fell near the railway at Glasshouses and missed the train by yards. Several cottages were hit by shell splinters which smashed their windows, and a sleeping boy in one bedroom woke to find his bed strewn with glass.

It is difficult now to imagine how dark it was on winter nights. No lights were permitted to show – any chink more than a hair's breadth was an offence. Doors could not be opened longer than absolutely necessary. Torches could only have a one-inch diameter circle of light visible. Big torches were reserved for officials such as air-raid wardens and police. Cars had headlamp covers with only five-inch slits.

Transport was at a minimum, cars were only allowed for essential purposes or where alternative means were not available; buses or bikes were the only means of transport for most. Only essential traders and people such as doctors could get petrol and they were allowed a very small amount above their average requirement for personal use. New vehicles were non-existent. Signposts were removed so that invaders would not know where they were. This could lead to dreadful detours in the blackout – one Pateley Bridge Dramatic Society group was returning from Shaw Mills, where they had been to present a play, and found themselves at Warsill, heading for Ripon.

If you had a car which was not in use, and you were lucky enough to find good storage, it went up on bricks 'for the duration'. The large empty flax-mill at Folly Gill stored a whole floor of 'West Yorkshire Roadcar' buses and one little Austin 7 car belonging to Mary Barley. What joy she had when she was able to drive that little car again!

Everything else was in short supply and shelves in the shops were almost empty. You might have to go to two or three shops for something, or order it for the future 'when available'. Packaging was minimal and loose groceries like sugar and flour were weighed out at the point of sale into bags. As a result of the rationing during the First World War the basic administration techniques had been refined. Consequently, the system was as fair as it could possibly be, although the diet was dreary. Again, although there was no great black market, country people did fare better than in the towns, since most people knew where they could get a little extra. Jack Burgess remembers visiting a friend whilst on leave, who was appalled how thin he was and promptly cut a couple of slices from a large ham.

Clothing, too, was rationed –'make do and mend' was the order of the day. When garments were outgrown or worn out they were passed on or adapted, using the best parts of two or three to make something new, or when too far gone, were utilised in peggy rugs or patchwork quilts. A woman from Skipton came regularly selling remnants of parachute nylon and other fabrics.

Of course, many local men and women were serving with the Armed Forces or working in reserved occupations far from home. For many of them it was a salutary experience, leaving the sheltered, relatively placid life of the dale to mix with strangers from totally different backgrounds and go halfway across the world, when they had never been further than Scarborough on a day-trip.

Interesting items of news about servicemen and women, such as medal awards, appeared in the local newspapers, but the exact posting was not given – it was usually 'somewhere in the Middle East'. Keeping in touch was important – Muriel wrote up to a dozen letters every week to friends and relatives. For overseas transmission there were air letters, which were written on a special form and then photographed, and the much-smaller film was sent

An air letter sent by Clifford Swires to his sister, Joyce.

over, then developed and printed at the destination, in order to save transport costs.

As so many people were posted overseas, weddings were often arranged at very short notice. Extra rations could be obtained for a reception on a banns certificate or special licence, and extra clothing coupons were given for the trousseau, although at short notice it might mean borrowing from friends and relatives and paying back later. Service people tended to wear their best uniforms.

Nevertheless, there was a lighter side to life. Most entertainment was inevitably in individual villages because of difficulties with transport, any which hoped to draw from other sources had to be timed to the bus service. Whist drives and dances were the most popular and the accepted means for young people to meet each other. Many girls met their husbands at the 6d. hop on Saturday night in the Drill Hall, and there were also more formal dances in the cinema. Socials which involved dancing and games were also popular. There was usually a faith supper, when everyone brought along a contribution and it was pooled, although regular meetings could have special ration allowances of tea, milk and sugar if a special permit was obtained.

Young people over the age of 14 were encouraged to join a youth organisation. Muriel was asked by the Congregational minister, Revd Woodmass, to start a youth club for girls, which she held in the Red Shield Club that was also used for rehearsing concerts and pantomimes.

Cinema was the mass entertainment. Pateley changed its programme twice weekly. Escapist, romantic films drew the crowds and there were also propaganda-type films such as *In Which We Serve*. The newsreels, which were part of every programme, brought events to life in a way that had never before been possible, although no doubt many of the battle scenes were faked.

Most seaside boarding-houses and hotels had been requisitioned for military use and the government encouraged people to stay in their own areas so local councils had to organise activities, such as sports days and galas, for holidays at home. To provide extra funds for wartime purposes, the government instituted a special week each year, such as 'Salute the Soldier' and 'Wings for Victory' weeks. The local council set its target using government guidelines. Everyone was urged to buy extra War Savings Certificates and special events were organised to raise further funds. The processions, sports and whist drives served as a way of improving public morale. In the week devoted to the Royal Navy, Bishopside and Bewerley bought a motor torpedo boat, whose plaque is housed in the museum.

Wartime activities drew communities together and all shared in grief when news of the loss of a loved one was received. Life was dour, but people made the best of it, finding resources within the area, both physical and emotional, which they had never known existed.

The slide in the Recreation Ground. This was part of the playground equipment presented by the City of Hull as thanks for the hospitality shown to the Sailors' Orphanage. The last remaining item is the rocking-horse, which is preserved outside Nidderdale Museum.

Local men at Brighton, with Private Sinclair Swires of Fellbeck winning a four-and-a-half-mile race, which had over 400 competitors.

Local men with their gun. The man on the extreme right is possibly Joe King.

Chapter 17

CELEBRATIONS

FEAST IN THE PAST
Eileen Burgess

At the time of writing Nidderdale Show is the major part still remaining of the earlier Pateley Feast which had its origins at the beginning of the fourteenth century. After a run of bad summers with failed crops and cattle plagues, the Scots came down into Yorkshire, plundering and burning. As a result, Nidderdale was left devastated. The lord of the manor of Bishopside was the Archbishop of York and, in 1319, as recompense for the great losses he had suffered from unpaid rents, the King granted him the right to hold a market and fair at Pateley Bridge (incidentally, this is the first mention of the bridge). This right was important as it encouraged trade and allowed the lord of the manor to collect tolls and taxes from those who attended.

There were no shops at this time, so markets were needed for local produce and small necessities. They drew people from a radius of about five or six miles, as far as a day's walk, and took place near churches, crossroads, bridges or other frequented spots. They were important places for gossip and the exchange of local information. There were rules as to the time for buying and selling and fair trading. Stallholders had to pay for their pitches and taxes could be imposed on goods sold. In the nineteenth century Pateley's market was held where the Bridgeway Stores stand at the time of writing, and across the road (next to where the Midland Bank is located in 2003) it ran up High Street. In the early days it was held on Tuesdays, but before 1821 it had changed to Saturdays.

A fair was a grander annual event, drawing traders and visitors from a much wider area. The best time to hold it was either between hay time and harvest, or soon after the harvest was over, before the weather deteriorated. Often, the local saint's day was chosen because it was already a holiday, with a special Mass held for the patron saint which parishioners were expected to attend. A religious procession drew people into the church for the service. In Pateley, the Feast of the Nativity of the Blessed Virgin Mary on 9 September was chosen, which became 17 September when the calendar was changed in the mid-eighteenth century, and it lasted five days – three days before, the Feast day itself, and the morrow.

Traders travelled from fair to fair with their wares, often over long distances, bringing goods which could not be obtained locally – finer fabrics and more-fashionable clothing, pottery and metal cooking pots, patent medicines, spices and dried fruit. Animals were bought and sold. Strolling players and preachers had a golden opportunity to display their talents. The inns and alehouses did a roaring trade and catered for strangers coming much longer distances – the amount of liquor taken would lead to much boisterous merriment in games and dancing.

Although Pateley's fair was small compared with those of larger towns on important trade routes, it was, nevertheless, the focal point of the calendar for much of the dale – probably the only time remote farmers came down into the town. Unfortunately, we do not have any accounts of what actually went on before the middle of the nineteenth century. It must, though, have been very lively to have lasted so long.

Thomas Blackah, the Greenhow poet, wrote at least two poems about the Nidderdale Feast or Rant as it was then called, describing how the entire population for miles around came into the town, and the merrymaking which enlivened it.

The preparations for the Victorian Feast started two or three weeks before the great day with a grand clean through the house and the making of pickles and preserves. Tarts were baked, and currant pasties and maids of honour made, to be placed on a large dish for all to help themselves. Each village had its 'Beef Day' when the meat and other items for preparation were bought. All the butchers attended and most families chose a large joint of beef – in 1886 many were between 28 and 60lbs in weight, according to the *Nidderdale Herald*. Three years before it had said:

The quality of the meat was equal to the occasion, but the quantity and number of buyers much less than fifteen or twenty years ago. Many... remember High Street so dense on Beef Tuesday that you might have walked on the heads of the crowd... a large proportion of the beef comes from Scotch cattle which have been fattening for months in Bewerley Park.

Sarah Anne Carling remembered:

It was real beef then. We used to get such a big piece it

would scarcely go into the oven. It was usual to roast half a ham. Pickles were a special item in those days. Folk used to take a horse and cart down to Pateley and pick up the meat, pickling onions, red cabbages and a hamper of plums.

In outlying villages such as Middlesmoor, other traders went along as well, offering pots and pans for the cooking, and drapery – tablecloths, aprons – anything which might need replacing.

The stallholders began to arrive and set up their pitches in the Feast Field, where the health centre stands at the time of writing, around Station Square and into the High Street. As more and more sideshows arrived the excitement mounted.

On Feast Saturday the trains arrived, packed with Pateley 'exiles' from the industrial West Riding, and the fair opened for business. Sunday was a quieter day, since religion was very strong in the dale and most people would be at church or chapel following serious pursuits. In 1885, on Sunday afternoon, the Independent (United Reformed) Chapel in Bridgehousegate held a service of song, 'The Torn Bible' and, in the evening, the Primitive Methodists held one based on 'The Life of John Ashworth', possibly one of their early leaders in Pateley. In the early-twentieth century there was a procession from St Cuthbert's Church up to St Mary's for an afternoon service, but whether this was a remnant of the medieval celebrations or a late introduction, we do not know. It was discontinued in the 1960s because of successive wet years.

Feast Monday was, however, totally different. Early in the morning the crowds began to walk down from every village and hamlet around, determined to make the most of their holiday. Special trains brought day-trippers – in the mid-1880s two trains brought a total of 33 carriages full of people. The focal point was the Feast Field, extending around Station Square, through the market-place and right up the High Street, with stalls on both sides. In 1883:

The [side] shows were more numerous than before, the influx of visitors wondrous large... The principal sights were a Bulgarian lady, her arms torn from their sockets in the well-known atrocities, who made her toes a good substitute for hands and demonstrated writing, crocheting, etc., a talking fish – a cleverly trained seal, performing monkeys and dogs, marionettes, etc. Taylor's mechanical exhibitions and wax works, etc.

Another year there were 'negro minstrels, a brass band, a drum and fife band, shying sticks and balls at coconuts on pegs and other means of amusement and losing money.'

Thomas Blackah said the lads 'laiked at cricket' in 1865. By the mid-1880s special matches were a feature of the Feast. In 1885, unfortunately, the game between Pateley Bridge and Tetley's Brewery

had to be called off because the weather was too wet. They were luckier when a team from Paddock Green came to play a local side, a match which included Peate, Lee and Peale from the Yorkshire County Cricket Club and Nash of Darlington. There was another match at Pateley on Thursday, and in Dacre Banks on Saturday, Tuesday and Wednesday, the last incorporating players who had taken part in the Monday match.

On Wednesday there was a gala on what is now the Recreation Ground and on Friday a Cricketers' Ball at the Royal Oak Assembly Rooms (possibly Dacre Banks Royal Oak, as it has larger premises than that at Bridgehousegate) and there were trotting races. These donkey and pony races were a feature of the Feast in Pateley for many years, taking place on Tuesday. Thomas Blackah's poem shows that they were active in the 1860s and they continued into the twentieth century, with an attempted revival in 1931. They took place on the flat land known as Hardesty's Field, occupied at the time of writing by the Recreation Ground, the caravan site and along to Bridge House with, it is said, gaps in the walls to allow the participants through. The animals were ordinary working ponies or donkeys, no thorough-breds were allowed. There was very good prize money, considering the number of entrants. In addi-tion, for several years there was a handsome silver cup, which Matthew Newbould won outright – it is now in Nidderdale Museum. No doubt there was much lively betting, bringing condemnation from the religious section of the community. On the Monday there were also trotting races at Harker's Farm at Ramsgill and on the Thursday for horses, ponies and donkeys at Fellbeck.

The Metcalfes of Nidderdale Brewery, Scotgate Ash Quarry and Glasshouses Mill gave their employees a week off for the celebrations, but probably without pay, as was usual at that time. However, Francis Thorpe at New York Mill did pay his workforce during the festival, although it may only have been for the latter part of the week.

Middlesmoor celebrated Pateley Feast with a Love Feast in the chapel. This was a series of revival meetings held all day Sunday and into the following week. Special hymns were sung, inspiring preachers engaged and everyone was encouraged to tell of the 'Goodness of the Lord'. A Loving Cup was passed around, in early days filled with ale but after Methodism became teetotal in the 1880s water was substituted. Love Feast Bread, a spiced currant loaf, was also distributed. On the Monday there was a service in the chapel, followed by a tea in the old chapel opposite, and then a meeting in the evening with a special speaker and devotions. In some years there was a public tea and a cricket match between Middlesmoor and Lofthouse. When Ramsgill Sports died out in 1918, Middlesmoor took over and held them on the Tuesday.

Wath held sports events on Thursday around the turn of the century, organised by Anthony Bland, the small man who features in some of the photographs. He was the landlord of the Sportsman's Arms and the land in front of his pub was the venue. He can also be seen in some of the Angram Sports photos – this event would have been in its heyday when the top reservoir was being built. These sports were lively with 'cock' (pillow) fighting astride poles, tug o' war and donkey hurdles among the events.

Ramsgill had sports on the Tuesday and a shooting match and sale of work on Wednesday, followed in the evening by a Foreign Missions meeting at Lofthouse. Greenhow held a Tea Festival with the brass band playing around the village and a musical entertainment in the evening, and Wilsill had a gala on the Tuesday with the Pateley Bridge Brass Band and a cricket match, pigeon-shooting match, races and trotting. Everything from Pateley transferred down to Dacre Banks for Wednesday.

With all these events, the Feast had an importance equal to Christmas for its enjoyment. In the industrial age of long hours and hard labour of mills, quarries and mines, it must have been the only prolonged relaxation the workers had, so they savoured it to the full.

The cockfight, Angram Sports in 1907.
Anthony Bland is the small man on the left.

The donkey hurdle race at Wath Sports in 1907.

PATELEY FEAST REMEMBERED
Muriel Swires

The highlight of the year in the 1920s and '30s was Pateley Show and Feast. Excitement mounted as the days drew near and there was activity in almost every household. Preparations were made in advance as families planned for the yearly gathering of friends and relations, in many cases not seen since the previous year.

I remember my mother and aunts buying large red cabbages to pickle. The week before the show huge joints of beef were roasted to eat cold with pickles. Innumerable 'Feast' tarts were baked, usually filled with either plum or apricot jam.

Children raced up the High Street to meet the incoming vehicles carrying apparatus for the Feast. When the large steam engine 'Big Bertha' arrived their excitement knew no bounds. Every day as the Feast Field gradually filled with caravans and stalls children watched and, whenever allowed, joined in the hustle and bustle of erecting all the amusements.

By the wall at Back High Street was the position of the swing boats and at the entrance to the field where the fortune-teller's caravan was parked. In the centre was a roundabout with cockerels that not only went round and round but up and down at the same time, as gaily painted figures in the centre beat out the tunes. It was later replaced by another – 'Noah's Ark'. There were coconut shies and rolling-penny stalls and hammers to test your strength by hitting a metal ball with hopefully enough force to make it

ring the bell at the top. There were brandy-snap and cinder-toffee stalls and rifle-shooting ranges.

When the weather was wet, as it often was, the field became a sea of mud so straw was spread about and planks of wood placed over the biggest pools.

People came from far and near. Trying to find anyone was impossible because the field was always crowded with people. Queues formed for all the amusements and it was often impossible to get on the big roundabout as people were waiting to grab seats even as it was slowing down. The air was hazy with smoke, but the bright lights and the music and the smells seemed to fill everyone with high spirits, making the atmosphere difficult to describe unless experienced. Friday night saw free rides for all, setting the happy mood for the weekend.

On Show Monday trains brought people into the town from Leeds, Harrogate and further afield. After the activities on the showground came to an end, crowds drifted to the Feast Field for the rest of the evening. On Tuesday morning the fair packed up and moved to Dacre and set up there ready to open on Wednesday evening. So after school and home-work on Wednesday, if we had any money left, it was on the bus to Dacre for more fun.

NIDDERDALE SHOW
Eileen Burgess

Although the Nidderdale Show as we know it was founded in 1895, it did have forerunners, as in September 1879, when there was a horticultural and

Nidderdale Show, c.1900. Anthony Bland is standing at the back and second from left is Thackray Summersall.

144

Longsters' stand at the Nidderdale Show in 1922.

poultry show in the Metcalfe's brewery, later the Drill Hall in Bridgehousegate. Then, on Whit Tuesday 1893 there was an agricultural show in Bewerley Park by invitation of Thomas Edward Yorke.

It was probably this which prompted Thirkill Holdsworth, the highway surveyor and a man prominent in local affairs generally, to call a meeting of Pateley men in order to organise a show to be held in August. However, it was postponed until Feast Monday and was staged at Grassfield, then tenanted by John H. Metcalfe, who was on the committee. There were 206 entries of cattle, sheep, horses, butter and eggs, with £50 in prize money. The Wyke Temperance Band was in attendance and a public luncheon was held at 2p.m. at a cost of 2s.6d. a head.

The following year, the Nidderdale Agricultural Society was formally established with representatives from each township and more farming members. Mr John C. Yorke was elected president and the show transferred to Bewerley Park. During the next few years the classes were widened to include dogs, honey, pigs and poultry. One of the reasons for establishing shows was to educate and enthuse farmers to improve their livestock and crops and to produce clean milk – dirty, infected milk was the chief reason for tuberculosis and infant deaths. Lectures were started and study visits made to farms outside the area.

Thirkill Holdsworth, who acted as first secretary, died suddenly in 1901 and was replaced by William Hardcastle, headmaster of Glasshouses School, who continued for 40 years and was then succeeded by his daughter, Mrs Gertrude Nettleton, until 1953.

In the early years there was acrimony between the Pateley Cricket Club and the show committee. The cricket matches had long been a feature of Feast Week and it was felt that the show was detracting from the game's support – the club asked for compensation of £10, but a compromise was found and the match became a focal point in the show, with many famous Yorkshire players taking part over the years, including Herbert Sutcliffe, Len Hutton, Freddy Truman, Brian Sellars, Hedley Verity, Maurice Leyland and Frank Smailes. Sheep-dog trials were introduced in 1904, only six years after the first competitions of this type were established, and from a slow beginning gradually gained support.

During the First World War the show was suspended, but it was revived in 1919, although medals were presented instead of cups. There was a record attendance and it was followed by a gymkhana and a greasy pig race.

In 1925 came the most important step the society took – it bought Bewerley Park, which the Yorke family had sold a few months before. The 70 acres were purchased at a cost of £65 an acre. The society quickly realised the advantage of letting the pasture and fishing rights, and the district generally benefited by being allowed to hold sporting and social events there, such as cricket, football, sports days and galas. Permanent facilities began to be constructed as money became available, starting with a grandstand in 1928.

The following year the Black Dyke Mills Band made its first visit, announcing its arrival by marching down the High Street – a tradition which

St John Ambulance members at the show, c.1970.
Left to right: Irene Beecroft, Joyce Robinson,
Madge Sutton, Margaret Burns, Sadie Beecroft.

has been kept by every band since.

With the depression in the early 1930s, shows throughout the country were struggling to survive, many being abandoned. Matters were not helped locally by a series of wet Feast Weeks – by 1933 there was a loss on the show and only £136 remained in the bank. The next year, however, the weather was even worse – the wettest on record – although there was an increase in entries and the gate money was up. Luckily, after that matters did begin to improve.

The Young Farmers' Club was started in 1932 and two years later was having its own classes, being encouraged as the next generation of agriculturalists. With better summers the show began to pick up and funds could be put into improving the ground – liming the land and replacing over-mature trees. A loudspeaker system was installed in 1936 and immediately proved its worth by helping the owners of a set of false teeth wrapped in a handkerchief and a wallet containing £170 to recover their respective properties. By 1938, the last show before the war, there were 1,565 entries and a balance in the bank of £627.

During the middle months of 1939 the government purchased over 19 acres of the Agricultural Society's land for an evacuation camp, although the plans for the show continued until only a fortnight before it should have taken place when, in common with almost all public entertainment in the next few months, it was cancelled. Shortly afterwards the park was inspected as a possible gun site and the Ministry of Agriculture ordered that ten acres were to be ploughed for food.

Between 1943 and '45 there were small local shows on Feast Saturday and at the end of the war German prisoners were employed to restore the park to its previous condition. In 1946 the show returned to Monday and attendance stood at 10,000.

Upper Nidderdale Women's Institute asked permission to have a demonstration tent and two years later they were allowed a marquee, although the classes were still organised for them by the men-only committee which was very patronising in its attitude.

When, in 1949, the annual dinner was revived, it also was for men only and it was some years before women were allowed to attend. What happened to Mrs Nettleton, the hard-working secretary for all those years, was she excluded too?

In 1955 the fair moved across from the Feast Field to the showground, and the following year Mr Brewster, who had been president since 1926, died. After that the office became a biennial tenure. Roger Worthy took over as secretary when Mrs Nettleton resigned in 1953 and continued for 29 years.

In 1960, because of the general adoption of tractors, the classes for agricultural horses were ended, but hunter classes increased. By 1963 there were 300 classes with £1,000 in prize money. Facilities continued to be improved, particularly roads and toilets. The show has continued to grow in strength and in 1995 it celebrated its centenary with many extra features.

There were problems in 2001, when the foot-and-mouth epidemic meant the show had to be cancelled, although a small event, without livestock, was hurriedly organised for the Sunday. The year of 2002, however, saw record crowds and wonderful weather with visitors returning in their thousands.

CHRISTMAS
Eileen Burgess

We often wish that we could have a peep back into the lives of our great-great-grandparents. This would be really interesting at Christmas, comparing it with our own lavish, spendthrift lifestyle.

Many of the nineteenth-century Christmas traditions in Upper Nidderdale had been passed down through countless generations, some going back to Viking times. Even the name used – Yule – was itself Norse.

The Yule log, if possible of oak, was lit on Christmas Eve, using a splinter saved from the previous year's, and was kept burning throughout the festive season. After dark, no one was allowed to take a light out of the house, not even a pipe. Each household had been given tall Yule candles by the tradesmen, often sufficient for each of the family to have one, and all were lit by the youngest person present. They were held in the hands for about ten minutes, when all but one were extinguished.

This was used to light the ceremony of cutting the cheese by the master of the house – it was a large one, of Wensleydale type, of course, at least 12lbs in weight. Each person was given a slice to eat with a Yule cake, which was a fruity, spicy rich teacake. The cheese was the size of a large plate, almost identical to Scandinavian ones served today, so they must have had a common origin, dating back to Viking times. The family sat around until midnight, telling stories.

The first person to enter after that time had to be a dark-haired man – a woman was an ill omen.

Soon after midnight, the local carol singers started their rounds. Sarah Ann Carling, née Beecroft, of Heathfield, remembered them coming in the night, and dropping money to them from the bedroom window.

A few years later, the local bands started their custom of going around the various houses. Mary Light, née Coates, said they played at almost every house in Middlesmoor and Lofthouse when she was a girl in the early years of last century, and were served refreshments in turn. She remembered also hanging up her stocking and being thrilled with an orange, apple, spice pig and a little book.

At about 5a.m. children holding a sprig of holly went visiting, knocking on the door and shouting 'Browt ye gud luck'. In return they were given a trifling present. If it was a boy and he was first he was the 'Lucky Bird' and he received sixpence, but if he were later, or a girl, only a penny or a halfpenny. In the 1880s at the top of the dale, this ended the festivities – they didn't even have a pudding, according to E.V. Lucas in his recording of the customs in *Studies in Nidderdale*.

For breakfast on Christmas morning, if they had not had it for tea on Christmas Eve, they had frume(n)ty – pearl barley or wheat boiled in milk with spices to make a porridge. The wheat was given in a little bag to each customer by the meal man who supplied the hen corn.

Around Pateley the midday dinner was probably a family affair – Sarah Carling mentions having fattened a goose for the meal. The tea, however, was communal. The chapels and church and their school-rooms had been decorated with evergreens, and anybody who wished to came along – presumably paying 1s. for a full meal or 6d. for simpler fare. One year, in the 1880s, the Pateley Primitive Methodists, whose chapel is the Playhouse at the time of writing, held their tea in the Oddfellows' Hall next door – up to 500 attended in several sittings. They sat at long trestle-tables, with a lady presiding over the tea tray at each end. Mr Wray the grocer supplied, cooked and carved a large ham. His wife baked spice cake and was 'cutter-up' with three other ladies. Afterwards there was a service of song in the chapel.

Another year, the Independents in Bridgehousegate followed their tea with a concert which was 'not dull or overtly religious, but produced much laughter.' As well as social events these were great money raisers – in 1881 the tea helped to pay for the Primitive Chapel roof which needed replacing after only 22 years.

Throughout the rest of the festive season the sword dance and mumming play were important features. In the 1830s and '40s there were eight to 12 in a group of young men. One was dressed as a clown, with a wooden sword. The others had white trousers and jackets of red, yellow or other bright colours, and caps decorated with ribbons. There was always a fiddler among them. The performers stood on one side of the room in a line, with their swords in their belts. The clown, as leading man, walked round and began telling the audience he was a great man, such as Samson. Then he asked the next, who claimed to be Alexander the Great, to follow him. The second man drew his sword and followed, and the rest did so in turn. They faced each other, clattering their swords above their heads. Then the

Scar Village Recreation Hall, prepared for the children's Christmas party in the late 1920s.

swords were lowered, the point held by the next man, and all jumped over in quick succession. This was followed by the making of a lattice which was carried around.

My husband remembers the mummers coming into his home in Summerbridge on New Year's Eve in the mid-1920s. They swept the hearth and dusted round and left without speaking a word. In the Nidderdale Museum is a coat from the Darley mummers. It is a tailcoat of glazed green-and-white chintz with portraits of the future Edward VII and Queen Alexandra at the time of their marriage in 1860. As far as we know, it was last used for a special production at Walker House in 1947, though the regular performance had died out years before.

A very old lady in Hampsthwaite remembered her Christmas and New Year in the middle of the nineteenth century:

We had the sword dance and cockfighting up Dicky Banks. At Christmas we had the mummers and wassailing, they usually came at 2.30a.m. and shouted 'Half past two and a very fine morning'. The muffin man came, he sold havercake [oatcake] and a man with pottery, and the sweet man, and the ting-a-lary man.

New Year was almost more important than Christmas at the top end of the dale. Watch-night services, started by John Wesley himself, were held in the Methodist Chapels, although Pateley Parish Church did not have one until 1880. First footing, where the first person (preferably a dark-haired man) to enter the house after midnight carried a piece of coal for good luck, was practised at New Year as well as Christmas.

Although the celebrations were much simpler, without the large-scale present-giving and the great fuss made today, the festival was nevertheless a focal point of the year, and with the emphasis on home and local pleasures, perhaps much nearer the true spirit of Christmas.

FUN AT CHRISTMAS
Muriel Swires

Long before Christmas, the cake was baked and the puddings mixed and put into white cloths and steamed for hours. Into each pudding mother stirred three-penny pieces wrapped in greaseproof paper, and what a thrill it was to find one in your helping on Christmas Day! One treat I looked forward to was helping to stir the puddings and the mincemeat. The yule bread and all the rest of the baking were done in the fireside oven. I spent weeks embroidering presents for my aunts, usually table centres, chair-back covers, runners, tea cosies or cushion covers.

As Christmas approached the excitement and activity increased. The week before, every picture had to be framed with sprigs and holly. All the rooms downstairs were adorned with greenery of every description. The brass candlesticks were given an extra polish and the tall red candles were brought out of store and put in – I don't recall them ever being lit. A real Christmas tree was decorated with baubles and sugar mice in pink or white and watches and other shapes of the same sugary mixture. Lots of tiny candles on metal bases were fastened on the branches. I don't remember any artificial lights.

The groceries delivered that week always contained a small packet of pearl barley or wheat to make frumenty. Then on the very top there was a sprig of mistletoe which was hung over the living-room door. During the week mother baked several batches of mince pies because freezers were unheard of and every visitor had to be offered a mince pie – each one you ate was believed to bring a happy month, so you can imagine the number of excuses that were made to visit friends and relations.

A collection of coppers and silver coins was made in readiness for the carol singers. Often children would come singing long before, but mother would not let them sing until the week before Christmas. It was not at all unusual to have seven or eight groups every night and the favourite ending was:

Christmas is coming, the goose is getting fat;
Please put a penny in the old man's hat;
If you haven't a penny, a ha'penny will do;
If you haven't a ha'penny, God bless you.

The children received coppers and the silver was reserved for the band and the choirs. Three half-crowns were also put aside as Christmas boxes for the coalman, postman and milkman.

On Christmas Eve all the family assembled at Grandma's house at night. She was dressed all in black with her beautiful white hair piled on top of her head, secured with large combs. There she sat proudly, with her family around, while Auntie Clara stood over the gas ring making the frumenty. She had soaked the pearl barley and was slowly boiling it in milk. When it was almost ready, it was seasoned with nutmeg and a splash of rum, and then served in small pudding dishes and eaten with a spoon.

After that it was time to exchange presents. As we sat in a semicircle round the open fire, the parcels were handed out and, one by one, we unwrapped them, as the rest of the family eagerly watched to see what was revealed. Later everyone attended midnight Mass. I think I was aged 11 before I was allowed to go. The church was always packed.

Christmas morning the postman delivered the mail and the milkman did his usual round. Uncle George was the milkman and I remember him telling us the happenings of one Christmas morning. His large milk churn was pushed on wheels and the measures hung inside. People met him at their doors with basins or jugs to fill, but because it was Christmas morning, he had to go inside and have a mince pie and a glass of sherry. Trying to refuse politely wasn't acceptable and so, not to hurt the feelings of his customers, he was prevailed upon to eat and drink. By the time he staggered up Ben Lane and reached School Hill he had taken on board so many glasses of sherry and mince pies he had to abandon his churn at the roadside and wrap himself round the lamppost outside the police station. There he propped himself up for about 20 minutes before he could continue his round.

Preparing Christmas dinner, which was eaten at about 1p.m., caused lots of excitement and we each had our part to play. One of my tasks was to set the table, but I loved to baste the goose most of all. When the meal was ready, a large damask table napkin was spread on a tray to cover the hot dishes containing a share of our dinner which I took to an elderly lady, Mrs Roberts. She would meet me at the door, wish me a happy Christmas and in exchange for the meal put a

neatly wrapped parcel in my hand. I could hardly wait to get home to open it and the joy I had from those quaint, old-fashioned gifts is hard to imagine. One year it was a little fur muff, another a brush and comb, and another little story-books. They were all old stock from pre-First World War days which she hadn't sold in her shop, but this, of course, I didn't realise at the time, and I thought they were just magical.

One Christmas Eve in the mid-1920s, the River Nidd overflowed its banks and the houses in Millfield Street were flooded to a depth of 3 feet. My neighbour, Peter, who lived there at the time, remembers vividly his brother grabbing a small Christmas tree from the table and rushing upstairs with it determined that it, at least, should survive the water. It was three days before they could venture down the stairs.

Recalling these homely, simple pleasures has brought back many happy memories of my youth.

Above: *The interior of St Cuthbert's Church, where midnight Mass was celebrated on Christmas Eve.*

Right: *St Cuthbert's Church choir, 1960s.*
Left to right: *Stephen Underwood, John Atkinson, John Watson, Geoffrey Brayshaw, ?, David Sykes, Jill Parker, Elaine Johnson, Janet Atkinson, Susan Bailey, Janet Watson, Elaine Sweeting, Mrs Wilkinson, Joyce Derrick, Lynda Robb, Heather MacFadden, Winifred Asquith, Walter Todd, John Wilkinson, Arthur Geldart, Revd Ronald B. MacFadden.*

Left: *King George V passing through Pateley Bridge, 15 August 1911.*

Below: *Coronation procession in 1911, near the bottom of High Street.*

Chapter 18

LEISURE

Above: *A decorated float outside Pateley Corn Mill. The occasion was possibly the coronation of King George V.*

Right: *The great flood of December 1969.*

Left: *Glasshouses cricket team, 1927.* Left to right, back row: ?, ?, ?, J.H. Shuttleworth, Alan May, ?, Harold Parker, ?, Fred Dunn; middle row: ?, Hilda Heaton, ?, Doris Dinsdale, ? Henson; front row: John Robinson, George Dinsdale.

Left: *Pateley Bridge gymnastic club, c.1933.* Left to right, back row: Jimmy Ross, Freddie Harrison, Wilf Surtees, Hilton Pickard, ?, John Nelson, Frank Atkinson, Harold Lowcock; middle row: Bernard Whitehead, ?, Peter Thorpe, ?, ? Knowles; front row: ? Green, Robert Longster, Sunny Simpson, ? Hudson (Bewerley), Clifford Swires, Bobby Longster.

Members of the Pateley Bridge tennis club in front of the pavillion in the Recreation Ground, c.1933.
Left to right, back row: *Mr Booth, Dr Flintoff;* middle row: *Wilf Surtees, Jack Sloan, Alan Thorpe, ?, Wilf Lawson, ?, Walter Todd, Reggie Walker, Jimmy Ross, ?;* front row: *Peg Summersall, Marjorie Chester, Mary Waddington, Bessie Summersall (with child), Mrs Lawson, Cassie Rayner, Kitty Thorpe, Peggy Boddy, Marion Rayner, Elizabeth Flintoff.*

Chapter 9

A MISCELLANY OF LOCAL VIEWS

Left: *The entrance to Wath Woods, once a local beauty spot with public access.*

Below: *Drawing water at the Lofthouse well.*

Right: *Low Woodale, the Wesleyan meeting-house until 1858, when it was replaced by Lodge Chapel.*

Left: *Hampsthwaite in the 1930s.*

Right: *Strawberry Castle, Glasshouses.*

Above: *Manor Farm, Hartwith, which was built in 1680 by William Knightson. It was once known as Hartwith Castle.*

Left: *Tourists admiring How Stean.*

Below: *Children at Wilsill, c.1900.*

Bibliography

A History of Nidderdale, edited by B. Jennings, 1967, was written by the Nidderdale History Group, to which three of the authors belonged. It provided much background information for this publication. Other sources include:

Chapter 1
Bowtell, Harold D., *Lesser Railways of the Yorkshire Dales,* 1991, Plateway Press.
Fountains and Byland Abbey Lease Book, Y.A.S Record Series, Yorkshire Archaeological Society, 1981.
Friends of Scar Village Association, *Scar Village Remembered,* 1991.
Howard, Christopher John, *Sir John Yorke of Nidderdale*, 1939, Sheed & Ward.
Lucas, Joseph, *Studies in Nidderdale,* c.1880, Thomas Thorpe, Pateley Bridge.
Masham Wills in Leeds City Archives at Sheepscar.
Professor Masahiro Takenaka, *The Cholmeley Players and the performance of King Lear in Yorkshire.* University of Tokyo, 2001.
Talks by Jack Haines.
Yorkshire Water Archives.

Chapter 2
Bruff, Harald, papers in Nidderdale Museum.
Cooper, Anne Ashley, *Yorke Country*, 1988, privately published.
Grainge, William, *Nidderdale*, 1863, Thomas Thorpe, Pateley Bridge.

Chapter 3
John Bradford papers in Nidderdale Museum, from Mrs Steel, Rugby.

Chapter 5
Medical Officer's reports and correspondence in the *Nidderdale Herald.*
Pateley Bridge Cocoa House records, Nidderdale Museum.
Robinson's Pateley Bridge Directory, 1900, Robinson, Leeds.
Speight, H., *Upper Nidderdale*, 1906, Elliot Stock, London.

Chapter 7
Alfred Barnard, *Noted Yorkshire Breweries,* c.1895.
Glasshouses School logbooks.
Metcalfe family papers, Dr G.C. Metcalfe.

Chapter 8
Court Rolls and Wills at Leeds City Archives, Sheepscar.
Fountains Abbey Lease Book.
New York Mill records in family papers.
Mr T. Skaife, personal papers.

Chapter 9
North Yorkshire and Cleveland Vernacular Buildings Survey 43.

Chapter 10
Bishop Thornton parish records.
Charity Commission reports.
Census returns.
Fountains Abbey Lease Book.
Hearth tax returns.
Honour of Knaresborough records.
Ingilby Papers.
Jennings, B. (Ed.), *History of Harrogate and Knaresborough*, 1970, Advertiser Press Ltd.
Knaresborough Wills, Surtees Society.
Lay subsidy, 1297.
Pamphlet on St Joseph's Church, Bishop Thornton, 1959.
Pateley Bridge Wesleyan circuit records.
Tithe evaluation, 1586.

Chapter 11
St Bede, *Ecclesiastical History of the English Nation.*
Bruff, Harald, papers in Nidderdale Museum.
Dawson, Joanna, notes from Methodist circuit records, Nidderdale Museum.
Friends Meeting-House Archives, York.
Grainge, William, *History of Harrogate and the Forest of Knaresborough,* 1871, Thomas Thorpe, Pateley Bridge.
Honour of Knaresborough records.
Ingilby, Sir Thomas, *Ripley Castle*, 2002.
Knaresborough Wills, Surtees Society.
Nidderdale Herald, Ackrill Newspapers, Harrogate.
Sessions, W.H., *More Quaker Laughter*, 1967, William Sessions, York.
Speight, Harry, *Nidderdale*, 1894, Elliot Stock, London.
Valor Ecclesiasticus, 1535, Borthwick Institute, York.
Weatherhead, William, *History of Netherdale,* 1839.

Chapter 12
Forest of Knaresborough records.
Fountains Abbey Lease Book.
Grainge, William, *Nidderdale.* Thomas Thorpe, Pateley Bridge.
Knaresborough Wills, Surtees Society.
Knaresborough Railway Report 1818–20.
Leeds Intelligencer.
Nidderdale Herald.
Metcalfe family papers.
Railway records, formerly at York.
West Riding Book of Bridges, 1752.

Chapter 13
Bewerley Township records.
Birstwith Township records.
Board of Guardians annual reports, Nidderdale Museum.
Forest of Knaresborough records.
Fountains Earth Township records.
Horrox, G.M., *A Study of the New Poor Law in Nidderdale, 1832–60,* 1984, MA dissertation
Pateley Bridge Board of Guardians, note book for minutes in Nidderdale Museum.
Poor Law Commission Report.
Stonebeck Down Township records.

Chapter 14
Fellbeck School logbook, Nidderdale Museum.

Chapter 15
Blackah, Thomas, poems published by Thomas Thorpe, Pateley Bridge.
Nidderdale Herald.
Pateley Bridge Choral Union minutes, in the possession of Nidderdale Museum.
Peter Barker monograph, Nidderdale Museum.
Ripon Chronicle.
Nidderdale Brass, Summerbridge and Dacre Silver Prize Band centenary publication.

Chapter 17
Blackah, Thomas, poems published by Thomas Thorpe, Pateley Bridge.
Dawson, Joanna notes from Methodist circuit records, Nidderdale Museum.
Lucas, J., *Studies in Nidderdale,* c.1880.
Nidderdale Agricultural Society, *Pateley Rant,* Nidderdale Show centenary publication, 1995.
Nidderdale Herald.
Pigot's Directory.

Subscribers

C. Max Abbott, Nidderdale

Norman Abbott, Nidderdale

Jan Antonovics, Dacre Banks, Harrogate

Win Asquith, Nidd Close, Pateley Bridge

Philip and Christine Atkins, Harrogate

Harold M. Atkinson, Nidderdale, Yorkshire

Peter and Frances Atkinson, Pateley Bridge

Mr Ron Backhouse, Hampsthwaite

Jean A. Bailey, Pateley Bridge

Peter Barnes, Harrogate

Dr and Mrs L.M. Barrett

Mr W.A. Baugh, Birstwith, North Yorkshire

Mr and Mrs M. Baul and Family, Watergate and Raventofts

John and Fay Beck, Nidderdale, North Yorkshire

C.N. Beecroft

Sadie Beecroft, Nidderdale, Yorkshire

Stan and Ann Beer, Pateley Bridge

Susan Behrens, Nidderdale, Yorkshire

Muriel C. Bell (née Gregg), Harrogate

Alfred W. Bickerdike, Hampsthwaite, Nidderdale, Yorkshire

John Francis Bird, Bewerley, Yorkshire

Jim Blackah, Lofthouse, Nidderdale

Major and Mrs D. Blaker, Pateley Bridge

Peter Boddy, Nidderdale, Yorkshire

Elizabeth A. Bowland, Ripon

John Bradley, Menwith Hill, Darley, North Yorkshire

William Bradley, Dacre, Nidderdale

Dorothy M. Bramley, Doncaster

John and Barbara Breckon, Pateley Bridge, Yorkshire

Dr David R. Britton, Lichfield, Staffs

Jesse and Esme Brockhill, Low Laithe, North Yorkshire

Patricia M. Brook, Ripon

Arthur Broomfield, Ripon, N. Yorkshire

Jill Brotherton, Acaster Malbis, York

Bob and Nora Brown, Glasshouses

Mr and Mrs H. Brown, Birstwith

W.C. and J. Brown, Heyshaw, Dacre

James S.S. Burrells, Birstwith

Pam Burton, Nidderdale

Ernest Busfield, Nidderdale, Yorkshire

Mr Stephen Harvey Caldwell, Shaw Mills, Yorkshire

Kevin, Valerie, Hannah and Finn Cale, Stean

Peter Calvert, great-grandson of Peter Calvert 1856–89

Philip Calvert, Upper Nidderdale

Mr Richard Campbell

Mr and Mrs P.L. Carr, Dacre Banks

David and Alice Cartledge, Milngavie, Scotland

Catherine and Peter Chadwick, Pateley Bridge, Nidderdale

Colin Chadwick, Harrogate, Nidderdale

Richard and Kathleen Chapman, Hamilton, New Zealand

G. Ian Charlton, Sunderland

Donna E. Clark, Nidderdale, Yorkshire

Brian and Barbara Clarkson

Helen Cobb (née Inman), Fareham, Hampshire

Lawrence C. Cockburn, Harrogate

Peter D. Cockburn, Nidderdale, Yorkshire

David C. Cockshott, Nidderdale, Yorkshire

Anthony Colbeck, Shaw Mills, Nidderdale, Yorkshire

Mr S. Coldwell, Holmfirth, Yorkshire

Anne Ashley Cooper, Hexton, Hertfordshire

Jill Coveney, La Parade, France

Mr and Mrs P.G. Cox, High Birstwith, Nidderdale

Mr and Mrs Richard W. Crosby

Stephen M. Dale, Nidderdale, Yorkshire

Brian C. Dean, Nidderdale, Yorkshire

Ronald Derrick, Shaw Mills, Nidderdale, Yorkshire

Bernice Dingwall, Wath, Nidderdale

Maurice Dinsdale, Norwood (formerly Glasshouses)

John Downey, Darley and Lofthouse

Audrey E. Downs, Leeds, Yorkshire

Peter E. Doyle, Knaresborough, Yorkshire

Fred Durance, Killinghall, Yorkshire

Mr D. Eggelton, Castlestead

Simon Elliot, Nidderdale

James W. Ellison, Nidderdale, Yorkshire

Dr Hazel Emslie, Bewerley, Yorkshire

The Enthoven Family, Hole Bottom, Bewerley

Douglas and Pauline Espie, Hounslow, Middlesex

The Evans Family, Summerbridge, Nidderdale

Vivien Evans, Ruckinge, Kent

S. Joan Fall, Glasshouses

Mr and Mrs Andrew Fallon, Hampsthwaite, Nidderdale

Mr and Mrs David Fallon, Glasshouses, Nidderdale

Mr and Mrs Richard Fallon, Vienna, Austria

John and Sheila Farndale, Pateley Bridge, North Yorkshire

Valerie Faulkner, Pateley Bridge, Yorkshire

Allen Firth, Bourton-on-the-Hill, Gloucestershire

Catherine Firth (née Burgess), Bourton-on-the-Hill, Gloucestershire

Robert W. Fisher, Nidderdale, Yorkshire

Sheila M. Fisher, Pateley Bridge, Yorkshire

Bill and Jean Fletcher, Bewerley, Nidderdale, Yorkshire

Olwyn Fonseca, York

Grace Forbes Bagley, Dacre Top

Imogen Forbes Bagley, Dacre Top

Anne Forgham, Nidderdale Hall, Bewerley

Ashley G. Fothergill, Lofthouse, North Yorskhire

Carl Foxton, Bewerley, Pateley Bridge, Harrogate

Mikki French, Hastings, Sussex

D. Galloway, Hampsthwaite, Yorkshire

Clare and Miles Gardner, Vale of York

Paul Garforth A.C.I.I., F.P.C., Pateley Bridge, North Yorkshire

Mrs Ann Gill, Summerbridge, Nidderdale

Barry Gill, New York/ Nidderdale

Mr and Mrs R.I. Goodall, Middlesmoor, Nidderdale

Martyn Gould, Birstwith, North Yorkshire

Jocelyn G. Goundry, Nidderdale, Yorkshire

Judith M. Grange, Nidderdale, Yorkshire

Mrs Connie Grayson (née Garnett), Ripon, North Yorkshire

Dawn and Ron Haida, Nidderdale, Yorkshire

E.M. Haines (née Ashby)

Geoffrey and Kathleen Hall, Darley

Ian and Margaret Hall, Rashdyke, Bewerley

Mrs Patricia Hall, Pateley Bridge

Wendy (née Marshall) and Clive Hall, Darley, North Yorkshire

Joan M. Hallums, Nidderdale, Yorkshire

Gordon Hanley, Fellbeck, Pateley Bridge

Harry Hardcastle, Harrogate, N. Yorkshire

Michael Hardcastle, Germany http://www.hardcastle.de

Dennis and Gillian Harling, Harrogate, Yorkshire

Steve and Sheala Harrison, Ripon

Kim Hatherly, Gymea, NSW, Australia

J.M. Hawkesworth, Nidderdale, Yorkshire

Mary Hayton, Glasshouses, Nidderdale

Linda Head, Tucson, Arizona, USA

Sylvia P. Hebblethwaite, Nidderdale, Yorkshire

Anthony Hebden, Nidderdale, Yorkshire

Chris and Sharelle Henderson, Old Church Lane, Pateley Bridge

Mrs Gladys Heptinstall, Nidderdale, North Yorkshire

Roy and Elizabeth G. Hesketh

Mrs Jean M. Highfield, Bewerley, Nidderdale, Yorkshire

Sue Hill

Colin J. Hodgson, Nidderdale, Yorkshire

Louise Hodgson, Nidderdale, Yorkshire

B. and E.A. Holdsworth, Pie Gill, Heathfield

Mike Hollingworth, Kettlesing

Joan Hollinworth (née Newbould), daughter of Henry, Green How, Pateley

C.F. Holmes, Harrogate

Clifford B. Hopes, Harrogate, North Yorkshire

The Late George Wetherald Horn, Middlesmoor, Yorkshire

Jim and Margaret Horrox, Low Laithe

Sue Horsman, Castle Donington, Derby

Canon Hoverley, Pateley Bridge

E.A. Howard, Dragon Avenue, Harrogate

Peter Howard, Darley, Nidderdale

Mr and Mrs M. Howell, Summerbridge, North Yorkshire

Shirley Hughes

James and Jane Hutchinson, Markington, North Yorkshire

Michael C.H. Hutchinson, Markington, Yorkshire

Anthony D. Hyett, Summerbridge, North Yorkshire

R.E.M. and W.J. Imeson, Pateley Bridge, Yorkshire

John Inman, Guildford, Surrey

R. Henry Ingle, North Yorkshire

Juliet Ingleby Wilson, Nidderdale, Yorkshire

Brian and Andrea Ives, Pateley Bridge

Eric H. Iveson, Summerbridge, Harrogate

Mr John Jacobs, Wormald Green, North Yorkshire

Mr Charles D. James, St Bees, Cumbria

Angela and Martin Jasper, Nidderdale, North Yorkshire

Peter Jefferson, ex Pateley Bridge

Mr R.C. Jennings, Hampsthwaite, Nidderdale

Colin Jordan, Greenhow Hill

Andrew Kaberry, Yorkshire

Ian and Linda Kendall

Ann and Michael Kent, Dacre Banks, Nidderdale, Yorkshire

Mary and Peter Kershaw, Harrogate, Yorkshire

Mary Kinsley, Eagle Lodge, Bewerley

Mr George Rodney Kirby, Harrogate, North Yorkshire

Mrs Joyce Knight (née Stoney), Berkshire

Marjorie Joyce Lamb, Harrogate

Ian Lambert, Nidderdale, Yorkshire

Joyce Latty, Sharow, Ripon

Ann and Arthur Layfield, Pateley Bridge

Mr C.E. Leahy, Bewerley, Yorks

Dinah H. Lee, Pateley Bridge, Harrogate

James Lee, Killinghall, Yorkshire

Mr and Mrs Don Leeming, Ramsgill

Felicity A. Leeson, Nidderdale, Yorkshire

Peter Lewis, Pateley Bridge

A.G. and C.A. Liddle, Pateley Bridge, Harrogate

Joyce M. Liggins, Pateley Bridge

Richard and Victoria Light, Bardsey, Yorkshire

Robert F. Light, Pateley Bridge

Richard and Maureen Lloyd, Scotton, Knaresborough, North Yorkshire

Bill and Brenda Lofthouse, Darley, Nidderdale

D. and V. Lofthouse, Summerbridge

M. and J. Lofthouse, York

S.R. Lofthouse, Norwood

J.K. Longster and Family, Bridgehousegate, Yorkshire

Peter and Ann Los, Woodmansey, East Yorkshire

W.A. Lowe, Pateley Bridge

Harry and K.M. (Molly) Lupton

Mrs Margaret Luty, Pateley Bridge

Trevor Lyons, Pateley Bridge

Betty MacArthur, Settle, N. Yorkshire

Mr and Mrs H.F. Mackay, Harrogate

Marguerite Maclellan, Pateley Bridge

Mr and Mrs K. Mansfield

Dennis Marshall

Dorothy Marshall, Nidderdale, Yorkshire

A.J. and Anne Martin, Woodlands, Bewerley

Annie McGrory (née Raw), Glasshouses, Nidderdale

Ronald T. McMillan, Felliscliffe, Nidderdale

Mr and Mrs P. Meech, Low Laithe

Chris and Barbara Mellor, Nidderdale, Yorkshire

Dr Chris Metcalfe, Ottery St Mary, Devon

Everald Mary Metcalfe, Heyshaw and Pateley Bridge, Nidderdale, Yorkshire

Michael A. Metcalfe, Boscastle, Cornwall

Win Metcalfe, High Birstwith, Nr Harrogate

Mr and Mrs A.H. Mills, Nidderdale

John V. Milton, Nidderdale, Yorkshire

John & Susan, Jack David, John Adam Mitchell, Fellbeck

David and Joanna Moody

Linda Moor (née Mackwell)

Paul and Jaki Moorhouse, Dukes Place, Nidderdale

Sheila Morgan, Nidderdale, Yorkshire

Joseph Selwyn Morris, Birstwith

P.H. and E. Moss, Pateley Bridge

Mrs D. Motley, Nidderdale, Yorkshire

Ellen C. (Hardcastle) Mullen, Charlestown, MA, USA

J.B. Munn, Castle Bolton, North Yorkshire

Paul and Anneliese Mustard, Bewerley, Yorkshire

Greg Nelson, Hampsthwaite, Harrogate

Adrian P. Newbould, Nidderdale, Yorkshire

Frank Newbould, Knaresborough, North Yorkshire

Anna and Roger Newman, Harrogate

Roger Newson Smith, Bewerley

Nidderdale Area of Outstanding Natural Beauty

Nidderdale Group, L.D.W.A., Knaresborough

North Yorkshire County Council's Libraries, Archives and Arts Unit

Mr Harry Oxtaby, Nidderdale, Yorkshire

Morag F.E. Pearson, Harrogate, Yorkshire

Alan Peel, Felliscliffe, Harrogate

Colin M. Pepper, Killinghall

S.D. and J.E. Pickering, Nidderdale

Val and Steven Pilkington, Low Laithe

Julie Plant, Birmingham

Tom and Peggy Pool, Pateley Bridge

G. and D. Portwood, Nidderdale

B. Potter, Nidderdale

Mrs Irene Powell, Nidderdale, N. Yorkshire

J. Alan Powell, Harrogate

Tom Price, Hampsthwaite, North Yorkshire

Linda and Doug Pridmore, Bewerley, North Yorkshire

Sylvia M. Pullen, Nidderdale, Yorkshire

Philip and Anne Rack, Bewerley

Paul and Judith Ransom, Lofthouse, Nidderdale

Alan and Barbara Ravenscroft, Bewerley

Joan M. Ravilious, Nidderdale, Yorkshire

Diana Read, Uppingham, Rutland

Paul Reinsch, Greenhow

Simon, Lisa and Max Reiter, The Knott

Brian and Doreen Reynard,
Darley, Harrogate, N. Yorks

Gabriella Louise Reynard-
Robinson, Darley, Harrogate,
North Yorkshire

D. Rhodes, North Yorkshire

Mr K.O. and Mrs A. Richards,
Harrogate

John Richmond, Pateley Bridge

Neil and Marion Richmond,
Harrogate, Yorkshire – ancestor
of Frederick Atkinson,
mill owner

Barbara Anne Rickards,
Nidderdale, Yorkshire

Doreen Roberts, Harrogate,
Yorkshire

Chris, Jenny and James Robinson

Eileen Robinson, Nidderdale,
Yorkshire

Eric and Maureen Robinson,
Dacre

Jan and Kirsty Robinson and
Byron Harrison, Middlemoor,
Upper Nidderdale

Sally A. Robinson, York

The Venerable Neil Robinson,
Ripon

Hardisty Rolls, Nidderdale,
Yorkshire

Ray, Bethan, James and
Rebecca Ross, Markington

Alan Rouse, Bewerley,
Yorkshire

Beatrice Rush (née Appleby),
Nidderdale

Mary Sara, Glasshouses,
Nidderdale

Gayle M. Saul, Smelthouses,
Nidderdale, Yorkshire

Sandra Sawyer, Leeds,
Yorkshire

Peter Seaman, Ripon,
Yorkshire

D. Shuttleworth, Pateley
Bridge, Nidderdale

Jacob Henry Simmons,
6 July 2000 Pateley Bridge

Alan and Hazel Simpson,
Oulston, Nr York

Doug Simpson, Killinghall
Moor, North Yorkshire

Jane Simpson, Low Laithe,
Harrogate

J.A. and E. Simpson,
Dacre Banks

Keith and Christine Simpson,
Laverton, Nr Ripon

Peter Simpson, Dacre,
Nidderdale

Ann Skelton, Washburn Valley

Chris and Elizabeth Smith,
Birstwith, Nidderdale,
Yorkshire

Dennis and Gloria Smith,
Harrogate, Yorkshire

Ian F. Smith, Glasshouses,
Nidderdale

Martin and Anne Smith,
New Close, Dacre

Peter Solomon, Bewerley,
Yorkshire

Kirsty Spalding, Shaw Mills,
Yorkshire

Richard James Spencer,
Thornthwaite

Walter and Sylvia Spencer,
West Ardsley, Wakefield

Peter W. Spittlehouse,
Pateley Bridge

Ronald P. Spragg, Ingerthorpe,
North Yorkshire

Jacky and Darell Staniforth,
Thornthwaite, Yorkshire

Pat and Allan Staniforth,
Pateley Bridge, Yorkshire

Malcolm Stannard Smith,
Nidderdale, Yorkshire

A.J. and H.M. Stewart,
Bewerley, Pateley Bridge

Andrew and Julia Stockham,
Summerbridge

Hazel Stothard, Harrogate,
Yorkshire

Mr T. Stott, Hartwith,
Nidderdale, Yorkshire

Norman and Pauline
Summersall, Harrogate,
North Yorkshire

Audrey Summersgill,
Nidderdale, North Yorkshire

Anne-Marie Swires,
Pateley Bridge

C. and E. Swires,
Pateley Bridge

Dayne and Heather Swires,
Summerbridge, Harrogate.
Founder members

Mrs Josie Swires (née Worsnop),
Beckwithshaw, Harrogate

Joyce Swires, Nidderdale,
Yorkshire

Douglas and Brenda Sykes,
Morley, Leeds

Frank and Marti Sykes,
Carpinteria, California, USA

Peter R. Sykes, Shawmills,
Yorkshire

Derrick and Margaret Tabrah,
Dacre

A.D. Taylor, Harrogate,
North Yorkshire

Ronald Terris, Harrogate,
North Yorkshire

Capt David J.V. Thackeray,
Nidderdale, Yorkshire

Patricia Boddy Tharp,
Dhahran, Saudi Arabia

A.G. Thomas, Nidderdale

Barbara M. Thomas,
Nidderdale, North Yorkshire

Clarice Thornton, Corby,
Northampton

Susan C. Tidswell, Dacre,
Nidderdale, Yorkshire

George Tinkler, Hew Green,
High Birstwith

Richard Tite, Littlethorpe, Ripon

Michael Turner, Hermitage,
Berkshire

David S. Tyrrell, Nairobi, Kenya

Margery Tyson, Low Laithe,
Nidderdale

Mr and Mrs Stephen G. Vasey,
Hampsthwaite

W.E. Verity, Hampsthwaite,
Nidderdale

Mrs Pat Voakes, Killinghall,
Yorkshire

Bill and Ros Wade,
Pateley Bridge

Mr David B. Walker,
Pateley Bridge

Pat Walker, Wharfedale,
Yorkshire

Richard B. Walker, Formby

John F.W. Walling,
Newton Abbot, Devon

Nevin and Christine Ward,
Summerbridge,
North Yorkshire

Elisa Wardman and Jim
Davenport, Copt Hewick,
Ripon

Pamela C. Warn, York

David Watson, Surrey

Edith M. Watson, Nidderdale

Brian and Judy Weatherhead,
Pateley Bridge

Christine and David
Weatherhead, Ivy House
Farm, Pateley Bridge

C. and R.H. Weatherhead,
Ivy House Farm,

Pateley Bridge

Ian E. and Andrew
Weatherhead, Book House
Farm, Pateley

Michael D. Weatherhead,
Brighton

Helen J. Webster,
Pateley Bridge, Nidderdale

Audrey E. Whalley (née
Maclellan), Bewerley,
Pateley Bridge

Paul Whitaker, Silsden

Ella Ward Whitaker

The Whitley Family,
White Oak Farm,
Summerbridge

Alison M. Whitney, Tewkesbury

Tim and Mary Whitney,
Pateley Bridge

Bruce Wilford, Nidderdale

Helen Wilford, Nidderdale

Ken and Ruth Wilford,
Nidderdale

Meryl Wilford, Nidderdale

A.L. Wilkinson, Harrogate,
Yorkshire

Charles Edmund Wilkinson,
Yorkshire

Jane Wilkinson, Trafoyle Drive,
Harrogate

John F. Wilkinson,
Pateley Bridge

Jo Williams, North Rigton,
Yorkshire

Thomas R.C. Wilson, Birstwith,
Harrogate

Mrs Sylvia Wilson,
Hampsthwaite,
North Yorkshire

Raymond Winder,
Pateley Bridge

John Witheford, Old Smithy,
High Birstwith, Yorkshire

Christine Wood, The Chapel,
Birstwith

M.A. and B.J. Wood,
Nidderdale, Yorkshire

Tony Wood, The Chapel,
Birstwith

Mr and Mrs W. Worsley,
Ranelands, Dacre

Joseph Robert Wray,
Nidderdale, Yorkshire

Rowland Yates, Darley

Gillian Yeadon, Pateley Bridge,
Yorkshire

D.J. Yorke, Hellifield, Skipton,
North Yorkshire

Community Histories

The Book of Addiscombe • Canning and Clyde Road Residents Association and Friends
The Book of Addiscombe, Vol. II • Canning and Clyde Road Residents Association and Friends
The Book of Axminster with Kilmington • Les Berry and Gerald Gosling
The Book of Bampton • Caroline Seward
The Book of Barnstaple • Avril Stone
The Book of Barnstaple, Vol. II • Avril Stone
The Book of The Bedwyns • Bedwyn History Society
The Book of Bickington • Stuart Hands
Blandford Forum: A Millennium Portrait • Blandford Forum Town Council
The Book of Bramford • Bramford Local History Group
The Book of Breage & Germoe • Stephen Polglase
The Book of Bridestowe • D. Richard Cann
The Book of Bridport • Rodney Legg
The Book of Brixham • Frank Pearce
The Book of Buckfastleigh • Sandra Coleman
The Book of Buckland Monachorum & Yelverton • Pauline Hamilton-Leggett
The Book of Carharrack • Carharrack Old Cornwall Society
The Book of Carshalton • Stella Wilks and Gordon Rookledge
The Parish Book of Cerne Abbas • Vivian and Patricia Vale
The Book of Chagford • Iain Rice
The Book of Chapel-en-le-Frith • Mike Smith
The Book of Chittlehamholt with Warkleigh & Satterleigh • Richard Lethbridge
The Book of Chittlehampton • Various
The Book of Colney Heath • Bryan Lilley
The Book of Constantine • Moore and Trethowan
The Book of Cornwood and Lutton • Compiled by the People of the Parish
The Book of Creech St Michael • June Small
The Book of Cullompton • Compiled by the People of the Parish
The Book of Dawlish • Frank Pearce
The Book of Dulverton, Brushford, Bury & Exebridge • Dulverton and District Civic Society
The Book of Dunster • Hilary Binding
The Book of Edale • Gordon Miller
The Ellacombe Book • Sydney R. Langmead
The Book of Exmouth • W.H. Pascoe
The Book of Grampound with Creed • Bane and Oliver
The Book of Hayling Island & Langstone • Peter Rogers
The Book of Helston • Jenkin with Carter
The Book of Hemyock • Clist and Dracott
The Book of Herne Hill • Patricia Jenkyns
The Book of Hethersett • Hethersett Society Research Group
The Book of High Bickington • Avril Stone
The Book of Ilsington • Dick Wills
The Book of Kingskerswell • Carsewella Local History Group
The Book of Lamerton • Ann Cole and Friends
Lanner, A Cornish Mining Parish • Sharron Schwartz and Roger Parker
The Book of Leigh & Bransford • Malcolm Scott
The Book of Litcham with Lexham & Mileham • Litcham Historical and Amenity Society
The Book of Loddiswell • Loddiswell Parish History Group
The New Book of Lostwithiel • Barbara Fraser
The Book of Lulworth • Rodney Legg
The Book of Lustleigh • Joe Crowdy

The Book of Lyme Regis • Rodney Legg
The Book of Manaton • Compiled by the People of the Parish
The Book of Markyate • Markyate Local History Society
The Book of Mawnan • Mawnan Local History Group
The Book of Meavy • Pauline Hemery
The Book of Minehead with Alcombe • Binding and Stevens
The Book of Morchard Bishop • Jeff Kingaby
The Book of Newdigate • John Callcut
The Book of Nidderdale • Nidderdale Museum Society
The Book of Northlew with Ashbury • Northlew History Group
The Book of North Newton • J.C. and K.C. Robins
The Book of North Tawton • Baker, Hoare and Shields
The Book of Nynehead • Nynehead & District History Society
The Book of Okehampton • Roy and Ursula Radford
The Book of Paignton • Frank Pearce
The Book of Penge, Anerley & Crystal Palace • Peter Abbott
The Book of Peter Tavy with Cudlipptown • Peter Tavy Heritage Group
The Book of Pimperne • Jean Coull
The Book of Plymtree • Tony Eames
The Book of Porlock • Dennis Corner
Postbridge – The Heart of Dartmoor • Reg Bellamy
The Book of Priddy • Albert Thompson
The Book of Princetown • Dr Gardner-Thorpe
The Book of Rattery • By the People of the Parish
The Book of St Day • Joseph Mills and Paul Annear
The Book of Sampford Courtenay with Honeychurch • Stephanie Pouya
The Book of Sculthorpe • Gary Windeler
The Book of Seaton • Ted Gosling
The Book of Sidmouth • Ted Gosling and Sheila Luxton
The Book of Silverton • Silverton Local History Society
The Book of South Molton • Jonathan Edmunds
The Book of South Stoke with Midford • Edited by Robert Parfitt
South Tawton & South Zeal with Sticklepath • Roy and Ursula Radford
The Book of Sparkwell with Hemerdon & Lee Mill • Pam James
The Book of Staverton • Pete Lavis
The Book of Stithians • Stithians Parish History Group
The Book of Stogumber, Monksilver, Nettlecombe & Elworthy • Maurice and Joyce Chidgey
The Book of Studland • Rodney Legg
The Book of Swanage • Rodney Legg
The Book of Tavistock • Gerry Woodcock
The Book of Thorley • Sylvia McDonald and Bill Hardy
The Book of Torbay • Frank Pearce
The Book of Watchet • Compiled by David Banks
The Book of West Huntspill • By the People of the Parish
Widecombe-in-the-Moor • Stephen Woods
Widecombe – Uncle Tom Cobley & All • Stephen Woods
The Book of Williton • Michael Williams
The Book of Witheridge • Peter and Freda Tout and John Usmar
The Book of Withycombe • Chris Boyles
Woodbury: The Twentieth Century Revisited • Roger Stokes
The Book of Woolmer Green • Compiled by the People of the Parish

For details of any of the above titles or if you are interested in writing your own history, please contact: Commissioning Editor, Community Histories, Halsgrove House, Lower Moor Way, Tiverton Business Park, Tiverton, Devon EX16 6SS, England; email: naomic@halsgrove.com